New Troy

MEDIEVAL CULTURES

Series Editors

Rita Copeland
Barbara A. Hanawalt
David Wallace

Sponsored by the Center for Medieval Studies at the University of Minnesota

Volumes in this series study the diversity of medieval cultural histories and practices, including such interrelated issues as gender, class, and social hierarchies; race and ethnicity; geographical relations; definitions of political space; discourses of authority and dissent; educational institutions; canonical and noncanonical literatures; and technologies of textual and visual literacies.

Volume 36
Sylvia Federico
New Troy: Fantasies of Empire in the Late Middle Ages

Volume 35
Jeffrey J. Cohen
Medieval Identity Machines

Volume 34
Glenn Burger
Chaucer's Queer Nation

For more books in the series, see pages 201–03.

New Troy

Fantasies of Empire in the Late Middle Ages

Sylvia Federico

Medieval Cultures, Volume 36
University of Minnesota Press
Minneapolis
London

An earlier version of chapter 1 appeared as "A Fourteenth-Century Erotics of Politics: London as a Feminine New Troy," *Studies in the Age of Chaucer* 19 (1997): 121–55; reprinted by permission of the New Chaucer Society. An earlier version of chapter 3 appeared as "Chaucer's Utopian Troy Book: Alternatives to Historiography in Chaucer's *Troilus and Criseyde*," *Exemplaria: A Journal of Theory in Medieval and Renaissance Studies* 11, no. 1 (1999): 79–106; copyright 1999 Pegasus Press; reprinted by permission of Pegasus Press, University of North Carolina, Asheville, NC 28804.

Published by the University of Minnesota Press
111 Third Avenue South, Suite 290
Minneapolis, MN 55401-2520
http://www.upress.umn.edu

Library of Congress Cataloging-in-Publication Data
Federico, Sylvia.
New Troy : fantasies of empire in the late Middle Ages / Sylvia Federico.
p. cm. — (Medieval cultures ; v. 36)
Includes bibliographical references and index.
ISBN 0-8166-4166-8 (HC : alk. paper) — ISBN 0-8166-4167-6 (PB : alk. paper)
1. English literature—Middle English, 1100–1500—History and criticism. 2. Literature and history—England—London—History—To 1500. 3. Chaucer, Geoffrey, d. 1400—Knowledge—Troy (Extinct city) 4. Arthurian romances—History and criticism. 5. English literature—Turkic influences. 6. London (England)—History—To 1500. 7. Trojan War—Literature and the war. 8. Troy (Extinct city)—In literature. 9. London (England)—In literature. 10. England—Relations—Turkey. 11. Turkey—Relations—England. 12. Imperialism in literature. I. Title. II. Series.
PR275.T74 F43 2003
820.9'358'0902—dc21 2003000197

Printed in the United States of America on acid-free paper

12 11 10 09 08 07 06 05 04 03 10 9 8 7 6 5 4 3 2 1

Contents

Acknowledgments

Many people helped me with this project, and in a variety of ways, from its beginnings as a doctoral dissertation to its present form. I am happy most of all to be able to thank Michael Hanrahan, Jean Taylor Federico, Jane Urban Taylor, Eileen Mitchell, and Veronica Hanrahan for their generous moral and material support at all phases of the process. My teachers at SUNY Purchase and at Indiana University, including Bob Stein, Richard Stack, Al David, Sheila Lindenbaum, Larry Clopper, Judith Anderson, and Linda Charnes, provided the models of rigorous and creative scholarship that got me started. My colleagues at the University of Leeds, especially Rory McTurk, Oliver Pickering, Mary Swan, Peter Meredith, and Catherine Batt, shared with me their expertise, humor, and good company as the project neared completion. I am particularly grateful to Steve Justice, David Wallace, Chris Baswell, and Mark Ormrod for reading all or parts of the manuscript and for suggesting many helpful corrections, and to Andrew Prescott, David Fairer, David Lawton, Carolyn Dinshaw, John Barnard, and Mary Carruthers for their encouragement and questions. My deepest intellectual debt is owed to Paul Strohm, my adviser. I have tried to live up to his standards of scholarship.

Photograph of Sophia Schliemann wearing Trojan diadem.
Reproduced by permission from AKG London.

INTRODUCTION

Troy and the Later Middle Ages

⁜

Upon discovering the ruins of Troy in April 1870, Heinrich Schliemann is said to have felt a singular joy, a kind of happiness imagined by one observer as a "fulfillment of a child's wish."[1] Schliemann's photographs of what he called Priam's Treasure are exultant: In one, the gems and precious plate of ancient Troy are piled high on the sideboard in his home; in another, his wife wears the Trojan diadem. For Schliemann, this moment of professional achievement—even conquest—was the fulfillment of a lifetime's expectation. As he wrote in one of his several accounts of the discovery, he considered himself, from a very early age, destined to find Troy.

Schliemann's *Ilios* begins with an "excavation" of his own childhood, implicitly borrowing from psychoanalytic assumptions:

> I begin this book with my autobiography... from a desire to show how the work of my later life has been the natural consequence of the impressions I received in my earliest childhood.[2]

These impressions include the memory of a foundational exchange with his father, who once presented him with a book illustrating Troy in flames, complete with Aeneas carrying Anchises on his back and holding Ascanius by the hand. This image provoked an argument between father and son, with the young Schliemann insisting that if the walls of Troy had indeed been as large as the picture showed, then ruins of them must survive somewhere. His father maintained the contrary, arguing that Troy was forever lost, until finally the two agreed that if the city survived, the son would one day excavate it.[3]

Schliemann's narrative is, on the one hand, an explanatory device for what he later became: His history is invoked to justify his future, to gloss that future as an inevitable consequence of the past. And yet on the other hand, this version of the past is obviously a motivated one: It is not necessary to doubt the veracity of the childhood memory to see it as a fabrication, a willed remembrance that suits a specific purpose and fills a specific need in the present. In the context of Freudian psychoanalysis, the difference between a true memory and a false one is less significant than the purposes to which that memory is put. In Schliemann's case, the desire for Troy "constitutes the very threshold of subjectivity;"[4] it is the moment at which his history, true or false, begins.

Schliemann created his identity retroactively, and in a sense, tautologically, by invoking Troy as his originary myth and then, in turn, offering himself as a fulfillment of that promising origin. Troy was for him an interpretive mechanism through which the past could be read in light of the future.[5] His father's gift made Schliemann the man who found Troy; but the gift of the Father (understood in psychoanalytic terms as that which represents and also grants the authority of the symbolic order) equally made Troy the signifier of origins. Theories of identity and of history thus converge around the specter of this ancient fallen city.

The observer who so vividly imagined Schliemann's happiness in finding Troy was Sigmund Freud himself, writing to his friend Wilhelm Fliess nearly thirty years after the discovery. Freud was fascinated by Schliemann. As Peter Gay writes, he was "the man in whose life history Freud took the greatest pleasure, and whom he probably envied more than any other."[6] Indeed, Freud attempts to claim a bit of Schliemann's magic when he describes the psychoanalytic process as a recovery of identity not unlike "the technique of excavating a buried city."[7] In a separate letter to Fliess, Freud elaborates on this metaphor in the course of describing a recent analytic success. With his help, the patient had unearthed a childhood scene

> which answers all requirements and into which left-over riddles flow; it is everything at once, sexual, innocuous, natural, etcetera. I still scarcely dare to believe it properly. It is as if Schliemann had dug up Troy, considered legendary, once again.[8]

Finding Troy, Freud imagines in this remarkable passage, is a phenomenon of fulfillment, of indescribable satisfaction, of being without end. It is, like his own new field of psychoanalysis, an interpretive key to the past with the power to "unlock" the identity of the present. Until Schliemann exposed its ruined foundations, Troy was a phenomenon of the imagination, a kind of aperture through which fantasies of the past might be glimpsed darkly. Similar to the archaeology that laid bare Priam's Treasure, Freud's work made visible to the trained scientist (though here, as with Schliemann's work, the results were designed ultimately for a popular audience) the mystery of history.

But the discourse that claims to find, discover, or disclose that which had been hidden is a bit of a ruse in its own right. The myth of origins resists attempts to dismantle its mystique and creates more narrative layers around itself in the face of such attempts. Indeed, the claims of elucidation themselves often become part of the obscuring process, part of the textual matrix in need of analysis. Schliemann's repeated narration of the discovery of Troy in his four large autobiographical volumes, for instance, suggests itself as a process of accretion—or even as a repetition compulsion—around the absence that persists in the place of the expected kernel of truth. The event of finding the city apparently is not enough to satisfy the monumental expectation it inspired; instead, the moment of anticipation must be revisited over and over again to affirm subjectivity. Desire (rooted, of course, in loss, in the absence of the thing anticipated) is more significant a phenomenon in the process of identity formation than is its satisfaction.

Jacques Lacan's elaboration of Freud's famous "*fort-da*" observation (in which a child repeatedly tosses a wooden spindle out of his cot, replaying symbolically the pattern of the presence and absence of his mother) is particularly fruitful here. Lacan maintained that symbolization (or the entry into language) occurs only at a cost, through the loss of the undifferentiated state between self and mother: When the child subsequently asks something of its mother, that loss will persist over and above anything she can possibly give or say in reply. Jacqueline Rose explains that

> demand always bears on something other than the satisfaction it calls for—and each time the demand of the child is answered by the satisfaction of its needs, so this "something other" is relegated to the place of its original impossibility. This is *desire*. It is

> the "remainder" of the subject, something that is always left over, but which has no content as such. Desire is like the zero term in the numerical chain—its place is both constitutive and empty.[9]

The desire for Troy is in many respects a similarly displaced and displacing phenomenon: It cannot be satisfied. Rather, like Schliemann with his books of himself, seekers of antiquity turn to narrative as an illusory remedy of self-definition in the face of history's absencing power.

The medieval fascination with Troy, and particularly the cult of "Trojanness" in late-fourteenth- and early-fifteenth-century England that is the subject of this book, places an individual claimant in relation to a fantasied history. The symbolic appropriation of Troy is at once a means of creating a past, present, and future in accord with specific ideals and also a means of mobilizing that imagined historicity in gestures of self-invention and self-definition. As is true for both Schliemann and Freud, medieval claimants to Trojanness invent not just Troy but also themselves in the process of imagining the ancient city.

The rights to the discovery or cultural ownership of Troy were contested in the later Middle Ages: Scores of European states and their rulers claimed Trojan precedent in efforts to achieve, consolidate, and maintain their power in relation to other states and often in relation to their own fractious constituencies. This plural aspect of "true" Trojanness stems from the popular medieval belief that following the fall of Troy, its handful of survivors were dispersed to the several corners of Europe to found individual new Trojan settlements. In an illustrated historical chronicle produced in France in the mid–fifteenth century, for instance, Aeneas's departure from Troy is shown as one of four trips away from the crumbling city; in indistinguishable portraits, he, Priamus, Turnus, and Helenus steer identical ships toward their separate destinies.[10]

But the acceptance of the principle of Trojan dispersal did not sanction the idea of simultaneous and equal new Troys; rather, as Virgil understood, the possibility of many Trojan settlements encouraged competing narratives of empire.[11] The appropriation of the Trojan past was always an imperial gesture for the European present. The emperors Constantine, Theodosius, and Charlemagne were linked to Troy through mythic genealogies that claimed Aeneas as their common forefather—a tradition that continued through Holy Roman Emperor Charles IV, Anne of

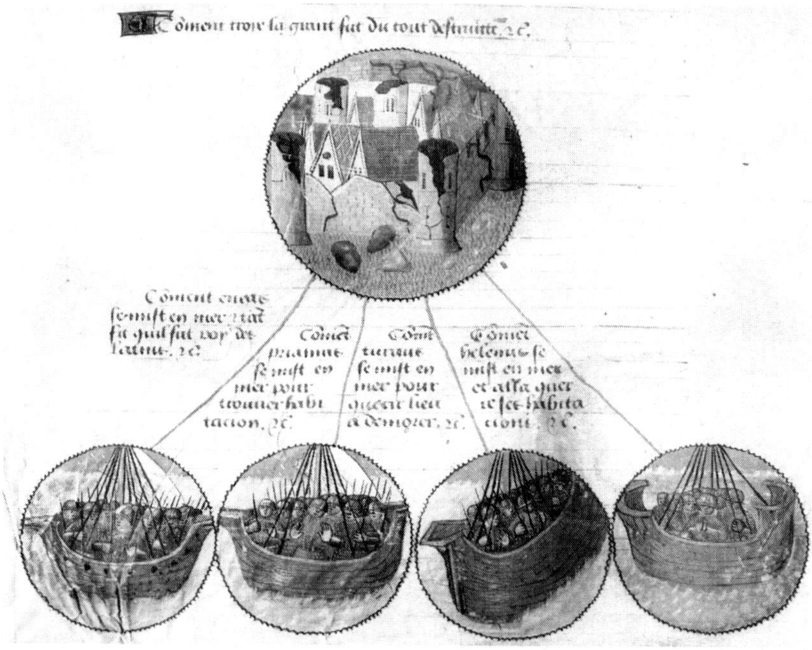

Illustration from Brotherton Library Special Collection Manuscript 100 showing survivors fleeing the ruins of Troy. Reproduced by permission of the Brotherton Collection, Leeds University Library.

Bohemia's father and father-in-law to England's Richard II.[12] The sacred pedigree passes from Noah to Saturn and Jupiter and then, via Dardanus, founder of Troy, reaches Charles through the Roman emperors, Clovis, and the Carolingians. According to this genealogy, the blood of the brothers Aeneas and Antenor, who established Trojan realms in Italy and Germany, meets in Charlemagne (who had a Roman mother and a German father) and culminates in Charles IV. In his castle at Karlstein, near Prague, Charles celebrated his descent from Troy by lining the walls of the royal reception hall with his ancestors' portraits.[13]

In England, Geoffrey of Monmouth's treatment of legendary history made popular the idea that London had ancestral ties to Troy.[14] In Geoffrey's *Historia Regum Britanniae* (History of the Kings of Britain), Diana appears to Brutus, a great-grandson of Aeneas, and explains that the *translatio imperii* from the ancient world to the modern one will be achieved through him and his heirs:

> Brute, past the realms of Gaul, beneath the sunset lieth an island, girt about by ocean. . . . Seek it! For there is thine abode for ever. There by thy sons again shall Troy be builded; There of thy blood shall Kings be born, hereafter Sovran in every land the wide world over.[15]

After searching the entire island, Brutus selects the site for the main city of the prophesied place and names it after Troy:

> When he came to the river Thames, he walked along the banks till he found the very spot best fitted to his purpose. He therefore founded his city there and called it New Troy, and by this name was it known for many ages thereafter, until at last, by corruption of the word, it came to be called *Trinovantum*.[16]

This version of the past, although disputed by clerical historians, was during the late medieval period a well-known and popularly accepted account of the founding of England.

In his discussion of the motives and effects of the myth of England's Trojan origins, Francis Ingledew suggests that the acceptance of the story in the later Middle Ages reveals a change in the intellectual values of the period. From its first mention in Gildas's early-ninth-century *Historia Brittonum* (on which Geoffrey of Monmouth draws) to its flourishing in the late fourteenth century, the idea of Trojan precedent represents a new historical consciousness, one Ingledew describes as

> associated with an aristocratic and lay cultural environment, at odds with the biblically oriented Augustinian-Orosian paradigm, which instead of claiming birth in Troy, confessed birth in the Fall.[17]

This shift in the paradigm of the historical imagination represents "a return of Virgil" in the Middle Ages insofar as Virgilian modes of narration (understood as the genealogical, the prophetic, and the erotic) were emphasized over Christian modes.[18] As Ingledew argues, "[W]hen the medieval Book of Troy quite distinctively reawakens the [Virgilian] issues of genealogy, prophecy, and eros, it thus opens up the question of history."[19]

History is opened specifically toward the political future through the adoption of this Virgilian perspective; its narrative is one of old empires lost, and more importantly, of new empires won. The return of Virgil, or of the Virgilian mode of historiography, allows for a self-consciously political present, one that looks backward at the past and forward to the future—and that imagines itself in relation to both. From this secular historiographical perspective comes the idea not only of nation but also of empire.

Troy, of course, was never an empire. It was only ever a city-state, its perimeters famously circumscribed by walls. But curiously, it was Troy and not Rome that signified "imperial" for English and French authors alike in the later Middle Ages. This avoidance of Rome, the true empire, in favor of the "false empire" of Troy is crucial to an understanding of the historical imagination of the period. For as this project will discuss, fantasies of empire took ideological precedence over actual military attempts at imperial conquest between 1380 and 1415. When colonializing impulses were manifested—say, for instance, in the English attempts to subdue the Irish, the Welsh, or the Scots—they were supported (and resisted) through reference to historical precedent rather than in the language of imperial right. Indeed, to claim imperial right was to assert dominion over all other states of Europe. This was a step too far for most late-medieval rulers, who tended to concentrate their political efforts regionally and often locally rather than "globally" or throughout Christendom.[20] As Bernard Guenée writes,

> [T]he Emperor claimed to be the heir of Rome. A State that insisted too much on its Roman origins could give rise to imperial claims, . . . whence the hesitation and reticence of the kings of France [or England] for things Roman.

A nation that claimed Trojan origin, on the other hand, "would not yield an inch to another nation, however glorious, on this issue."[21]

And yet it is not only modesty or reticence that kept European states from claiming imperial right over each other; as Guenée's discussion seems accidentally to suggest, the claim on Troy, with its mythic imperial flavor, was a more perfect vehicle than the true empire of Rome for the development of medieval national identity.[22] As we shall see, it is precisely the fantasied quality of Troy as an empire that permits equally fantastic visions of new Trojan greatness and specifically encourages the creation of the idea of England as a nation. The writers of this period, in turning collectively to Trojan stories, help create an empire of English letters that is just as fantasmatic and just as ultimately definitive: the canon of the medieval matter of Troy and, more broadly, English literary history in the later Middle Ages. The "new historicism" of the Virgilian perspective thus created the boundaries for many of the political and disciplinary territories that remain largely definitive today.

James Simpson, however, in an important response to Ingledew's article, points out that late-medieval redactions that respond to the "other book of Troy"—that is, to Guido delle Colonne's *Historia destructionis Troiae* rather than to Geoffrey's *Historia*—do not use a Virgilian template. Guido's text and its fourteenth- and fifteenth-century English translations are, according to Simpson, part of a tradition that is "resolutely anti-imperialistic."[23] This tradition, which includes John Lydgate's *Troy Book, The Laud Troy Book,* and the alliterative *Destruction of Troy,* is

> intensely historical, but history holds no promise of transition from catastrophe to empire; history is instead the story of societies imploding under the pressure of poor decisions and the cumulative weight of events.

These texts, Simpson continues, "are in no way imperialist or propagandistic, not even covertly, not even when they try to be."[24]

But the question of whether Guido's Troy tradition is historical in the Virgilian ("imperialist") sense or historical in the clerical (true?) sense is complicated by the fact that his text is itself a translation of a secular romance. Copying and adapting Benoît de Sainte-Maure's 1160 *Le Roman de Troie* from French verse into Latin prose, while claiming faithfully to follow Dares Phrygias and Dictys Cretensis, Guido's 1287 *Historia* can be considered history only in the most qualified way. Although Dares and Dictys were considered legitimate historians during the period, their texts were later proven forgeries. Even more discrediting, however, is the *Historia*'s false attribution of its source: Insofar as Guido maintains his work to be something other (and especially something more authoritative) than it is, he must be seen as one of the initiators of the propagandistic tradition of Trojan interpretation.[25]

This controversy over true and false histories of Troy resonates in the ongoing discussion regarding the generic, disciplinary, and theoretical boundaries of medieval studies. The vehemence with which these boundaries are asserted and defended both by medieval authors and by their modern readers affords an opportunity to bring some interpretive pressure to bear on medieval notions of historicity as well as on our own assumptions of methodological propriety. Most at stake in this discussion are those concerns created by and around competing definitions of the categories of "history" and "literature." Medieval authors, like modern critics, are careful to distinguish between records of the "truth" of events and their misleading representation in rhetorical figures.

Often, as we see in the example of Guido, historiography's claim to be distinct from false textuality is crucial to its work. The authoritative status of history resides in its ability to convince us that causality flows from its direction: Literature is *its* bastard, in other words, rather than the other way around. Clearly, however, and particularly in the case of the legendary matter of Troy, historiography and literary practice draw on and reproduce many of the same generative assumptions and ideological purposes: Before the dig at Hïsarlik—when, arguably, the facts of a Trojan settlement were brought into contact with mythologies of the place—Troy both was and was not a historical phenomenon. Qualified and contested (as well as rewritten), the "records" of the Trojan War are readerly and writerly texts, sometimes explicitly fictional, often contradicting each other, and always claiming veracity. Histories of Troy frequently use tropes and conventions typically thought to belong exclusively to literary practice (such as nonsequential narrative, character analysis, descriptions of the natural world, and moral exempla), while the poems often pose themselves as witnesses to events, even as unmediated records of experience. It makes sense for us as readers to acknowledge these points of intersection.

Gabrielle M. Spiegel notes although literature and history obviously cannot be approached in precisely the same way, they nevertheless share many features of textuality that have been overlooked by scholars on both sides of the disciplinary aisle. She points out that "historical contexts do not exist in themselves; they must be defined, and in that sense constructed, by the historian."[26] It will not come as news to many of us that history is a motivated textual construct, but it is worth keeping in mind that

> if texts bear within them layers of discursive displacements and heterogeneous meanings, so too does history. Events are not necessarily any more logical, less ridden with contradiction and hidden intentions, than speech or writing.[27]

Literary historians of the Middle Ages would do well to respond to Spiegel's call for a theoretical approach that acknowledges the separate yet interdependent methodologies of historical and literary practice. Rather than granting literature's purely (and merely) reflective status, we might instead probe the ways historiography both calls upon and disclaims mimetic literary genres and devices as its models. I would suggest that we consider the possibility that multiple genres fall under the rubric of historiography and are as varied, overlapping, competing, and difficult to categorize as are the genres that belong to literature. These genres of history, furthermore (and again like their literary counterparts), are defined and contested by parties with a stake in their interpretation.

One way into such an approach is to consider, with Carolyn Dinshaw, how "appropriation, misrecognition, [and] disidentification," terms that queer theory has highlighted in extremely productive ways, "all point to the alterity within mimesis itself, the never-perfect aspect of identification" that obtains equally in both literary and historiographical practice.[28] When Guido tried to pretend that he was engaging in a historical rather than a merely literary enterprise, he was of necessity doing both. But his claim to truth can only be realized (and then only partially and temporarily) through the failure of identification that such a subterfuge attempts to conceal. His attempt to "Other" the discourse of literature reveals the historiographical mode in the process of creating itself. Such attempts at self-definition necessarily require the discrediting of others' attempts to claim authoritative status.

Similarly, much recent scholarly debate on theoretical issues in medieval studies centers on (usually unspoken) assumptions regarding what constitutes a "real" medievalist and what, by contrast, bears the mark of the aberrant, of the false claimant to a true tradition. Like the critical discourse that asserts one state rather than another to be the true inheritor of Trojan precedent, this discourse also is of necessity biased; but it is also central to the formation of fantasmatic territories—in this case the formation of professional boundaries. This discourse of belonging and Otherness is especially pronounced in discussions of the gulf that is assumed to exist (and that participating scholars on both sides insist *must* exist) between historicism and psychoanalysis. As Lee Patterson's recent review of the situation demonstrates,[29] the tone of this debate is noticeable both for its combative quality and also for its "nation-building" impulses; that is, all too often one cannot choose the one approach without losing one's "home," or membership in an intellectual tribe, in the other. One is either a historicist, or one "does Theory." The reductive nature of such a binarism is so obvious (as though historicism were not a theory and as though psychoanalysis were synonymous with theory) that it is shocking not only that we participate in it but also that it is permitted to pass for professional discourse at all. As in medieval debates regarding the veracity of competing claims to Trojan precedent, the motivation for such claims of theoretical exclusivity is transparent, though no less fascinating for that.

My assumption is that historicism and psychoanalysis have much to gain from the other. In the case of Trojan legend in the late-medieval period, the construction of "history" is rooted in fantasies about the past that are continually reconstructed and contested in the present. Psychoanalytic insights about the nature of fantasy, memory, and identity are thus not only relevant but vital for an analysis of the particular stories (or histories) that nations tell about their past. Insofar as the process of remembering or renarrating is a process of becoming, psychoanalysis *is* a theory of history. The central assertion of this book is that representations of the matter of Troy were vital to authorial, regnal, and national identity formation in late-medieval England. Historicism and psychoanalysis are both crucial to the elaboration of this central point, and throughout, I shall interpret from the position that these two central methodologies are mutually formative rather than mutually exclusive.

Narratives that participate in the multiple identifications that constitute Trojanness invoke a number of different modes, or genres, of creative historiography as they link medieval England to its supposedly imperial past and for the sake of its national future. Sometimes specifically invoking Virgil, Geoffrey, and Guido, though just as often disguising their sources, Geoffrey Chaucer, the *Gawain*-Poet, John Gower, and John Lydgate use the Trojan myth to construct versions of their monarchs and also of themselves as specifically English inheritors of the *translatio imperii et studii*. Medieval redactors of Trojan legend transform themselves individually as writers and collectively, as a nation, through reference to the ancient city.

Particularly for Chaucer, whose reputation was very much in flux between the 1380s and the 1420s, "memories" of Troy permit new interpretations of his poetic and political identity, both during his lifetime and afterward. The metaphorical excavation of Troy in the Ricardian and Lancastrian eras locates Chaucer as an *auctor* on the continuum of literary history, but it further invests the nation as the inheritor of a vexed Chaucerian precedent. Digging up Troy in the late fourteenth and early fifteenth centuries not only creates an image of Chaucer that is variously problematic for his later readers but also creates an image of imperial Britain that will continue to haunt even while it defines the collective identity of the English.[30]

Just as important as what late-medieval authors made out of their narratives of Troy, and why they did it, is *how* their textual strategies speak to the operations of the medieval historical imagination. Poets who write about history and historians who narrate the past play in an imagined space between what is necessary and what is hoped for, between generic categories of history and literature, and between chronological categories of past and future. This study will consider these dynamic categories of genre, place, and time under the rubric of utopianism. Like Troy itself, a utopia is a site "with no real place" and yet with "a general relation of direct or inverted analogy with the real space of society."[31] Occupying an unreal space and time, a utopia nevertheless represents, contests, and inverts the real. As Michel Foucault writes, placeless places of this kind are like a mirror, insofar as the play between the real and the not real, as exists in a mirror (or in a narrative), describes identity formation. The subject finds a version of himself through the alienating prospect of utopian representation:

> Starting from this gaze that is, as it were, directed toward me, from the ground of this virtual space that is on the other side of the glass, I come back toward myself; I begin again to direct my eyes toward myself and to reconstitute myself there where I am.[32]

The process of reconstituting identity through narrative is one that shapes not only the observer in his place but the very definition of that place itself.

The literary strategies of the late-medieval historical imagination reconstitute subjects of English identity, and of England as a subject, at a particularly contestatory moment. The late fourteenth century witnessed a large-scale social revolt in 1381, a lingering and seemingly hopeless war with France, and fierce factional struggles in royal politics and London civic government that left many officials exiled or executed. Each of these domestic or international struggles revolved around the concept of English identity: The rebellion of 1381 was not simply a challenge from below to the hierarchical structure of social relations. Instead, it engaged members from every stratum of English society against one another. The war with France was, of course, bound up with perceptions of national identity, and within London and at the court of Richard II, the controversies centered on who rightfully could claim power in the city or access to the king and who on the other hand was a usurper, outsider, or traitor to the kingdom. Following the revolution of 1399, these problems were repeated rather than resolved: Regional rebellion, war with France, and dangerous factionalism returned in the early fifteenth century and came to define the Lancastrians as much as they had marked the Ricardian era.

All parties engaged in these struggles sought to justify their actions by claiming historical precedent. Such instantiations of the historical imagination figure the competing assertions of authorial legitimacy, nationhood, and rule that characterize the Ricardian and Lancastrian era. Crucial within this enterprise is the claim upon Troy. The right to wield its precedent and the operations necessary to reground and justify political motive in relation to an imagined antiquity become in themselves manifestations of a theory of symbolic historiography. To return just for a moment to the nineteenth century: We can readily see how Schliemann's text creates its author through historical reference. But when paired with Freud's response, we might further see how Schliemann's autobiographical impulse—its invocation and analysis of the childhood memory—retroactively confirms the Freudian future. Schliemann's Trojanness, including the search, the joy, the everything, is for Freud a mode of description that makes sense of the emerging discipline of psychoanalysis. Paradoxically, Troy can look forward to the future, can represent its awesome Freudian "etcetera," precisely because of the force of its historicism. In medieval terms, the matter of Troy was crucial for contemporary constructions of Richard II's regnal identity and of Chaucer's poetic legitimacy. But as this project will discuss, it is how these claims on Troy are remembered that defines what comes to be called the Ricardian era and, with it, Chaucerian poetry. Each of the chapters in this book will reflect on the ways in which Trojanness is invoked in the service of national memory and literary history, and the Conclusion will further elaborate the significance of gender as a structuring model for both.

Chapter 1 introduces the extraordinary signifying power of Troy for the late-medieval period by focusing on how London, the new Troy, is imagined as a subject during two discrete moments in the city's troubled history: the Great Rising of 1381 and the 1392 "quarrel" with Richard II. Like several contemporary chroniclers, Gower and Richard Maidstone fashion their city in the image of a sexually misbehaving woman: In Gower's *Vox clamantis,* London is a wanton widow, and in Maidstone's *Concordia,* she is a withholding wife. The charged imagery with which new Troy is described in these texts permits new and often surprising corresponding roles for the men who live in and around the city. The invading rebels, the mayor of London, the aldermen and guildsmen, Richard II's advisers, and the king himself occupy textual positions of exemplary identity in the civic crises Gower and Maidstone address. This productive deviance of Troy as a particularly feminine fantasy space constitutes the textual unconscious of many of the self-historicizing English narratives of the late fourteenth and early fifteenth centuries.

The necessity of Troy's flawed morality frequently, though illogically, is located in the figure of Dido, who is supposed to present an obstacle to European empire and yet is also the means by which that empire is accomplished. Even in the most self-consciously revisionary literary treatments of Aeneas's treason, a remainder—or residue—of this trauma persists, often in the guise of an unfaithful or otherwise sexually dangerous woman. *Sir Gawain and the Green Knight* and Chaucer's *House of Fame* articulate a concern with England's "wounded" Trojan history by revisiting in their respective heroic figures the flaws that accompanied Aeneas's famed settlement of the west. The transgressions of Aeneas, however, are reenacted textually as well as historically: As Trojan liars, traitors, and transgressors of bodies complicate the heroic lineage of Britain, so the translation of ancient *stories* into the medieval present is marred by stained transmitters. The *auctores* themselves are complicit in the transmission of Trojan deviance into an emerging empire of English letters that is always aware of its own literary and historical inadequacy even as it asserts its arrival. The conclusion to the second chapter marks a transition to the project's sustained examination of how medieval redactors of the *translatio imperii* transmit not only their matter but themselves, their monarchs, and their nation into the record. Particularly at stake in this transmission is the reputation of Chaucer and of "his" king, Richard II, both in their own lifetimes and in their Lancastrian afterlives.

Troilus and Criseyde speaks to the seductive impossibility of historical revisionism: The narrator's willful and hopeless belief in an innocent Criseyde figures the contemporary cultural nostalgia (equally fantastic) for a new Troy made clean. Chapter 3 considers Chaucer's meditation on the "moral" and "philosophical" crisis provoked by an awareness of the necessity of history, but it also shows how this crisis is itself necessary to his arrival as the authoritative poetic voice of 1380s London for his present and our future. Whereas here, unlike the abrupted ending of *House of Fame,* Chaucer manages to draw out a conclusion placing himself in the canon of "poesye," the ambivalence with which the poem as a whole announces its *auctor* underscores the point that literary production in new Troy is only possible because of the deviance of its past. The problematic history of Troy, as Chaucer seems to foresee in the end of the poem, is to become his own history, as he and his text come to be glossed in the fifteenth century as Ricardian problems.

Chapter 4 turns to the explicitly politicized and purposefully constructed versions of the Ricardian (and Chaucerian) past produced by Lancastrian sympathizers before and after the revolution. These texts assert specifically English views of history that depend as much on history's recent and flagrant disruption in the usurpation as on any mythic source of empire. This chapter discusses the specter of Troy as a foundational imaginary, a utopian site of longing and fantasy that serves the interest of contemporary political discourse. Gower's *Confessio amantis* and Lydgate's *Troy Book* transmit knowledge of the Ricardian past before and after it happened. More significantly, they invoke this past in their transmission of the Lancastrian empire—and with it, Chaucer's reputation—to our future. At the same time, and with similarly effective results, Lancastrian chroniclers narrate the fall of Richard II as inevitable, historically necessary, and morally justified. His history is, in short, a version of the fall of Troy.

Running throughout the project is a focus on Trojan and post-Trojan women and on their central role as mediating figures in the enterprise of *translatio imperii*. The Conclusion collects and extends the analyses of Helen and Criseyde as "causes" of the fall of Troy, of Dido as a sexual lure for the translation of Aeneas toward his imperial destiny, of Lady Bertilak's and Morgan's roles as obstacles to Gawain and to the Arthurian court, and of London and Anne of Bohemia "under" Ricardian rule. In these cases, as with Lancastrian revisions of them, "~~the~~ woman does not exist" (to borrow Lacan's famous phrase). Rather "she" serves as a means to interpret the past for the purpose of the present: The category of woman not only maintains the illusory distinction between deviant and exemplary narratives, or between false and true stories of Troy, but even creates that distinction for masculinist historiography.

Ultimately, the distinction between true and false versions of the Trojan legend is unhelpful, since, inherently, all versions of it were known to be false (whether acknowledged as such by their redactors or not). For a medieval Christian, the only true history is salvation history, and this view did not change with the influence of Virgil. Furthermore, because Troy was forever gone and buried, never seen (not unlike the position of the medieval period itself from our perspective), its mythic status was heightened. But poets and chroniclers in the late Middle Ages nevertheless found the false, unreal place of Troy useful as an explanatory device. Not despite but because of its admittedly mythic status, Troy was seductive for a range of writers who found its very illegitimacy useful for motivated constructions of English identity.

Our own search, as medievalists, for the truth of the past is a historical exercise not unlike that which looks for Troy. This is not to suggest that the plural (and thus "indeterminate") results of such a search undermine its usefulness—just the opposite. As Kathleen Biddick observes, the alterity of the Middle Ages is such that the period can be "everywhere, both medieval and modern, and nowhere, sublime and redemptive."[33] This utopian vision of the past underscores the wealth of medieval and modern reading practices in creating modes of analysis and in shaping the ways in which such alterity may be understood. Of course, such practices are political and propagandistic insofar as they are inflected by specific circumstances and pressures, but they are also always productive fantasies. In all cases, the return to Troy, whether archaeological, literary, or critical, relies on and creates cultural memory through interpretive acts disguised as (and functioning as) history.

1

Late-Fourteenth-Century London as the New Troy

Nicholas Brembre, former mayor of London and associate of Richard II, was hanged in 1388 after being charged with treason by the anti-Ricardian Lords Appellant. Rumored among his purported crimes, as narrated by Thomas Walsingham in the *Historia Anglicana,* was that he had thought to destroy the name of the Londoners by renaming the city "Little Troy" and that he further had thought to style himself duke of London.[1] The late-fourteenth-century alliterative poem *Saint Erkenwald* uses the name "New Troy" to describe the city's current status as a center of moral virtue and economic success. The anonymous author boasts that, unlike in Saxon times, when the city was the seat of Satan, "[n]ow þat London is neuenyd hatte þe New Troie, / þe metropol and þe mayster toun hit euermore has bene."[2] Whereas Walsingham's comment is made with the benefit of hindsight, written after Richard's party had been defeated, the *Erkenwald*-Poet claims the city's present identification with Troy as evidence for its continuously glorious history (that is, *now* that London is the new Troy, it evermore *has been* a praiseworthy place). These two texts, different in many ways in genre, purpose, style, and date, articulate in their different views of Troy the central problem that is the subject of this chapter. On the one hand a mark of a citizen's capital treason, and on the other a mark of the capital's civic progress, London's Trojan precedent had an extremely ambivalent political currency in the last twenty years of the fourteenth century.[3]

Geoffrey of Monmouth's founding myth implies that new Troy is destined to replicate, and perhaps even surpass, the glory of old Troy.

The *Erkenwald*-Poet's reference to Trojan precedent to justify his claim that London is a "metropol" and a "mayster toun" demonstrates the use value of this Galdfridian version of the Troy myth. But London's attachment to Trojan precedent was complicated by the treachery that, according to medieval versions of the story, undid Troy from within. As D. W. Robertson noted some time ago, England's Trojan origins "provided inspiration, but also served as a warning for the English." Along with the precedent of a grand (though mythic) empire, "it was remembered that Old Troy was burned by the Greeks, having first weakened itself through lust."[4] The Trojans were considered a noble society, but they also were considered lecherous and traitorous; their ultimate defeat was but the natural result of their unnatural desires.[5] The troubling implication of this aspect of the Trojan legacy was that London, too, was full of deviant rulers whose passions would lead to the destruction of the city. The Appellants' charge that Brembre had thought to destroy the name of the Londoners ("nomen Londoniarum delevisse meditatus fuerat") by calling the city "Little Troy" ("Parva Troia") can be seen as a capitalization on this other, unsavory association of Troy with destructive passion and a mobilization of this association for political gain.[6] Although it is impossible to say just what the former mayor hoped to achieve for himself or his king by using the name "Little Troy," or even, for that matter, if he really said it, the volatile signifying power with which the idea of Troy was invested made it possible for Trojan deviance and destruction, and not the glory of a new Trojan empire, to adhere to him.

These two principal Trojan determinations reiterate the split, noted recently by Elizabeth Bellamy, in which the European idea of the *translatio imperii* "represses and flees from the destruction of Troy, even as it nostalgically yearns to recuperate the tragic *Troiana fortuna* into a narcissistic re-vision of imperial 'wholeness.'"[7] The fantasy of imperial wholeness is both permitted and threatened by Trojan precedent, an interpretive impasse that leads to what Bellamy calls the "neurosis" of the latter-day empires self-fashioned in the image of ancient Troy: European imperial identity is forged through the process of rejecting the same Trojan heritage it rests on. Unnatural desire, and especially unnatural sexual desire, not only caused Troy's fall but was also the fortunate flaw that permitted the establishment of later empires. To put this from an English perspective, the fall of Troy is productive, leading to Brutus's voyage and the founding of the new empire. But so, too, is the eastern deviance that caused the fall productive of English political identity. As we see in the case of Brembre, this split in the understanding of Trojan precedent opens up a space of imaginary activity within which multiple and even mutually exclusive possibilities coexist and often clash. Constituting himself in the image of imperialism as the duke of new Troy, the former mayor then was constituted in turn as a deviant traitor to the realm.[8]

But the specter of a grand Trojan empire ruined by passion was not simply a convenient device for the calculated construction of exemplary identities for some and deviant identities for others. It could and often did exceed the realm of its designated use, producing associations of empire and ruination outside their intended targets. What Troy meant for London was split between prophesied glory of empire and doomed destruction by treason and lust. Similarly, how Troy made meaning in London was fragmented by the strategic, controlled uses of its associations, the uncontrollable excesses of these associations, and the inevitable clash these conflicting impulses produced.

This irrepressible volatility stems from Troy's liminal location between history and fantasy. The ultimate unreal city, Troy is (and was) always already obliterated, always only a place-name and never a place. In this way, Troy can be seen as a textual phenomenon, a voided signifier open for multiple re-inscriptions. But at the same time, the ancient city is also designated as a historically and geographically "once real" place. Hovering between historical truth and utter fiction, Troy "exists only retroactively in the imaginations of belated observers."[9] Similar to the status of recovered memories of the primal scene in the context of psychoanalysis, the idea of Troy is more significant for the way it operates than for its actual truthfulness. The reconstructed primal scene is an occasion for interpretation that, regardless of its veracity, produces the truth of and for the subject in analysis.[10]

Invoking London's mythical past by terming the city "New Troy," John Gower's *Vox clamantis* and Richard Maidstone's *Concordia facta inter regem Riccardum II et civitatem Londonie* construct a space that is neither London nor Troy. It is in this fantasy place, where historical memory and imaginative construction vie with one another for such interpretive ascendancy, that translations of identity can occur. Some of the identities constructed and destroyed in Gower's and Maidstone's interpretive texts are obviously motivated and traceable to certain specific political aims, but many are contrary to their own presumed intentions. What makes these "failures" of intended Trojan association productive is that they permit new possibilities of identity that—although presenting a challenge to Gower's and Maidstone's stated ideologies—promise and deliver a release from the writers' otherwise restricted positions. London in disguise as new Troy is a realm that frees political thought to envision the city in ways that had not been possible before.

Both poems specifically address moments of great crisis in London's semblance of civic order. Gower, who lived across the river in Southwark, added Book I as a preface to his already completed *Vox clamantis* shortly after the Great Rising of 1381. Although the rising was spread over a wide area and was diverse in its aims and practices, the siege of London that occurred over the course of three days in June particularly captured the imagination of contemporary observers, whose narratives of events in the capital came to define the rebellion as a whole. Between June 13 and 15, thousands of rebels, primarily from villages in Kent and Essex, converged on the city, where they were joined by even greater numbers of like-minded Londoners. Among their most notorious crimes, the rebels slaughtered Flemings wherever they found them, leaving piles of headless corpses in the streets; they broke into the Tower of London, dragged out the archbishop of Canterbury, and beheaded him; and they burnt John of Gaunt's Savoy palace to the ground. Groups of rebels met with Richard II on three occasions, presenting grievances that were addressed through hastily written charters of manumission (later revoked). Through all of this, London officials were seemingly paralyzed, and they offered little or no resistance to the rebels until the third day of the siege: During a meeting with the king at Smithfield, at which Wat Tyler was slain, the rebels were finally subdued after Richard rode out among them, exhorting them to follow him.[11]

Maidstone, a Carmelite friar,[12] wrote his *Concordia* after witnessing the August 1392 street pageant that celebrated the reconciliation of Richard II with the citizens of London after their so-called quarrel. This quarrel, which probably started over the citizens' refusal to lend money to the Crown, culminated in the king taking away the liberties of the city, arresting the mayor and other city officials, and removing the royal bench from London to York.[13] The quarrel did not end definitively with the pageant, however. Rather, it represents the first serious sign of the irreconcilable differences between Richard II and the city that were to continue to the end of his reign.

At issue in both the 1381 rising and the 1392 quarrel is a compromising of London's cohesive corporate identity. The rebels' physical entrance into the city and the king's abrogation of its freedoms eleven years later were invasions from without that provoked questions about the city's physical and legal integrity. Furthermore, these invasions highlighted the degree of internal cohesiveness, or lack thereof, that characterized the space called "London" in the late fourteenth century.[14] In the case of the rebels' invasion, London's integrity was able to be violated from without because of pervasive divisions within the city walls. The king's invasion in 1392 was prompted by the Londoners' exclusion of him from their benefit, manifested in their unusual show of solidarity in joining together to refuse Richard a loan. The potential conflicts and surprising alliances that contributed to the crises of 1381 and 1392 include those between rival mayoral parties, citizen and noncitizen merchants, freemen and disenfranchised workers, competing guild and trade interests, and the royal court and the citizens, as well as factions within the court. Clearly, talking about London as a unified city-subject is impossible—as impossible as talking about seamless and whole human subjects.[15]

But as theories of psychoanalysis often assert, the fantasy of psychic wholeness is the very thing upon which "real" identity is constructed. In particular, Lacan's understanding of the gendered dynamics at work in the construction of identity asserts that the idea of woman exists to bolster the idea of man as a unified entity:

> As negative to the man, woman becomes a total object of fantasy (or an object of total fantasy), elevated into the place of the Other and made to stand for its truth. . . . The absolute "Otherness" of the woman, therefore, serves to secure for the man his own self-knowledge and truth.[16]

Constructed in language as different and set up as that which man is not, "she" becomes the defining counterpoint for masculine identity and in this way can be said to produce what man is. Such an identity, however, is as fantastical as that which asserts London to be new Troy. Lacan is concerned not with repeating the binary construction of woman versus man but with articulating the triangulation and interdependency that obtain among the categories of woman, man, and fantasy.

Masculine identity, from the point of view of Lacan's work, is always in danger of being exposed as a construction by woman's excessive status insofar as the possibility of something outside the signifying system undermines that system itself and everything constructed in and by it.[17] Like the idea of Troy, the idea of woman is an always voided signifier, one that simultaneously supports and threatens to destroy masculine identity.

Gower's and Maidstone's poems can be seen as engaging the issue of the fantasy of London as an integrated whole. Tellingly, the vehicle that permits fantasies of integration and disintegration is a woman, or rather, an idea of a woman: Gower's new Troy is a widow, and Maidstone's is a wife. London's corporate identity is represented as a woman's corporeal identity. The city is a fantasy feminine body capable of being open or closed, invaded or protected, common or chaste. This city-as-woman offers numerous possibilities for political commentary on the men who are inside or outside "her." The men who enter into London, the rebels in 1381 and the king in 1392, are portrayed in these poems as occupying gendered positions of identity that correspond to the licit or illicit sexual behavior of the city-as-woman. By allegorizing his city as a chaste and vulnerable widow, Gower attempts to smooth over London's internal conflicts in a mirage of completion, to construct cohesive boundaries, and to explain away violations of those boundaries in terms of the sexual impropriety of outsiders. Maidstone's portrayal of London as a penitent spouse attempts to gloss the king as an ideal ruler and to stabilize a political fiasco by translating it into a domestic rift, thereby allowing the relationship between sovereign and city to continue for the benefit of both parties. When these two London writers represent their city as a feminine new Troy, they construct an idea of the city and of the men in it—an ideology of masculine "self-knowledge and truth" based on feminine Otherness—that, when controlled, could produce specific, politically motivated, exemplary, or deviant identities (however temporary and illusory).

But the slippages that accumulate in the process of trying to construct masculine identity in the feminine city generate a host of excessive associations that literally have no place in the ordered schemes favored by Gower and Maidstone. These placeless political associations, generated by the necessarily unstable eroticization of city space, represent utopian possibilities for new forms of civic behavior and identity, a kind of political *jouissance*. Only in the fantasy space of a feminine new

Troy, with the multitudes of unresolved erotic and political associations embedded within it, could these alternative visions of an Other London arise.

GOWER'S UTOPIANISM

The first book of Gower's *Vox clamantis* is a space particularly suited to the entertainment of fantasies and alternative identities. First, Gower's own name is written in a riddle:

> If you should ask the name of the writer, look, the word lies hidden and entangled within three verses about it. Take the first feet from "Godfrey" and add them to "John," and let "Wales" join its initial to them. Leaving off its head, let "Ter" furnish the other parts; and after such a line is arranged, the right sequence of the name is clear.[18]

This rather precious obfuscation of the identity of the poet sets the stage for the more serious confusions of generic identity found in Book I of *Vox:* Gower claims to have had a dream that will "furnish memorable tokens of a certain occurrence" (50), but he then proceeds to narrate some of the events of the 1381 rising as though he had witnessed them personally. Along the way, he invokes elements of classical myth, pastoral idyll, apocalyptic prophecy, beast fable, travelogue, and moral exemplum. Furthermore, he refuses to identify exactly what kind of dream, or vision, or waking nightmare he is having: "In this dream I did not spend the hours which sleep requires, although I do imagine seeing this calamity in my dreams" (95) ("Non dedimus sompno quas sompnus postulat horas, / Tale licet sompnis fingo videre malum").[19]

These confusions of identity, genre, and levels of consciousness contribute to the general sense of nightmarish instability that Gower is trying to invoke, and they have been discussed as aspects of his literary achievement.[20] But the sheer elusiveness of the terminology at work in Book I places both the poem and the poet in a chaos of shape-changes, a place where Gower's stated project frequently eludes him. Between and across the boundaries of the several established genres, as well as between the boundaries of competing authorial personae, curious gaps and symptomatic links emerge to reveal something other than what Gower says he means.

Gower's first fantasy[21] is that England was a paradise before the revolt. The land was fertile, meadows grew with flowers, birds sang with untutored throats, and fountains flowed from brooks, "just like the gardens of Paradise" (52):

> This sole region laid claim to all that land, air and sea fostered and held good. Here was the ornament of the globe, the flower of the world, the crowning glory of things, containing every delight that enjoyment seeks. It was planted with trees, sown with greenery, and surpassing in every gift which man asks for himself. (52)

Exemplifying the perfect accord between man and nature, England is described here as a Cockaignian realm of plenty. The bountiful, open paradise provided its inhabitants with all they could possibly desire.

Moving from a mode of exaggerated pastoral topography to the explicitly fantastic generic structure of a dream vision, Gower begins his discussion of the revolt itself by transforming the rebels into animals. The already unsettled vision narrative is augmented by a perverse catalog in which the rebellious bands are depicted as nightmarish mobs of asses, oxen, swine, dogs, cats, foxes, birds, flies, and frogs. These unnatural beings, neither fully human nor fully beast, trample over the English countryside and ruin everything in their path.

In the course of this generic shift, London is transformed into a feminine new Troy:

> On my right I then thought I saw New Troy, which was powerless as a widow. Ordinarily surrounded by walls, it [she] lay exposed without any wall, and the city gate could not shut its [her] bars. (69)

> A dextrisque nouam me tunc vidisse putabam
> Troiam, que vidue languida more fuit:
> Que solet ex muris cingi patuit sine muro,
> Nec potuit seras claudere porta suas.
> (I, 879–82)

The vulnerable, open widow is caught unawares; "stunned at the coming of such a strange calamity" (70) ("stupet ignotum tale venire malum" [I, 894]), she is defenseless and eligible for the rebels' bestial plunder.

The fantasy of the city as an utterly powerless widow turns the invading rebels into rapists: "[T]he savage throngs approached the city... and entered it [her] by violence" (70) ("adeunt vrbem turbe violenter agrestes, / Et...ingrediuntur eam" [I, 911–12]). The previous description of the rebels as generally brutish is extended here into a realm of ferociously masculine sexuality as the physical bounty of the feminine city is plundered by the animals; the madness "plunged into any—and everything forbidden" (70) ("in vetitum quodlibet ipse ruit" [I, 900]). The initial shape-change of the rebels into animals is revised again as the invaders take on a human, criminal form to correspond with the city's transformation into a vulnerable woman.

This description in *Vox* of the hypermasculine rebels forms part of a contemporary discursive network linking deviant political behavior with deviant sexual behavior and is in accord with a similar tactic used by Walsingham to describe the rebels' entrance into the private apartments of the king:

> Who would believe that peasants, and not just regular peasants, but the lowliest kind, not only in groups, but even individually, would dare to plunge into the bedroom of the king, and that of his mother, with the nastiest of sticks,...and that when they had done all these things (both, like we said, in crowds as well as individually having gone into the rooms), they grew haughty and started sitting, lying, and joking around on the king's bed; then, on top of this, they propositioned the mother of the king with kisses.[22]

The sexual depravity ascribed to the rebels, who are represented here poking their nasty sticks into places they do not belong, is in keeping with other contemporary opinions that asserted the debauchery of the rustics. Walsingham reports that some people, in trying to determine the causes of the revolt, held the peasantry as a whole morally responsible for it because of their generally dissolute way of life. They are said to spend their nights drinking and swearing false oaths ("noctes insomnes in potationibus, ebrietatibus, et perjuriis transigentes"), and their days fighting with each other ("rixando, litigando, cum proximis contendendo").

They are given to wantonness, accustomed to fornication, and stained with adultery ("libidini dediti, fornicationibus assueti, adulteriis maculati"), and finally, their sexuality is bestial. In a significant twist on an old phrase, Walsingham reports that every single one of them "whinnied after" his neighbor's wife: "[U]nusquisque post uxorem proximi sui hinniebat."[23] The chronicler's assertions that people generally had a low opinion of the peasants and that they were associated particularly with sexual wrongdoings place Gower's suggestion that the rebels were animalistic rapists of the chaste city in a tradition of innuendo-laden political discourse.

But the peasants were not the only ones blamed for the revolt. Walsingham also reports that some people thought the rebellion was due to the moral failures of the lords, who provided a bad example for those under them by living in incest and violating the sacrament of marriage ("Alii peccatis dominorum ascribebant causam malorum, qui in Deum erant fictae fidei . . . vivendo incesti, violatores conjugii")[24] That sexually immoral behavior could be blamed for contributing to the Great Rising of 1381 indicates not only how intertwined the two discourses of erotics and politics were but also the extent to which these discourses were widely available for appropriation within and across social boundaries. That is, despite his notorious hostility toward the rebels, Walsingham concedes via these reports that what happened in 1381 may have been partly the result of the misgovernment of the upper tiers of society and not necessarily solely attributable to the generally sinful nature of the lower tiers.

Although Gower explicitly blames the revolt on the innate grossness of the rabble in Book I of *Vox,* he also frequently admits to other causes and thus contradicts the blame he places on the peasants elsewhere in the poem. For example, in the midst of his description of England's perfection before the revolt, when all kinds of birds sang wonderful songs, he notes that

> Philomena recovered her lost property of speech and by her notes proclaimed what had been done. And Procne sang too of her sister's lost virginity—for so great are the tricks in love. (53)

As a demonstration of the triumph of good over evil, no doubt the example of Philomena and Procne is meant to suggest the free-flowing nature of truth before the revolt perverted everything. But it is a particularly unfortunate example, suggesting as it does that reports of a vicious rape and mutilation were declared throughout the supposed paradise. Gower's manufactured "before and after" sequence, the narrative stance that claims to tell an already fulfilled prophecy, requires him to ignore England's prerevolt imperfections even as he discloses them.

The portrayal late in Book I of the postlapsarian England, after the idyllic "second paradise" was ruined by the rebels, further reveals that the country had been imperfect long before the revolt. Gower's presumed point is that the rising corrupted England's "natural" hierarchies of political, social, and religious order. The rebels single-handedly destroyed the place to such a degree that the narrator does not even recognize his homeland. He asks an old man, "Tell me, what island is this?" The man answers by describing the ravaged land, but with a special emphasis on the historical division of the English people:

> This once used to be called the island of Brut, an exile. Diana gave it to him out of pity. The people of this land are wild. Their way of life involves far more quarreling than love. Because this people sprang from different tribes, it has faults of a varied nature. . . . This land, which bloodshed and slaughters and wars always control, was born of mixed stock. The unsightly fields bring forth bitter wormwood, and by this fruit the land shows how harsh it is. (92)

> Exulis hec dici nuper solet Insula Bruti,
> Quam sibi compaciens ipsa Diana dabat.
> Huius enim terre gens hec est inchola, ritus
> Cuius amore procul dissona plura tenet.
> Nam quia gens variis hec est de gentibus orta,
> Errores varie condicionis habet
> . . . .
> Hec humus est illa vario de germine nata,
> Quam cruor et cedes bellaque semper habent:
> Tristia deformes pariunt absinthia campi,
> Terraque de fructu quam sit amara docet.
> (I, 1963–68, 1977–80)

The language here suggests that England's problems are historical, perpetual, and perhaps even genetic. So it is not the case that Gower's

England is a place transformed by the rebellion. Rather, the country was never in accord to begin with. Even Geoffrey of Monmouth's founding myth has a revised emphasis: Instead of a place divinely prophesied to surpass Troy's glory, Gower's England is granted to Brutus out of a gesture of divine pity.

Just as he gives in to this backdating impulse, which allows England's problems to be traced to its very founding moment, Gower admits to additional extenuating circumstances that may be seen to shift the burden of blame away from the rebels. The supposed rapists of new Troy are not simply hypermasculine criminals. Their misdeeds are attributed to deviant feminine sexuality when Gower suggests that the "beasts" are goaded into misbehaving by an evil woman:

> And time and time again the cruel Coppa, following on foot, urged her cock on toward various things which she had an idea were mischievous. The chatterer made up in talk for what she could not do in deeds, and she alone incited a thousand to general wickedness. And when the gander coupled with her, he deserted his own goose and aspired to new game everywhere. (62)[25]

> Multociensque suum fera Coppa pedisseca gallum
> Prouocat ad varia que putat esse mala;
> Quod nequit in factis ex dictis garrula suplet,
> Ad commune nephas milleque sola mouet.
> Ancer et ipse suam, cum qua se miscuit, aucam
> Linquit, et in predam spirat vbique nouam.
> (I, 545–50)

The rapists are the (henpecked) dupes of a monstrous feminine symbol of misrule.[26]

Gower's vision of London as a widow likewise underscores the instability of the commonplace association of political and sexual misbehavior. On the one hand, widows were acknowledged to be an especially vulnerable group in late-medieval London, and special city customs related to their financial protection. But widows were also an important part of the city's economic structure, and they were granted their dead husbands' property and goods not simply out of charity. Instead, they were expected to participate in the economy of the city by continuing their husbands' businesses, often even by becoming members of the guilds to which their deceased husbands had belonged.[27] During this period, the image of an economically independent widow was frequently conflated with the image of a sexually voracious woman (witness Alison of Bath)—an ambivalence that Gower himself had helped to reinforce in his earlier *Mirour de l'omme:*

> But those merry widows—wearing green with little flowers of pearls and embroidery to attract new love affairs to their bedrooms—do not at all resemble the turtledove.... I distrust the old hag who is prettified when her breasts are dried up.[28]

It is this image of the deceitful, sexually consuming widow to which Gower reverts in Book I of *Vox clamantis.* Just as the monstrous rebels are revised into victims of feminine misrule, so too is the victimized chaste city, the widowed new Troy, transformed into a sexually voracious, monstrous woman. London as the new Troy is not vulnerable. She is a lascivious widow who willingly opened her gates for the rebels: "Everything was surrendered. We unlocked our doors to the enemy and faith was kept only in faithless treason" (70) ("Omnia traduntur, postes reserauimus hosti, / Et fit in infida prodicione fides" [I, 903–4]).[29] The moral blame for the rape/invasion thus lies within the city, the erstwhile victim, herself: "O the degenerate nature of our former city, which allowed the madly raging rabble to take up arms!" (71) ("O denaturans vrbis natura prioris, / Que vulgi furias arma mouere sinis!" [I, 979–80]). The indiscriminate city is too common, its entrance open to all.[30]

But Gower's blaming of the victim for her own rape disguises the ultimate target of his censure. London as a defenseless widow should have been protected, and as a promiscuous widow she should have been controlled. The men charged with these duties utterly failed to perform when the moment came:

> No boldness of a Hector or Troilus defeated anything then, but instead those who were defeated suffered the whole affair without courage. Priam did not shine then with his usual honor; instead, the master put up with whatever the servant did to him. (72)

> Hectoris aut Troili nil tunc audacia vicit,
> Quin magis hii victi rem sine corde sinunt;
> Nec solito Priamus fulsit tunc liber honore,
> Set patitur dominus quid sibi seruus agat.
> (I, 993–96)

This pathetic catalog of defeated Trojan War heroes is not so much a lamentation for the loss of the city as it is a condemnation of London's leading men, who are as effectively absent as the widowed city's dead husband.[31] The protectors and controllers of the feminine city failed to do their masculine jobs: "The peasant attacked and the knight in the city did not resist" (71) ("Rusticus agreditur, miles nec in vrbe resistit" [I, 991]). The men in charge of London are, at best, not men.[32]

At worst, though, these unmanly men are traitors. Gower's comparison of the London rulers with notorious traitors from Troy crystallizes the suggestive undertones found elsewhere in the poem into blatant criticism of the upper tiers of English society. Not content merely to emasculate them, Gower likens the rulers to deceitful Trojans who helped destroy their own city:

> Behold, even the old man Calchas, whose wisdom was greater than everyone's, then knew no course of action. Antenor did not know then by what means to arrange peace treaties; instead the great frenzy destroyed all his efforts. (71)

> Ecce senem Calcas, cuius sapiencia maior
> Omnibus est, nullum tunc sapuisse modum:
> Anthenor ex pactis componere federa pacis
> Tunc nequit, immo furor omne resoluit opus.
> (I, 961–64)

Calchas, a prophet who switched sides and joined the Greeks, and Antenor, a self-server who helped the Greeks orchestrate the horse trick, are represented here in surprisingly sympathetic language, as though Gower were unaware of the men's notoriety as traitors.

An even more striking example of the way Gower's Trojan metaphor resists his supposed point is his depiction of the death of Simon of Sudbury, archbishop of Canterbury, at the hands of the rebels. Sudbury is introduced "as if through a symbol" ("quasi per figuram") as "the high priest Helenus, who served Troy's Palladium at the altar" (72). But Helenus not only served the Palladium, he *sold* it to Antenor and Aeneas in an act widely thought to be instrumental in causing the destruction of the city. The rebels charged Sudbury with treason and executed him for it. Gower, surprisingly, reasserts the rebels' interpretation of treason by figuring Sudbury as Helenus.

These and other slippages that occur in Gower's poem make for a confusing and seemingly confused interpretation of the revolt. Troy is a supersaturated symbol with such a wide range of references that it often seems as though Gower sat down to write "Troy style," as though he pulled out some mythological names at random and fit them into his poem without considering what they meant. In addition to this instability of the Trojan overlay, we have noted how Gower's eroticization of the city's relationship with the rebels further contributes to the creation of masculine identities that are far from what we may assume he intended. The poet is at all points undermining his condemnation of the rebels to such a degree that his "mistakes" might be seen as systematic—perhaps unconscious, but with a consistent logic behind them nevertheless. The logic behind Book I is found in the rest of the text of *Vox clamantis,* composed before the revolt.

The "mistakes" in Book I are in keeping with the strategies and motives of the rest of *Vox,* a long-winded poem in which Gower attacks the moral laxity of all the social groups and subgroups of England, but with a special emphasis on the corruption rife among the leadership of the two higher estates. Aligning his authorial persona with the lower classes, Gower claims that his *Vox clamantis,* or "voice of one crying," is a representation of the *vox populi.* His is the voice of the little people, crying out in the wilderness against the injustice of the secular and clerical governors of the country. The passages in Book I that criticize these leaders and that indicate that their perversion contributed to the rebellion are thus not mistakes at all. Instead, they represent a continuation of the moralist's original thesis: that the rulers are primarily responsible for the damage being done to England.

In its call for reform in the upper tiers of society, the bulk of Gower's *Vox* consistently veers toward and draws upon many of the same generative assumptions as do the voices of the rebels themselves. Book I, added as a preface to the poem immediately after the revolt, can be seen as an attempt to address this disquieting similitude by distancing Gower's *vox* from the riotous *vox populi* of the rebels in 1381. Steven Justice, for example, has recently remarked that Gower's depiction of the rebels as beasts in Book I constitutes a "virtuoso mockery" that keeps Gower's own voice from being too similar to theirs. His characterization of them as "hopelessly undiscursive" successfully "erases any trace of verbal performance on the part of the rebels and disembarrasses Gower's own claim—to represent the popular voice—of a discrediting similarity."[33] But Book I is a compensatory act in the extreme and, like all compensatory acts, embarrassingly traceable in its intent. The many slips that accompany Gower's attempts to discredit the rebels are equally significant for the way they reveal his strategy of self-justification as a social critic.[34]

Until the revolt presented him with an opportunity to identify with his audience of outraged and victimized Londoners, Gower had been squarely on the outside of the contemporary political scene. Not only did he live in Southwark, a place that functioned as "a dumping ground and exclusion zone for early modern London,"[35] but he was ideologically in the suburbs as well. *Mirour de l'omme* and *Vox clamantis* often seem like the same poem written in two different languages: They both catalog the sins of the estates, with variants, examples, and correctives. They both argue that English social life should return to its moral center, obey its time-honored hierarchies, and stop deviating from the old, good ways. The man Chaucer called "moral Gower" seems to have been fond of announcing the same moral perspective, repeatedly, over a number of years; there was no currency to his message. But with the outbreak of the revolt, suddenly this message reads less like outdated moralism and more like dangerously relevant social criticism. Depicting himself wandering across the countryside hiding from the violent mob, Gower elaborates on his difficult position:

> I was not at liberty to confide secrets to anyone; on the contrary, my silent lips withheld their words.... Whenever I was on the point of speaking, I considered myself to be in ambush; and looking upon the ground, I uttered only a few words. When my lot forced me to say something to somebody, I passed the time idly with glib talk. Again and again a soft answer turned away wrath, and my very safety depended upon agreeable words. (82)

> Non michi libertas cuiquam secreta loquendi
> Tunc fuit, immo silens os sua verba tenet.
> . . . .
> Memet in insidiis semper locuturus habebam,
> Verbaque sum spectans pauca locutus humum:
> Tempora cum blandis absumpsi vanaque verbis,
> Dum mea sors cuiquam cogerat vlla loqui.
> Iram multociens frangit responsio mollis,
> Dulcibus ex verbis tunc fuit ipsa salus.
> (I, 1493–94, 1505–10)

But Gower is not afraid of the rebels here; he is afraid for the reception of his *Vox* after the revolt, when his customary blaming of the two higher estates is no longer a tired truism but is instead dangerously seditious, in accord with what the rebels themselves had been saying. By publishing *Vox* anyway, with Book I added as a lubricating preface, Gower takes the risk of establishing himself as a voice crying out for good reason—and as a social critic who is not behind the times but painfully in tune with them. The revolt permits Gower to speak, for once, with real contemporary relevance.

With a renewed sense of being called, Gower constructs himself as a prophet and a leader at the end of Book I of *Vox*. Just as Cassandra's unheeded prophecy about Troy came true, so had Gower's own warnings (in his earlier poetry, including the bulk of *Vox clamantis*) about the impending doom of new Troy fallen on deaf ears. His prophecy having been fulfilled in the form of the revolt, Gower boldly ventures to offer himself as a moral leader: Fleeing the burning new Troy in a ship, buffeted by storms "more grievous than Styx" (85), passing by a sea monster "brother to Scylla, raging more than Charybdis" (87), losing the steersman (87), and finally putting in at an unrecognized but eerily familiar place (92), the poet figures himself as a type of Aeneas.

But just as Aeneas initially met with opposition in Italy, so does Gower's leader persona see that he has a lot of work to do to renew England. Coming out of his dream, and with a new sense of the importance of his mission, he sets his sights on writing for the sake of the new society:

> O wakeful sleep, whose difficult meaning my writings must now tell! . . . Let the task of long standing which is wontedly mine now yield, and let my former care be banished by this new one. (95)

O vigiles sompni, quorum sentencia scriptis
Ammodo difficilis est recitanda meis!
. . . .
Quod solet esse michi vetus hoc opus ammodo cedat,
Sit prior et cura cura repulsa noua.
(I, 2145–46, 2149–50)

Although Gower is not writing anything new (it is still the same old *Vox,* after all), he is reinterpreting how his work should be read: The long *Vox clamantis* is, according to the postrevolt Gower, a manual of advice for the postrevolt England. Similarly, Gower's authorial persona is no longer that of a single voice crying (unheeded) in the wilderness of Southwark. His is a London voice bravely crying for obviously necessary social reform.

Gower's social criticism, like the rebels' own demands for change, rests on a backward-looking idealism and imagines a future defined by an illusory golden age of relations between and among the estates. The vision of the future is an idealized fantasy of the past, when kings were kings (and neither besotted old men nor boys) and knights were knights (and not traitors), when the rulers of the country were responsible for and protective of the people under them, and when the clergy was not made up of mercenaries, buying and selling their offices. Gower has not succeeded in erasing any of these retro-radical ideas from his poem. On the contrary, his addition of Book I to *Vox* reasserts the need for radical reform and ultimately serves to reassert the rebels' grievances.[36] It is in this sense that Gower's political vision is utopian: Not despite but because of the rising of 1381, the retrospective idealism of *Vox clamantis* becomes a plausible plan for the future.

Ricardian Imperialism Yields to Rome

Eleven years later, political and social conditions had not improved along the lines Gower had called for. As chapters 3 and 4 will discuss in more detail, the 1380s and '90s witnessed continued violence and discord in London, fierce factional struggles and vindictive squabbles among civic and royal government officials, and—from Gower's disappointed perspective—the maturation of Richard II from a boy king with great promise to a willful, embattled, and erratic ruler.[37] A prominent example of Richard's difficult later years is the quarrel he had with the city of London when the citizens refused to lend him large sums of money. The king retaliated by suspending the city's customary freedoms, removing the mayor and the sheriffs of London from their offices and putting them in jail, and replacing them with men hand-picked by himself to act as wardens and keepers of the city. He imposed huge fines on the city for mishandling its affairs and finally placed the "entire income" of London at his own disposal.[38]

In August 1392, the citizens of London put on a sumptuous pageant in an effort to convince Richard to relent and restore their customary liberties. The pageant was wildly extravagant: The conduits flowed with white and red wine, the streets were decorated with banners and flowers, and parades of guildsmen and city officers in costume turned out to greet the king. Expensive gifts were lavished on Richard and his wife, Anne of Bohemia, and a tableau of John the Baptist in the wilderness and a chorus of angels were staged for the king's pleasure, all at considerable cost to the Londoners.[39]

Richard Maidstone's *Concordia facta inter regem Riccardum II et civitatem Londonie,* written and dedicated to Richard II in 1393, records the events of the pageant as though the author had witnessed them in person. Unlike Gower, Maidstone claims his poem to be an account of what actually happened, not a dream or an explicitly fantastic space. The *Concordia* emphasizes the enthusiasm of the Londoners for their task and Richard's goodness and grace in accepting their apologies. The author's perspective is that of a loyalist to the king, a view announced in his dedication: "O Richard, as you are allied to me by the double bond of name and authority, I am impelled by Friendship and honored to recount for you in meter the splendid sights which I beheld of late in Trenovant."[40] Maidstone's poem thus declares itself a celebratory narration of an exemplary moment in the relationship between city and sovereign. The king is "more handsome than Paris," "peace-making, clement, and careful to destroy nothing good" (167). London is decorated in splendid finery as the "entire city unites" (171) ("tota cohors sociatur")[41] to greet its king.

Like Gower before him, Maidstone calls on a sexualized metaphor to describe the relationship between new Troy and the men in the city. The pageant celebrates the reunion of Richard and London as husband

and wife. Richard's is an idealized masculine identity in relation to this city-as-woman, which is portrayed here as one who erred against her lord by refusing him services. In keeping with Maidstone's allegiance to Richard, London's misbehavior—and not the king's—caused the "bridegroom to forsake his bridal chamber" (167) ("desereret thalamum sponsus ut ipse suum" [24]). But because of the city's fine display, lavish gifts, and demonstration of utter subjection to Richard, he now desires to come again to his spouse.

When Richard, the groom inclined but not yet committed to forgiveness, comes (in)to his chastened, decorated bride, he is presented with the emblematic sword and keys of London—tokens signifying his right to enter the city, his wife, whether by force or by consent, respectively. Upon presenting the king with these patently phallic symbols, the keeper of the city says to him, "Let not the most beautiful walls in the kingdom be rent nor torn, for they are the king's own and whatever is in them" (181) ("Non laceret, non dilaniet pulcherrima regni / Menia, nam sua sunt, quicquid et exstat in hiis" [145–46]). The keeper's words suggest that the city walls constitute a "vaginal symbol" complementing the phallic tokens of entrance presented to the king, thereby showing Richard that he is entitled to London's goods and services just as a husband is entitled to sex with his wife under the terms of the marital *debitum* (debt). Acknowledging that the king can enter his wife with or without her consent, the city here asks not to be raped.[42] To reinforce the image of the city's sexual submissiveness, the gifts she gives are announced as signs "that the citizens now yield themselves—bodies, riches, the Trojan citadel, their all" (189) ("dantur in hoc signum quod se reddunt modo cives— / Corpora, divicias, Pergama, queque sua" [213–14]).

Anne of Bohemia's role in the pageant further demonstrates how a good wife ought to behave with her king. The queen models an ideal of civic behavior by throwing herself at the king's feet and begging for the city to be forgiven: "'Beloved,' she says, 'my king, my spouse, my strength, my life... who among all kings possesses a city that has honored him like this one this day?'" (217). The king responds to the pleas of his queen and declares himself ready to forgive London her waywardness. The citizens, taking their cue from Anne, then fall to their knees rejoicing and praising Richard: "Long live the king! May the king live forever!" (225). The celebratory narrative concludes with the citizens united in posture and in speech, all agreeing that to be subject to Richard is to be fulfilled.

Maidstone's poem demonstrates to the king that the citizens accept his authority wholly and that his identity as a masculine ruler is secure.

But of course the Londoners are not putting on this dramatic display of abjection unprompted. Their liberties having been removed (along with their elected officials and their legal means of redress, the royal court) and under threat of even greater violation and restriction, the citizens are participating in what Louise Fradenburg calls a communitarian experience: a ritual that "helps to obscure constraint" through "a remaking of the subject to enable identification with, and idealization of, an authority experienced as liberating and unifying rather than repressive and divisive."[43] The remaking of the subject of authority is evident in the pageant when throngs of notoriously competitive guildsmen join together in one parade:

> Here are the Silversmiths, the Fishmongers, and beside them are the Mercers and the Vintners; here the Apothecaries, the Bakers, the Painters, and the Masons; here the Cutlers, Shearers, and Armourers; here the Carpenters, the Tailors, the Menders.... Each guild is clearly delineated by its own livery. Whoever should witness these squadrons, I think, would not doubt that he was seeing the forms of an angelic order. (173–77)

As recorded in the *Letter-Books,* however, guildsmen in the victualling trades were famously opposed to their counterparts in the nonvictualling trades, and vice versa—a relationship symbolized by the fierce competition and often violent strife during the early and mid-1380s between Mayor Brembre, who was a grocer, and his arch-rival, Mayor John Northampton, a draper.[44] The pageant's collection of bakers and vintners marching alongside painters and masons, and fishmongers alongside mercers, although not impossible to imagine, constitutes an unusual and purposeful alliance.[45]

The guildsmen's unity is matched by other unlikely social and political unions: Men and women parade together, leading citizens and aldermen brush shoulders with a criminal from Southwark (185–87), and "every order" of "the clergy of the entire church" (169) forms in procession. Separate and often hostile bands of Londoners reconstruct themselves here as loving subjects of the king. In this way, the pageant does "essential work for sovereign love"; as Fradenburg notes, such spectacles are "a way of securing desire for hierarchy."[46] Richard operates as a source of unifying pressure on the Londoners. His threats to their autonomy impel them to put aside their differences, however temporarily, and show themselves to the king as his faithful subjects.

At the same time that the Londoners' identities are being transformed by the obligatory *communitas* of the pageant ritual, however, they are also working to transform Richard's identity. Communitarian experience helps shape the *object* of sovereignty as well as its subjects and should be thought of as a form of interpellation that not only calls the citizens loving subjects but also calls Richard a deserving object of that love. In other words, the apparently spontaneous demonstration of the citizens' affection for the king is not so much a record of their love as it is a construction of Richard as a lovable king, and the narrative of this demonstration is likewise not so much a record of the past as it is a prescription for the future. The orderly unity and easy compliance of the once riotous and willful city exerts pressure on the king to respond in complementary fashion. By playing the role of a wayward but penitent wife, the city invites Richard to play a stern but forgiving husband in language often bordering on a command: "Let not the bridegroom hate the bridal chamber which he has always loved" (181) ("Non oderit thalamum sponsus quem semper amavit" [147]).[47] The pageant constructs an ideal identity for the king through its elaborate insistence that he is not a tyrant: He *will* be forgiving, and he *will* give them back their liberties, because, as everyone knows and says, he is just, fair, and good.

In Maidstone's account of the happy ceremony, the feminine space of the city is used to construct an exemplary regnal identity for Richard.[48] He can be all forgiveness and love as long as the city is all culpability and humble remorse. The Londoners' demonstration of their desire and their entreaties for his forgiveness—mirrored in and augmented by the tableau of Anne on her knees—help create the king as a paragon of masculine virtue. He loves and respects his wife and his city, and he will forbear. Through the use of the metaphor of sexual relations, Maidstone shows the city applying the gentle pressure of abjection in an effort to influence the man with the power that no one disputes or resents.[49]

This interpretation, however, ignores the wider array of choices available to both women and cities in the late-medieval period. On the one hand, as Fradenburg notes, the city is "created" by the king (in the sense that he grants its privileges) and is therefore dependent on the aristocratic order. But the city is equally defined by its separateness from that order:

> The gift given to the city by the king is the gift of difference: the city is demarcated, contained, and inside it special activities are pursued. The creation of the city is thus an act of divisiveness.[50]

The problem with women and cities is that they had an unsettling "margin of freedom" within which to bestow their goods. They could trade as *femmes sole* (single women) without their husbands; buy, sell, and profit on their own; sue and be sued independent of their husbands; train their own apprentices, and participate in their own mysteries. As Caroline Barron notes, the balance of power in marriage would correspond to these economic realities.[51]

If we see London, the feminine city, as a woman engaging in business—a wife who has something Richard wants and needs—then the tenor of the extreme lavishness of the pageant is quite changed. It becomes not an apology for her own bad behavior but instead a show of wealth, a powerful display of the wares she could choose to bestow, if *Richard* were to behave properly. Although Barron is careful to distinguish between economic and political power, arguing that the possibilities of increased status for London women "were entirely economic and in no way political,"[52] there is a convincing argument for the conflation of the two on the symbolic level. In the narrow context of participating in civic government, holding ward office, or any of the other privileges afforded to freemen of the city, of course Barron is right: Women did not participate in London's governance. But as the case of the quarrel between London and Richard shows, economic power is a representational form of political power. The citizens' refusal to lend money to the Crown, money that they had available to lend, was a political act; it was an assertion of their independence from the king.[53]

The parades of impressively organized and outfitted guildsmen, for example, emphasize not only the economic productivity of the city but also its own internal hierarchical structures, which compete with the hierarchy of subject to king, city to sovereign.[54] Moreover, there is a martial quality to the "mighty force" of the guildsmen, arranged in "squadrons," each guild like a "phalanx" (177) ("tam valido" [99], "turmas" [97], "phalangas" [101]). This language suggests that the guildsmen, with their considerable economic power, are setting off to do battle with an enemy—not to meet a husband on their knees. The parade represents a threatening force. As Maidstone acknowledges, the guildsmen are fully capable of destroying what gets in their way:

> First one guild and then another wends its way back to the city: the road was scarcely sufficient for such an army. Throng presses on throng—here a man lies thrown to the ground, there one falls, here one collapses. (185)
>
> Illa prius, hec posterius ars, tendit ad urbem:
> Vix exercitui sufficiebat iter.
> Turba premit turbam—iacet hic, ruit hic, cadit ille.
> (169–71)

The intimidating and even dangerous unity of the guildsmen, finally, is exactly that which threatens Richard, since the problem leading to the quarrel in the first place was the "entire city uniting" to refuse the king his loan. The show of unity during the pageant thus could easily be interpreted as a taunting gesture that demonstrates to Richard just how united the citizens can be, whether in acquiescence or in opposition to his desires.[55]

Further unruliness in the feminine space of the city is revealed in Maidstone's comment on a group of ladies whose cart turns over during the procession:

> When one of the ladies thereupon exposed her womanly thighs, the people scarcely were able to hold back their laughter. And that fall is pleasing; may it come to pass, I pray, what that fall signifies to me: All extravagance and cupidinous love will tumble down. (193)
>
> Femina feminea sua dum sic femina nudat,
> Vix poterat risum plebs retinere suum.
> Casus et ille placet; veniat, rogo, quod michi signat:
> Corruat ut luxus et malus omnis amor.
> (253–56)

Two seemingly opposed interpretations of the exposure of women's bodies are offered here: that of the people on the street and Maidstone's own. But they really are not all that different, for both ultimately approve of the uncontrollable sexuality represented by the glimpse of intimate flesh. The Londoners' raucous laughter and Maidstone's remarkably contrived moralization both call the fall pleasing. London's unseemly "extramarital" sexuality continues to thrive in the midst of the official wedding ceremony and suggests that there are a host of alternative arrangements possible between men and women and kings and cities.

Anne's model behavior can likewise slide into something other than a show of submissiveness. The queen interprets the symbols of the pageant and the behavior of the citizens and tells Richard that they honor him. On her knees, she occupies the position of moral authority over her husband. As the keeper of the city remarks, "What a man does not dare, the woman alone can" (213) ("Quod vir non audet, sola potest mulier" [442]). Paul Strohm is right to point out that "the actual thrust of her speech is practical and advisory" and that Anne is "anything but abject"[56] when she suggests to Richard that it is "acceptable now to return the city's ancient rights and to restore its liberties" (219). The queen's important role in the pageant as a successful intercessor discredits the very form of institutionalized subservience in marriage that the pageant is supposed to celebrate, and it further suggests that if Anne is a model for the city's behavior, London might similarly advise Richard as to what to do and why.

Anne's prominent role as intercessor between Richard and his city/bride involves the queen in a complicated dynamic: She gives her husband a second wife, effectively acting as a bawd by arranging services for him. In a triangulated exchange of procurement, the keeper of the city gives Anne gifts of considerable expense and asks her to be the broker of the new relationship between her husband and another "woman," London. These unsavory sexual undertones are the by-products of Maidstone's attempts to construct Richard as a masculine ideal in relation to an imperfect feminine city. Competing with the poem's portrayal of a just and good husband and king is the image of a sexual deviant, even a criminal.

The queen's beauty is praised by Maidstone with a choice of metaphor reminiscent of Gower's unhappy example. Here, as in *Vox clamantis,* the invocation of Trojan precedent causes more interpretive trouble than it resolves: "Very beautiful herself, she stands surrounded by beautiful maidens; the New Troy conquers under these Amazons" (179) ("Pulchra quidem pulchris stat circumcincta puellis; / Vincit Amazonibus Troia novella sub hiis" [123–24]). Anne as an Amazon allied with new Troy is probably a figure for Penthesilea, the warrior queen who came to the aid of the Trojans. With the introduction of this metaphor, Richard, who is supposed to appear in the poem as a patient and ultimately just ruler, is suddenly on the wrong side of the Trojan War. His intervention in London's autonomy is likened to the Greeks' invasion of Troy. Maidstone produces an upside-down revision of the battle between the Greeks and the Trojans in which Richard comes into new Troy and is conquered, defeated by a woman warrior in league with an impressive civic army.

Maidstone's depiction of a perverse imperialism, defined by the adherence of Ricardian deviance to what is supposed to be an image of new Trojan glory, is further elaborated by reference to Rome, that other locus of civic glory and the true empire stemming from the fall of Troy. Drawing a false comparison between Richard's treatment of new Troy and fair rule in Rome, Maidstone notes that "[l]ike Rome, London is ruled by these men [the aldermen] in accordance with the senatorial law, and a mayor, whom the people elect, presides over them" (173) ("Iure senatorio urbs hiis regitur quasi Roma, / Hiisque preest maior, quem populus legerit" [73–74]). But London at this moment was of course *not* ruled by its elected officials, since the king had replaced them with his own men. Maidstone's "comparison" thus serves instead to contrast the ideal of elected, senatorial rule with the actual practice of Richard's tyranny and suggests that Ricardian London represents not a fruition of destined glory but rather a regressive episode.

Far from congratulating Richard for his wisdom and good governance, the *Concordia* instead is warning a deviant king to look to the future of his city and perhaps to that of his own reign. The poem's allusions to post-Trojan history place Richard along a continuum of noble descent that compliments his lineage even while anticipating a future without him. The ambivalence of imperial chronology is indicated in the words of the keeper to the king:

> Since you take after your father, you have brought to the name "Richard" whatever was honorable. Thus, from excellent kings and noble forbearers noble offspring follow. Destiny gave as was fitting. (209)

Prole patrissante, "Ricardi" quod fuit ante
Nomen, adhuc repetit quicquid honoris erat.
Regibus ergo probis patribusque bonis bona proles
Successura fuit; sors dedit ut decuit.

(399–402)

While filling the name "Richard" with idealized content, the keeper simultaneously puts Richard in his (chronological) place. The king with great ancestors (and incidentally, without heirs)[57] will soon enough be a memory himself.

Anxieties over treacherous precedents and usurping rulers underlie the terms of the quarrel between the king and the Londoners. Richard was extraordinarily careful to adhere to protocol and to established legal procedures when he moved against the city, suggesting that he was very much aware of the validating function of precedent and that he knew he might need to call on it to justify his actions.[58] His final speech in Maidstone's poem focuses on his willingness to return to the old ways and further indicates that he had always practiced the ancient customs until the Londoners violated them: "You shall administer this city according to the ancient laws. As long as justice exists in not changing the customary way, let what was lawful before be so now" (225) ("Legibus antiquis hanc regitote plebem. / Antea quod licuit, liceat modo, dum tamen equm / Extiterit solitum non variando modum" [534–36]). Richard's idealized vision of civic history pretends an ancient absence of conflict between city and sovereign and obliquely asserts that London's newly deviant behavior, rather than his own, is responsible for initiating the quarrel.

Maidstone's account of the king's "primal scene," in which Richard (falsely) remembers London as perpetually obedient, depicts a willful reinterpretation of the past designed to permit the future everyone desires. Of course the citizens wanted their liberties restored, but Richard, in turn, needed London in the 1390s, and he especially needed the economic potential of this profitable spouse at his disposal.[59] The *Concordia* presents an image of how a good city could behave with a good king, and it rather generously glosses Richard on his best behavior. But the poem also shows the full capability of either party to deviate from the mutually beneficial relationship. Through the metaphor of marital roles,

Maidstone's text revises civic roles to allow London her independent profit-making abilities "under" the king. This new dynamic for city-sovereign, wife-husband relations is one that puts on a display of traditional feudal and baronial ties in order to achieve a return to modern business as usual—business that is good for everyone.

The *Concordia,* dedicated and presumably presented to the king in 1393, shows Richard how he can relent with his dignity intact and get his money, too. But by describing the pageant as that which ends the quarrel and reconciles the king with his city, Maidstone is engaging in a bit of premature representational closure. The quarrel did not end until 1397, when Richard finally restored the liberties of the city *in perpetuum,* after having kept them predicated upon his own interpretation of the citizens' good behavior for five years. The poem's premature resolution of the quarrel is perhaps an indication of a wishful fantasy closure, but it also functions as a form of symbolic pressure in itself.[60] Reminding Richard of his precarious position along the continuum of imperial history, the poem presents the king with a prognostic record of his own best policy already enacted—and suggests that he follow it. But as we shall see in the following chapters, Richard II's relationship with London was to follow quite another script.

Before the Lancastrians' ultimate revision of Ricardian London, however, Gower and Maidstone imagine the city as a place of possibility. "Remembering" the precedent of Troy in both its glory and its deviance and relying on the similarly split image of woman as both idealized and debased, these two poets envision the city of London as its fantastic Other, the feminine new Troy. Their figuration of London in the future perfect constitutes a utopian historiography, one that depends upon, even as it condemns, the generative, productive deviance of the past.

2

Arthur's Court and Britain's House of Fame

The versions of London as the new Troy found in *Vox clamantis* and the *Concordia* serve as two discrete instances of the operation of the medieval historical imagination. Prompted by the political disruptions of 1381 and 1392, respectively, Gower and Maidstone re-imagine contemporary events and persons in relation to ancient Troy and, in the process, re-imagine themselves as social poets. Although they are to varying degrees coy and cautious in this role, both consciously participate in late-fourteenth-century London political life. Chaucer's *House of Fame* and the anonymous *Sir Gawain and the Green Knight,* on the other hand, are more concerned to develop and to play with history as a theoretical concept: Each embeds an ancient myth within a frame that explores how narratives of the past are transmitted into the discursive systems of the present and how these already worked-over narratives then face an uncertain projection into the future as authoritative discourse.

The theoretical nature of these texts does not make them any less significant for our understanding of the contemporary scene in new Troy. Instead, Chaucer and the *Gawain*-Poet offer intellectually dense and emotionally nuanced responses to the trauma of history in their own moment. The two poems raise questions about the many possible definitions of authority and purposes of textuality and, as the conclusion to this chapter will show, thereby implicate themselves in the cultural and textual environments of the later fourteenth century.

House of Fame and *Sir Gawain and the Green Knight* suggest that the route of transmission of ancient narratives is a circuitous one masquerading as a line of descent and that the terms that serve to separate the authentic from the imposter (such as "storie" and "fable") are subject to motivated readings and misreadings.[1] The corresponding validity of chronological descent is also thrown open for reconsideration. The supposedly authoritative past is as subject to projected fantasies as is the usually discredited present, which, in turn, becomes the launching area for competing fantasies of the future.[2]

Aeneas's ghost lurks productively in the background of both poems, driving their literal progress: His famous journey westward is refigured in the movements of Geffrey and Gawain. The process from Troy through Carthage to Rome and beyond (via Brutus's translation to Britain) is recapitulated in Geffrey's dream-and-eagle transport from London to Venus's temple, through Fame's castle and on to the wicker house of tidings. Likewise, Gawain's journey from Camelot through the wilds of Wales to Bertilak's castle and on to the Green Chapel is an echo of his famous ancestor's odyssey. Finally, both Geffrey and Gawain return at the end to their starting points, their origins, from which the "real" journey, that of narrating the past, begins. As with Aeneas, the protagonists of these two Middle English poems find their greatest adventures in narrative; but as was also true in the *Aeneid,* the occasion for narration in both texts is necessarily marked by the treachery that inevitably accompanies cultural translation.

As Gawain's physical journey and Geffrey's dreamed progress retrace the steps of Aeneas, so do the poems themselves retrace the texts of the *translatio imperii* from Troy to Britain. Attaching their narratives to the list of literary authorities who came before them, including Virgil, Ovid, Geoffrey of Monmouth and his followers Laȝamon and Wace, Guido delle Colonne, and a number of unnamed "olde bokes," the narrators of *House of Fame* and *Sir Gawain and the Green Knight* self-consciously return to a past that already has been told. This backward-moving adventure, a textual odyssey that revisits and revises the past, is at once a self-authorizing and self-destructive expedition. The act of attaching oneself to the fame of Aeneas or to the fame of earlier Trojan narratives paradoxically authorizes one's own journey or narrative while simultaneously ensuring its status as an imposter.[3]

Medieval adventurers and narrators, whose progress is always in the wake of the glory of their Trojan and post-Trojan predecessors, face the problem of the ignobility of these same predecessors. The figure of

Aeneas in the Middle Ages was invested not only with his personal heroism and political and nationalistic success but also with deceit, treason, and sexual transgression.[4] Likewise, textual treatments of Trojan legend typically were viewed as unreliable, mutually contradictory, and politically motivated even as they were accepted as foundational. To revisit such texts is to struggle between the suppression of Trojan deviance and the reenactment of Trojan glory, but it is also, at best, to subject one's own text to misreading and, at worst, to guarantee its placement in a long line of compensatory poetry and prose that in seeking to overcome its traumatic foundation, inevitably reinforces it.

This textual lineage (or rogue's gallery, as Chaucer imagines it in the *House of Fame*) is of course the canon, that vexed and vexing body of "seminal" texts said to contain and transmit the authority of the past. As these two Middle English poems demonstrate, issues of canonicity, such as which texts qualify for entry and why, and who decides, were as complicated and as politically charged in the late fourteenth century as they are today. Then as now, hostile or frustrated responses to the perceived ossified nature of the canon inevitably end up as part of it—proving, of course, that it is precisely the dynamic aspect of canonicity that is so troubling. Michel de Certeau expresses the mutually dependent relationship between old and new narratives when he notes that "the trace, or the 'wound,'" of objectionable material in a body of knowledge (for example, the "canon" of Trojan legend) functions like a grain of sand in an oyster: It "irritates" new texts into being.[5] In this case, the trouble with Aeneas, and with texts about Aeneas, aggravates or incites post-Trojan texts that are themselves stained, or "wounded," by their heritage. As de Certeau writes, a wounded origin "can only be 'represented' by a discourse that in turn is wounded," thus prompting even more proliferation of compensatory texts.[6]

Geffrey's and Gawain's respective journeys to what they think is a definitive endpoint articulate this problem: Both conclude with the frustrating realization that the perversion of truth is the necessary concomitant to fame. Geffrey's unsatisfying search for the real locus of tidings is promised, deferred, disappointed, and finally and permanently curtailed at the moment of its greatest (though illusory) possibility, when the "man of gret auctorite" appears on the scene only to end the poem. Gawain's mission to the Green Chapel ends with a series of riddles in place of the expected revelation: The Green Knight was not the Green Knight, just

Bertilak testing Gawain. Bertilak was not testing Gawain; Morgan le Fay was. Morgan was not interested in testing Gawain after all; she only wanted to scare Guenevere. Geffrey's and Gawain's quests re-present, rather than address or solve, the instability and the questions that provoked them in the first place, particularly insofar as both protagonists' narratives of themselves are destined to be misread in the future. These journeys are those of their creators (and their creators' predecessors) writ small: Medieval redactors of the Trojan legend project themselves into the past and find nothing but themselves and their own textual practices to transmit to the notoriously unfaithful future.[7]

Jacques Derrida's playful interpretation of a postcard's illustration of Socrates and Plato suggests that intellectual legacies flow in a surprising chronology—not really even backward, but circuitously from the present to the past and then "back" to the future. In Derrida's example of this process, Plato has not simply recorded Socrates' wisdom and shared it with posterity. Instead, "plato has made Socrates write whatever he [Plato] wanted while pretending to receive it from him."[8] Plato is in this sense the author of Socrates' "message," not its receiver, since,

> if to plato, his addressee, Socrates had addressed some message, it is also that plato would have had to be able to receive, to await, to desire, in a word to have called in a certain way what Socrates will have said to him, and therefore what Socrates writes.[9]

The future audience, or addressee, of a narrative thus pre-interprets what is written. To put it another way, the future anticipates, and even creates, the textual authority of the past.

Narrators and "authors" of adventures—whether to Fame's castle or to Bertilak's—insist on being misread at the very moment of claiming authenticity. Geffrey wakes up after a strange dream and, inspired to write it down, sends out his interpretation for a certain kind of reader: One he presumes will pervert his meaning. Gawain comes back to Arthur's court after his strange journey and is expected to recount for the knights of the Round Table what happened to him and what it means. Interpreting and misinterpreting the signs of his experience, he narrates a story of himself that is destined to be misread by his audience of willful courtiers. Sending out letters of themselves, under the guise of (dutifully or merely) retelling a received history, Geffrey and Gawain construct not just the past but also their future interpreters. Similarly, moving backward in a retroactive explanation of or compensation for elusive or objectionable sources, and forward in visions of ideal readers and paranoid fantasies of misreaders, English Trojan letters come back from the future to create their *auctors*.

Gawain's Body of Knowledge

Since Geoffrey of Monmouth popularized the myth in the twelfth century, it was widely repeated—though not universally accepted—that King Arthur was descended from Brutus, the founder and namesake of Britain, who, in turn, was descended from Aeneas. William Caxton's 1485 preface to Thomas Malory's *Morte Darthur* expresses the ambivalence common in the late medieval period toward the veracity of Arthurian legend. According to Caxton, some noble gentlemen approached him and asked him to publish the story of Arthur and his knights. The publisher was initially reluctant, arguing

> that dyvers men holde oppynyon that there was no suche Arthur and that alle suche bookes as been maad of hym ben but fayned and fables, bycause that somme cronycles make of hym no mencyon ne remembre hym noothynge, ne of his knyghtes.[10]

The men reportedly responded that it was folly to doubt the truth of Arthur's historical existence and then provided enough "evidence" that Caxton was finally persuaded that "there can no man resonably gaynsaye but there was a kyng of thys lande named Arthur." As further justification for publishing the project, Caxton notes that the Arthur story is more popular "beyonde the see" than it is in England and that, therefore, it must be told in English and for England's sake.[11]

The importance of Arthurianism as part of the national founding narrative, coupled with the claim for its relative scarcity in English literature, provides a provocative backdrop for a close look at the *Gawain*-Poet's treatment roughly one hundred years before Caxton's comments.[12] Opening with the vexed genealogical history that translated Troy to Britain, the *Gawain*-Poet announces a focus on ambivalent precedents:

Siþen þe sege and þe assaut watz sesed at Troye,
þe borȝ brittened and brent to brondez and askez,
þe tulk þat þe trammes of tresoun þer wroȝt
Watz tried for his tricherie, þe trewest on erthe.
Hit watz Ennias þe athel and his highe kynde,
þat siþen depreced prouinces, and patrounes bicome
Welneȝe of al þe wele in þe west iles.[13]

As Alfred David notes, there is a history of critical dissent concerning the identity of the "tulk" whose "tresoun" and "tricherie" helped the Greeks win the war: Do lines three and four describe the Aeneas of line five, or do they refer to the silent specter of Antenor?[14] Asking such a question, David argues, betrays a desire among modern critics to preserve Aeneas's reputation as the founder of Western civilization and to counter his reputation as a traitor to his own origins. And yet, of course, Aeneas was both a founder and a traitor: He had to be the latter in order to be the former.

The authority for the story of Aeneas as a traitor originates in the supposedly eyewitness accounts of the Trojan War by Dictys Cretensis and Dares Phrygias, who in the late Middle Ages were considered historians and thus more reliable than poets such as Virgil.[15] According to this tradition, Aeneas and Antenor plotted against the city once it became clear that the Greeks would soon rout it (and once Priam had decided to have them murdered for speaking out against his policies: Aeneas and Antenor had infuriated the king by advising him to return Helen and negotiate a settlement). After the destruction of the city, in Dares' account, Aeneas was banished by the Greeks for having tried to save Polyxena in a last-minute impulse to salve his conscience, while Antenor stayed on in what remained of Troy. In Dictys's account, both traitors remained in the city after the Greeks' departure until Aeneas tried to take it through treachery from Antenor, who subsequently forced him out.[16] These were the unsavory "facts" that were preferred to Virgil's more palatable fiction.

The *Gawain*-Poet repeats the common wisdom of Aeneas's betrayal and thus, as David notes, anticipates Gawain's own stained honor.[17] In between this compromised Trojan ancestor and his descendent is an intermediary link in the genealogical chain who further complicates the *translatio*. Geoffrey's *Historia regum Britanniae,* which exults in Brutus's divine calling to the founding of Britain, also recounts the irregular circumstances of his birth and his prophesied Oedipal drama.[18] Not surprisingly, Brutus's participation as the mediator between Rome and Britain results in the founding of a stained empire, characterized in *Sir Gawain and the Green Knight* as full of "werre and wrake and wonder" and "oft boþe blysse and blunder" (16, 18).

"Arthur þe hendest" (26), the great king descended from Brutus, has a similarly antiheroic background and forms another compromised link in the noble descent from Troy. Begotten on his mother out of wedlock, under the auspices of a sorcerer, Arthur was not only the king who beat the Romans but also the one who would eventually destroy his own kingdom.[19] Indeed, it was while he was away claiming imperial right in Rome that he lost his power at home. Deceit, treason, sorcery, and adultery brought the Trojans to Britain on a path characterized by illegitimacy and corruption, and a perverse desire for empire ruined its most famous king.

In *Sir Gawain and the Green Knight,* the issue of compromised human authorities folds into one of compromised textual authority, as we see in regard to the narrator's own contradictory admissions regarding his source. Right after his catalog of corrupted Trojan and English rulers, the narrator acknowledges his source to be a rumor, something he heard around town:

> Bot of alle þat here bult of Bretaygne kynges
> Ay watz Arthur þe hendest, *as I haf herde telle.*
> Forþi an aunter in erde I attle to schawe,
> þat a selly in siȝt summe men hit holden
> And an outtrage awenture of Arthurez wonderez.
> If ȝe wyl *lysten þis laye* bot on littel quile,
> *I schal telle hit* astit, *as I in toun herde,*
> *With tonge.*
>
> (25–32, emphasis added)

With these lines, the narrator opens up the text's central concern with the process by which oral knowledge crosses into authoritative, textual "truth." He does so not by trying to pass off a rumor as true but by demonstrating how its textualization transforms rumor into trustworthy narrative. He claims he will repeat a heard story to an audience who listens; and yet at the end of the poem, the narrator authorizes his text by retroactively attaching to it a previous, written source. He credits an unnamed book of romance and a Brutus book as his text's predecessors: "As hit is breued in þe best boke of romaunce" (2521); "þe Brutus bokez þerof beres wyttenesse" (2523). The process of repeating something heard turns what is heard into something already written and thus "true."

Gawain will enact this theory of textual construction and transmission on his body. Beginning with the Green Knight's challenge to the court and up through the return to the scene of this trauma—when the adventure is narrated at the end to the knights of the Round Table—Gawain's physical being is called upon to demonstrate the ruses, pleasures, and dangers of textuality. His body is variously exerted, transported, dressed, undressed, seduced, threatened with sodomy, girdled, cut, scarred, and ultimately returned (sent back to explain itself). These many physical postures and scenarios work to define Gawain's body in relation to the poem's two tests, the beheading game and the exchange of winnings, but they suggest themselves more broadly as metaphors for the poem's concern with textual interpretation.

When the narrative opens at Christmas, the king is waiting on dinner until he hears a good story; he will not eat "er hym deuised were / Of sum auenturus þyng" (92–93). Although he might settle for an actual joust, Arthur prefers "an vncouþe tale / Of sum mayn meruayle þat he myȝt trawe, / Of alderes, of armes, of oþer auenturus" (93–95). The king's reliance on discursive pleasures is symptomatic of the larger problem of his court: The knights of the Round Table are famous only in words, or rumors, and have not proven themselves in physical deeds to be worthy of their fame. At least, this is what the Green Knight implies when he arrives with a challenge to the authority of Arthur's court. As in the earlier muddled distinction between rumor and written authority, here the poem again calls into question the unimpeachable nature of textuality: The assumption of the primacy of the body (the need variously to control or exert it) in this paradigm disguises the far more difficult enterprise of controlling a reputation.

Pretending to fail to perceive which of the men in the hall is the king, the Green Knight asks, "[w]her is . . . / The gouernour of this gyng?" (224–25). Assaulting the dignity of Arthur, he brings into sharp relief the difference between the "berdlez" (280) physical appearance of the court and its impressive reputation, which is what has brought him to the feast:

> Bot for þe los of þe, lede, is lyft vp so hyȝe
> And þy burȝ and þy burnes best ar holden,
> Stifest vnder stel-gere on stedes to ryde,
> þe wyȝtest and þe worþyest of þe worldes kynde,
> Preue for to play wyth in oþer pure laykez,
> And here is kydde cortaysye, *as I haf herd carp.*
> (258–63, emphasis added)

The Green Knight questions whether Arthur's court deserves its reputation through the backhanded process of saying he has heard tell of it. Like the narrator's initial insistence that his source is oral, the Green Knight's emphasis on what he has only heard underscores the lack of authority behind the rumors of the Round Table knights' prowess. His offer of the beheading game challenges the court to prove, in something impossibly other than words, that it deserves its rumored status.

The beheading challenge is a taunt, implying that none of the "chylder" (280) in Arthur's company is "so hardy" or "so bolde in his blode" (285, 286) to take up the game.[20] The overwhelming silence with which the Green Knight's request is answered prompts even more taunting, this time with remarks specifically tailored to slight the court's ability to live up to its rumored fame. Now they cannot even speak, let alone act:

> What, is þis Arþures hous . . .
> þat al þe rous rennes of þurȝ ryalmes so mony?
> Where is now your sourquydrye and your conquestes,
> Your gryndellayk and your greme and your grete wordes?
> Now is þe reuel and þe renoun of þe Rounde Table
> Ouerwalt wyth a worde of on wyȝes speche!
> (309–14)

But Gawain and Arthur both mistake the nature of this challenge. Presented to them in taunting words, and suggesting that they have only words, the Green Knight's game hinges not on textuality's transcendence but on its awful persistence. He has "ouerwalt" (314) them not with his body but with his speech, a point literalized in the terrible joke of the first fitt when he speaks out of his severed head. The heavy ax, in turn, which should have dispatched its fleshly target, ends up instead as a conversation piece; it provokes discourse rather than serving deeds.

The firm presence of deeds and of strong bodies (as opposed to mere rumor) is an illusory solidity, rather like the myth of a pure textual origin. Whether the king and his nephew assume that the Green Knight will die when his head is struck off, or that Gawain will die when the Green Knight strikes him, they both fail to perceive that the court is being tested as much for its way with words as for its way with an ax. The persistence of textuality is clear even in passages that lavish an almost fetishized attention on Gawain's physical being. The ornate outfit (566–618) Gawain puts on to meet what he perceives as a challenge to his body functions as a set of signifiers providing information about his identity. The shield, for example, is decorated with a pentangle (619–39), announcing that Arthur's sister's son is devoted to the Virgin Mary and to the "five fives" of Christian virtue. But like the shield decorated with scenes from Rome's past and future glory for his legendary kinsman, Aeneas, Gawain's is an insistent sign of more than his personal identity.[21] "Gawain" means "trawþe," chivalry, chastity, honesty, and humility, but—as the purpose of his quest requires—he also means Arthur's court. And Arthur's court, as the poem's frame indicates, means Britain itself as the inheritor of the Trojan legacy. Gawain's body is never only his. Rather, it is always part of the language of textual transmission and is thus always available for multiple interpretations by a wide range of readers.

When Gawain arrives at Bertilak's castle, his identity as a Christian knight is literally dismantled when he is stripped of his special clothing and gear. In place of this virtuous identity, and attaching itself to Gawain's seemingly anonymous body, is a body of knowledge about him—one that has preceded his physical presence at Bertilak's. After he is clothed, fed, and comforted by his host's servants, it is discovered "þat aþel Arthure þe hende haldez hym one, / þat is þe ryche ryal kyng of þe Rounde Table, / And hit watz Wawen hymself þat in þat won syttez" (904–6).[22] But this "Wawen" is different from the Gawain who set out on the journey. In this case, as the people at Bertilak's murmur, because he is the one called "Wawen," he is expected to speak well about love:

Now schal we semlych se sleȝtez of þewez
And þe teccheles termes of talkyng noble
. . . .
I hope þat may hym here
Schal lerne of luf-talkyng.
(916–17, 926–27)

This expectation of discursive prowess from Gawain directly contradicts the physical prowess that is supposed to provide the point of his mission.

The particular kind of reputation the people whisper about, moreover—that of a love-talker, a smooth courtly ladies' man—directly contradicts the martial and Christian virtues Gawain had clothed himself in. The Continental Arthurian literary tradition, which was relatively unbothered by the ill-repute of the English king and court, often depicted Gawain as a womanizing abuser of the chivalric code.[23] Although the words attesting to Gawain's seductive skills do not appear explicitly in *Sir Gawain and the Green Knight,* they are given a quiet voice here in the form of the readerly expectations of the company at Bertilak's.

Gawain in this poem, with his virtue, pentangle, and quest for the physical truth behind discursive fame, is at odds with who he is in the body of literature that precedes him. And the lords and ladies at Bertilak's are readers who, in privileging the Continental reputation of Gawain as a womanizer over the present, physical appearance of Gawain as the Virgin's knight, graft onto Gawain's body a textual interpretation of their own. He is not a man opposed to text but is instead implicated in the process of textuality itself. In the case of Gawain's "luf-talkyng" reputation, a textual challenge—in which "Gawain" symbolizes seductiveness, selfishness, and stubbornness—is presented not only to Gawain's body but also to an alternative textual tradition about him: the one under construction in the present poem, in which his "outtrage awenture" symbolizes the glory of the English court and of Britain itself. Multiple textual bodies here struggle for interpretive ascendancy in a poem whose conflicts revolve more around the competition for discursive prowess than around the outcome of any physical battle.[24]

The primacy of the text is again inscribed on Gawain's body in the form of the bedroom challenge. Bertilak and Gawain have agreed on an exchange-of-winnings game: The host is to bring back whatever he finds on a hunt, and Gawain, in return, is to give him whatever he finds during his host's absence. The terms of the game make it clear that full disclosure is required:

> "ȝet firre," quoþ þe freke, "a forwarde we make:
> Quatsoeuer I wynne in þe wod hit worþez to yourez
> And quat chek so ȝe acheue chaunge me þerforne.
> Swete, swap we so; sware with trawþe,
> Queþer leude so lymp lere oþer better."
>
> (1105–9)

The legalistic emphasis on true words indicates that Gawain is to remain faithful to his pledge of "trawþe" and to meet his host's gifts with his own gift of true speech. Bertilak has not asked Gawain to do anything—or to refrain from doing anything—in his absence; he has only asked him to tell the truth.

But when the host's wife appears in his bed chamber the next morning, Gawain cannot help but be led away (seduced) from the discursive nature of the game. The lady's beautiful body, as Gawain noticed when he first saw her (943–45), makes her even more lovely to him than Arthur's queen. The poem's juxtaposition of Bertilak's aggressive hunting forays with his wife's aggressive bedroom tactics has often been understood as a purposeful parallel, showing Gawain trapped like the cornered animals.[25] The lady's assaults on him in the bedroom are portrayed as a siege—"Ful erly ho watz hym ate" (1474)—as she offers her body to him in no uncertain terms:

> ȝe ar welcum to my cors,
> Yowre awen won to wale,
> Me behouez of fyne force
> Your seruaunt be, and schale.
>
> (1237–40)

Gawain's nudity and vulnerable position in bed, and the lady's physical attractiveness and seductive words, lead to the understanding—his and the reader's—that the knight's chastity is being tested.

But like the Green Knight's challenge, Lady Bertilak's assault is discursive rather than physical. She presses Gawain with sexy chatter. Moreover, the topic of her assault is itself focused on words. She insists that he fulfill his reputation as a love-talker. She remarks that he must not really be Gawain, since the knight she has heard about knows how to talk to a lady: "Sir, ȝif ȝe be Wawen, wonder me þynkkez" (1481). Gawain's reputation is so alive that it—like the Green Knight's talking head—speaks without the body that usually carries it: "And ȝe ar knyȝt comlokest kyd of your elde, / *Your worde and your worchip walkez ayquere*" (1520–21, emphasis added). Word and worship (in other words, fame) have a life of their own, creating a textual body that threatens to overtake not just the physical person of Gawain but his identity as a true knight as well.

Insofar as Gawain is able to disappoint the lady's apparent desire for him, he considers himself as having safely negotiated the threat. His mistake is in assuming the primacy of his physical integrity, as he dutifully kisses his host every night in exchange for the only tangible losses he sustained in the bedroom hunt.[26] But the lady's interpretation, and thus seduction, of him is complete when she gets him to perform with words. "True" to his famous but erroneous reputation, Gawain parries her charms with winning phrases of his own, flirting and chatting with her just as he is supposed to:

> Scho made hym so grete chere,
> Þat watz so fayr of face.
> Þe knyȝt with speches skere
> Answared to vche a cace.
>
> (1259–62)

Gawain is so taken in by the verbal jousting that he worries at one point that his words are not charming enough; he "ferde lest he hade fayled in fourme of his castes" (1295).

On the second day of the parallel hunts, Gawain gladly rises to the occasion and uses words as a means of delaying a physical encounter, or even, he hopes, as a ruse with which he can avoid sexual seduction altogether:

> Þus hym frayned þat fre and fondet hym ofte,
> For to haf wonnen hym to woȝe, whatso scho þoȝt ellez;
> Bot he defended hym so fayr þat no faut semed,

Ne non euel on nawþer halue, nawþer þay wysten
Bot blysse.

(1549–53)

"Representation mingles with what it represents"[27] when Gawain here not only interprets the lady's and the host's texts but becomes them. In a Derridean sense, Gawain's love-talking and nice kisses are supplements[28] to his physical body, just as the court's reputation is supplementary to the knights' deeds of chivalry: In both cases, the pretense is that talk has been merely added, or attached, to the thing itself, whereas in truth, talk has only ever been the only thing there is. Gawain's gestures, for example, pretend to be the means of both referring to and avoiding the forbidden contact they represent. Instead, they constitute Gawain. He has become his mythic reputation as a love-talker, and he has confirmed that the reputation of the court rests, as it only can, on a discursive base and not a physical one.

Gawain's "entrance into textuality" is complete when, approaching the dreaded Green Chapel, he remarks that now he will "talk" with the man who is going to strike him with an ax: "Bot I wyl to þe chapel, for chaunce þat may falle, / And talk wyth þat ilk tulk þe tale þat me lyste" (2132–33). For once, and perhaps unwittingly, Gawain has correctly articulated the nature of his dealings with the Green Knight. The blows from the ax do not kill Gawain or even hurt him that much, but the verbal rebuke he receives damages his understanding of himself and of the court. Gawain learns, however, to counter the Green Knight's threat to his identity with texts of his own making. The two opponents trade interpretations of Gawain's experience in a battle that culminates not with the death of either but with the generation of multiple possible meanings for a single event.

The accusation of faithlessness is especially devastating to Gawain, who prided himself on his chivalric virtues and, above all, on his "trawþe." Whereas the Green Knight prefers to dismiss the importance of the failure to be faithful, since Arthur's knight was justifiably afraid for his life, Gawain's interpretation underscores the severity of his fault. His cowardice and covetousness, he says, made him forsake his "kynde," "þat is larges and lewte, þat longez to knyȝtez" (2381). He has betrayed his host and jeopardized his own knightly stature, but he has also failed the court and his king as their chivalric representative. Further rejecting

Gawain's abject remorse and denial of his own chivalric worth, the Green Knight tells him to take the girdle back to the court, where it will serve as a token "of þe chaunce of þe Grene Chapel" in the dwellings of "cheualrous knyȝtez" (2399). The girdle, like his ax the year before, will be a conversation piece in the great hall, prompting Arthur's renowned knights not to great chivalric deeds but to great stories about the Green Knight's own prowess. Writing himself into the narrative life of the Round Table, the Green Knight offers an interpretation of Gawain's experience that promises to serve his own fame.

Gawain, in turn, refuses this interpretation and instead reaches for an old standby, the one that blames women for leading men astray. Many scholars have been puzzled by this antifeminist outburst, properly noting that it does not seem to fit with Gawain's character or with his experience at Bertilak's.[29] But Gawain's exegetical historicism—Adam, Solomon, Samson, and David, he notes, were all deceived by women—functions more as a means of creating a place for himself in that history than as a simple repetition of a lesson from the past. This is a noble company of men, according to Gawain, who excuses himself for similarly falling prey to a woman and thus conveniently places himself in the canon of beguiled heroes: "For þes wer forne þe freest, þat folȝed alle þe sele / Excellently, of alle þyse oþer vnder heuen-ryche / þat mused" (2422–24). He will accept the girdle, but on his own, newly revised terms. It will not stand as a symbol of the Green Knight's championship nor for "wele ne for worchyp, ne for þe wlonk werkkez" (2432). Instead, Gawain receives it as a sign of his sin and thus as a sign of his worthiness to join the ranks of great men undone by women.

But, generating ever more interpretive matter, the Green Knight rejects Gawain's place in the canon when he reveals that Morgan le Fay had devised the whole test "For to assay þe surquidre, ȝif hit soth were / þat rennes of þe grete renoun of þe Rounde Table" (2457–58). And behind this motive lies another: Morgan ultimately wanted to grieve Guenevere and make her die of fright when she saw the Green Knight (2460–62). These multiple explanations and counterexplanations spiral ever further away from the adventure and from the idea of the thing itself. The challenge has only ever been one of discursive prowess (rather than physical), and the poem has only ever been one of imaginative skill (rather than historical accuracy).

Back at Arthur's court, Gawain tries to secure interpretive control over the meaning of his experience through the critical practice of revealing and explaining the symbols of the adventure. The walking wounded text "ferlyly" (2494) tells all to his audience of knights:

> þe chaunce of þe chapel, þe chere of þe knyȝt,
> þe luf of þe ladi, þe lace at þe last.
> þe nirt in þe nek he naked hem schewed
> þat he laȝt for his vnleute at þe leudes hondes
> For blame.
>
> (2496–500)

As he tried to do with the Green Knight as his audience, he attempts here to gloss his experience in a Christian context. But like all texts—as he just learned in Bertilak's castle and at the Green Chapel—Gawain's is (and Gawain is) immediately available for alternative explication. He loses control over his own story as soon as he stops telling it. And because his story is a text of himself, one that defines his identity, "Gawain" is nothing without his story. As Derrida notes, the letter (the text) is a signifier whose proper place (proper meaning) is "occupied successively by all those who possess it."[30] The interpretive process of the girdle, for example, as it passes from hand to hand and acquires different meanings along the way, shows just how unstable the symbols of textuality can be. To Bertilak and his complicit wife, the girdle is what makes Gawain break the rules and thus lose the game. Later, to the triumphant Green Knight, the girdle is a souvenir memorializing his own reputation. Gawain, in turn, here interprets his text differently from all of the above. The belt, he claims to his audience at Camelot, is a sign of his sin:

> "Lo! lorde," quoþ þe leude, and þe lace hondeled,
> "þis is þe bende of þis blame I bere in my nek.
> þis is þe laþe and þe losse þat I laȝt haue
> Of couardise and couetyse, þat I haf caȝt þare;
> þis is þe token of vntrawþe þat I am tan inne."
>
> (2505–9)

Trying to connect the significance of the belt with his identity as a Christian knight, the very identity undermined in the poem, Gawain provides his own revisionist gloss of himself.

In response to his demonstration of abject sorrow and remorse for his sin, the knights laugh and make of his interpretation what they prefer, a sign of the glory of the court:

> Þe kyng comfortez þe knyȝt, and alle þe court als
> Laȝen loude þerat and luflyly acorden
> Þat lordes and ledes þat longed to þe Table,
> Vche burne of þe broþerhede, a bauderyk schulde haue,
> A bende abelef hym aboute, of a bryȝt grene,
> And þat, for sake of þat segge, in swete to were.
> For þat watz acorded þe renoun of þe Rounde Table
> And he honoured þat hit hade, euermore after.
>
> (2513–20)

Perverting Gawain's text, and Gawain as a source for the text, the knights read the story of his failure in a way that ensures their own future fame.

The motivated misreading to which the Round Table knights subject Gawain's text returns our attention to the poem's concern with compromised authorities. In the final framing lines, as I noted before, the narrator quickly forecloses alternative interpretations by merging his tale—which he had earlier attributed to an oral source—with a body of authoritative literature. Despite the knights' clearly contentious reading of Gawain, the poem's narrator attaches their interpretation to the specter of an unassailable precedent and thus produces his own "truth" of the text.

But the poem does not end with this univocal assertion. As the experience of Gawain has demonstrated, readers will add to the identity of the text as soon as the tale is told. In this case, the motto of the Order of the Garter[31] has been added to the poem: *Hony soyt qui mal pence*, roughly translated as "Shame on him who thinks evil of it." Too little is known about the *Gawain*-Poet and the manuscript tradition of the poem to say with any certainty who inscribed this phrase or when. But it is clearly a warning against those who would engage in a misinterpretation of some kind. Coming on the heels of a poem so concerned with the mutability of textual authority and with the ways in which willfully misinterpreted narratives are retroactively attached to the past and disseminated as truth, the motto's warning serves as a haunting residue of the violence inflicted on textual bodies in the name of history.

BODIES IN MOTION

Chaucer's *House of Fame* exhibits a similar focus on the inevitability of misinterpretation,[32] the compromised authority of the past, and the persistence of textuality over the truth. Picking up where *Sir Gawain and the Green Knight* leaves off, Chaucer's poem begins with a crisis of interpretation. Already having experienced his adventure, Geffrey, like Gawain back at court, must now attempt to say what it means. Even more than *Sir Gawain and the Green Knight, House of Fame* engages the ways in which the process of writing authoritatively is complicit in the dissemination of falsehood. Geffrey is a writer (whereas Gawain is a text already written) confronted with the impossibility of guaranteeing a stable meaning for, or a proper reading of, his experience. His text is a dream, in the obvious sense that the poem's genre is the dream vision but also in the sense that what he writes is as illusory, unstable, and subjective as the texts that have come before it. Likewise, his dream is of a text: The poem explores the fantasmatic qualities of literary authority, of pure sources and interpretations, and of an immutable afterlife for letters.

Such issues of literary instability are underscored by the conceit of narrative chronology in *House of Fame*. Unlike *Sir Gawain and the Green Knight,* which separates a distinctive narrative voice apart from the hero, Chaucer's poem poses the narrator as the hero, asserting that the dream was dreamt and then written by the same person. And of course, the name "Geffrey" interferes with any attempt to separate this narrator-dreamer from the figure of the poet himself, as the conclusion to this chapter will explore in more detail. In this and other respects, *House of Fame* locates itself even more precisely than *Sir Gawain and the Green Knight* in that particular late-fourteenth-century moment concerned with the rightful place of post-Trojan English letters.

The narrating Geffrey begins by acknowledging the many difficulties inherent in the interpretation of dreams, but he then peevishly announces that nobody had better misread his own:

> And whoso thorgh presumpcion,
> Or hate, or skorn, or thorgh envye,
> Dispit, or jape, or vilanye,
> Mysdeme hyt, pray I Jesus God
> That (dreme he barefot, dreme he shod),

> That every harm that any man
> Hath had syth the world began
> Befalle hym therof or he sterve,
> And graunte he mote hit ful deserve.
>
> (94–102)

Coming after his dreamed experience, in which he witnessed the precariousness of the reputation of men and of texts, this warning against future "mis-deeming" is not only unreasonable but willful as well. Expressing a desire for what Derrida calls "a letter without partition,"[33] Geffrey's willed insistence on the immutability of his text is rather like the motto tacked onto the end of *Sir Gawain and the Green Knight:* Both betray an underlying conviction that the text will be misread. In Geffrey's case, the trip to Fame's castle has taught him a lesson that he would just as soon forget, a lesson about the illegitimacy embedded in textuality and about the awesome generative powers of that illegitimacy itself. For him essentially to announce "Shame on him who thinks evil of it" here at the start of the text suggests that he has, indeed, ignored the lesson of his experience.

Like the line of Trojan imperial descent outlined in the opening lines of *Sir Gawain and the Green Knight,* the genealogy of Trojan letters is, as shown to the dreamer in Fame's castle, stained with illegitimate transmitters: Bastard offspring, incestuous allegiances, competing legitimate authorities, and outright usurpers mar the smooth translation of narratives to their descendants. Homer, Dares, Dictys, Lollius, Guido, and Geoffrey of Monmouth are initially presented as authorities only to be then revealed as pseudo-authorities:

> But yet I gan ful wel espie,
> Betwex hem was a litil envye.
> Oon seyde that Omer made lyes,
> Feynynge in hys poetries,
> And was to Grekes favorable;
> Therfor held he hyt but fable.
>
> (1475–80)

This criticism of Homer is but a single example of the kind of allegation commonly levied against poets of the Trojan War. As we see here, Homer's account was widely thought to be false because of his allegiance to the Greeks. Virgil's account, in turn, although praised for correcting Homer's bias, was considered slanted in favor of "the fame of Pius Eneas" (1485), and Ovid was highly suspect in Chaucer's day as one whose passions prevented him from writing the truth.[34]

As the knights of the Round Table demonstrated in response to Gawain's text, the transmission of narrative is dependent upon readerly desires. In this case, the medieval redactors' treatment of the already problematic classical narratives adds an extra layer of indeterminacy to the matter of Troy, especially in light of the several instances of mistranslation and misattribution involved in this descent. Benoît de Sainte-Maure, for example, who used a compiled Latin edition of Dares' and Dictys's two accounts as the source for his metrical romance *Le Roman de Troie,* thought he was working from a translation by one Cornelius, nephew of the Roman historian Sallust. But this is a false identity stemming from a mistranslation of the proper name "Cornelius Nepos," who wrote a letter *to* Sallust (who was not his uncle).[35] Similarly convoluted in its acknowledgment of alleged sources is Guido's extremely influential *Historia destructionis Troiae,* which claims faithfully to follow Dares and Dictys even though—as we have seen—it is really a paraphrased, prose translation in Latin of Benoît's vernacular poem. Guido's text pretends to be history ("historia") while it suppresses its own origins as an adaptation of a verse romance.

The patently fabricated nature of Geoffrey of Monmouth's *Historia regum Brittaniae,* in turn, further clouds the field. His sources are culled partly from Welsh folk legend and from the historical writings of the Roman Britons Gildas and Nennius, but his work is just as often simply invented as part of a calculated political strategy to justify the Norman invasion for Geoffrey's audience of aristocratic conquerors.[36] Wace and Laȝamon, who use Geoffrey's *Historia* as a major source for their vernacular retellings of the story, similarly add and omit material according to the political contingencies of their own circumstances. And Chaucer himself will again participate in this "ruse of the source" when he claims the nonexistent Lollius as his *auctor,* rather than Boccaccio, in *Troilus and Criseyde.*[37]

Like Gawain, who—for all his struggles against others' interpretations of his identity and experience—concludes his narrative with a willful gloss, Geffrey is complicit in the literary tradition of misreading the past, despite the lesson learned in his dream. Regardless of his pronouncement that his own text should remain impervious to the whims of future misreaders, Chaucer's narrator systematically denies the good fame of Aeneas (despite Virgil's assertion of the Trojan's heroic stature) and sends out a misreading of the *Aeneid* as an authoritative letter in its own right. The "perversion of the letter" is accomplished in *House of Fame* through the construction of a set of frames that bracket Virgil's story in a way that emphasizes both the prior authority of the classical source and the radical way that the process of reading that source can alter it for the future.[38]

Virgil's letter arrives under conditions that are at once foreign and familiar, the dream device and the disorienting terrain of Venus's temple. But despite this disquieting occasion for a reading of the *Aeneid,* the authentic text makes an undeniable, almost literal appearance in Geffrey's account:

> But as I romed up and doun,
> I fond that on a wall ther was
> Thus writen on a table of bras:
> "*I wol now synge, yif I kan,*
> *The armes and also the man*
> That first cam, thurgh his destinee,
> Fugityf of Troy contree."
> (140–46, emphasis added)

The appearance of these transliterated words from the *Aeneid* asserts the presence of Virgil's text in no uncertain terms and, furthermore, implies that what is to follow will be as faithful to it as are these parroted lines. But buried in the middle of this apparent borrowing from Virgil is Geffrey's first corruption of the *Aeneid,* when he has Virgil mouth his own lack of authority with the phrase "yif I kan." Posing as a faithful translator, Geffrey not only permits the false assumption that he is following the classical source practically to the letter, he also asserts (through an act of ventriloquism) that his own version is better.

The next one hundred or so lines of the poem comprise a fairly accurate retelling of Virgil's version of Aeneas's flight from Troy and arrival in Carthage. But Geffrey's account soon diverges again from its source. The narrator emphasizes Dido's pitiful plight and portrays Aeneas as a womanizing liar, a cheat, and a traitor. Even as he introduces this very un-Virgilian[39] rendition of the story, Geffrey continues to assert his fidelity to his monumental predecessor by relying on conventional words of attribution:

> And after *grave was* how shee
> Made of hym shortly at oo word
> Hyr lyf, hir love, hir lust, hir lord.
> (256–58, emphasis added)

This insistence on the authority of written material and on the primacy of the one best classical source, Virgil, sits oddly in a poem that everywhere else emphasizes the lack of authority of "graven" sources, especially Virgil's *Aeneid*.

The poem further undermines written authority in the reason given for the dream itself: to take Geffrey away from the poverty of writing and into the wealth of immediate tidings. His dull occupation as a maker of administrative texts, slouched over his "rekenynges" (653) by day, is matched by his dull hobby of reading and writing literary texts at night. As the eagle tells him, when Geffrey comes home, "also domb as any stoon, / Thou sittest at another book / Tyl fully daswed ys thy look" (656–58). Jove has granted Geffrey's visit to the house of Fame to show him "mo wonder thynges" (674) than he can experience from mere written authority.

But of course this distinction is in itself a fiction. Not only does the dream device provide for an unsettling, "extra-real" experience, but—rather like the false distinction between discursive and "actual" prowess in *Sir Gawain and the Green Knight*—the presumed primacy of unmediated experience invoked in Chaucer's poem ultimately serves the continued primacy of written culture. Geffrey is left frustrated at the end insofar as the tidings he hears are fabricated and haphazardly dictated and disseminated, not corresponding with "truth." This nagging problem prompts him to write another text (the record of his dream) which represents the same problems of dullness and indeterminacy that were supposed to be solved on his journey.[40]

A similar disingenuousness characterizes Geffrey's false representation of his source material. Pretending to read the *Aeneid* as he finds it written, Geffrey laments Aeneas's falseness to Dido as though sanctioned to do so by Virgil:

Allas! what harm doth apparence,
Whan hit is fals in existence!
For he to hir a traytour was;
Wherfore she slow hirself, allas!
(264–67)

Although the false appearance in question here is Aeneas's guise as a faithful lover, or even a husband, to Dido, the false guise of texts as authoritative receptacles or neutral containers of truth is equally lamentable. Geffrey's condemnation of Aeneas's faithless sexual practices is a reflection of his own faithless textual practice.

The similarities between Aeneas and Geffrey thus include more than the fact that both are adventurers. More unsettlingly, according to Geffrey's own account, they are both liars, having their way, respectively, with Dido and with Virgil's text about Dido. When the queen of Carthage complains that her good reputation is ruined by Aeneas, she voices a fantasied reader's complaint against what Geffrey did to Virgil:

O wel-awey that I was born!
For thorgh yow is my name lorn,
And alle myn actes red and songe
Over al thys lond, on every tonge.
(345–48)

This imaginary reader, complaining about the misuse of his name, is a kind of projection of Virgil himself, back from the dead and speaking in a future that has come to malign him. Dido, originally spoken by Virgil, now speaks for him in a text that Virgil would not recognize as his own.

After Geffrey has had his way with Virgil's version of Dido and Aeneas, he gives short shrift to the rest of the *Aeneid,* "which is longe to telle" (446). He mocks Virgil's epic with the implications that it is too long and that it is just as well read in another redactor's version. Whoever wants to know the rest of the story—which includes such signal moments as the triumph in Italy and the fulfillment of divine prophecy—"moste rede many a rowe / On Virgile or on Claudian, / Or Daunte, that hit telle kan" (448–50). In a final blow to the primacy of Virgil's text, Geffrey skims over the main thrust of the classical epic even as he acknowledges his debt to the written authority of the *Aeneid:*

> But to excusen Eneas
> Fullyche of al his grete trespas,
> *The book seyth* Mercurie, sauns fayle,
> Bad hym goo into Itayle,
> And leve Auffrikes regioun,
> And Dido and hir faire toun.
> (427–32, emphasis added)

Denying the imperial significance of the *Aeneid,* Geffrey's version effectively obliterates the good fame of the classical author.

As Christopher Baswell points out, Geffrey and Aeneas are both misreaders of Trojan texts.[41] Although Aeneas's misreading of his past, which is inscribed on the murals depicting the Trojan War at Juno's temple at Carthage, has often been understood as part of Virgil's expression of a divine imperative, both Virgil's and Chaucer's heroes can be seen as misreading in their efforts to secure their own fame. Aeneas reads the murals that trace the fall of Troy as signs of the glory of his destroyed homeland and of his personal sacrifice and struggle, but he inevitably fails to see that his fame is elsewhere, in the future glory of Rome. This necessary misrecognition of the nature of his own fame is the means by which he secures Dido's love, the abnegation of which in turn will make Rome possible.

As Chaucer's narrator demonstrates, the deconstruction of classical authority is a prerequisite for medieval letters even as they claim to rely on and honor that precedent. The very act of enshrining the texts of the past is a means of bracketing their relevance to make room for revisionary treatments. This process enables the creation of new heroic narratives, for, as de Certeau observes,

> writing places a population of the dead on stage . . . and speaks of the past only in order to inter it. Writing is a tomb that . . . both honors and eliminates.[42]

In this case, "exactly by emulating Aeneas Geffrey can abandon him."[43]

Eliminating the past and the authority of past writers permits the construction of a mythology of the present as well as a mandate for sending these contemporary letters out to the future. De Certeau articulates this process with a metaphor of especially appropriate domestic architecture: "[N]aming the absent of the household and inserting them into the language of the scriptural gallery is equivalent to liberating the apartment for the living."[44] Such a house of Fame (like Arthur's court) is both a container for the preservation of disembodied discourse *and* an imaginary locus for the transmission of willfully revised discourse.

Chaucer's treatment of the Dido episode in his *Legend of Good Women* similarly demonstrates an impulse to jettison the past in order to please the present. Under strict orders from the God of Love to tell stories the way he likes them, Chaucer's narrator perverts his ancient sources to suit the restrictions of Love's literary tastes. The narrator, as Lisa Kiser notes, is a "bad translator of the Legends,"[45] working with a willful misreader as his ideal audience. But in this case, a bad translator is nevertheless a purposeful one.[46] Engaging in the same feigned reverence for his predecessor as was evident in *House of Fame,* the narrator here pretends that Virgil portrayed Aeneas as a liar and a betrayer of women:

> Glorye and honour, Virgil Mantoan,
> Be to thy name! and I shal, as I can,
> Folwe thy lanterne, as thow gost byforn,
> How Eneas to Dido was forsworn.
> (*Legend of Good Women,* 924–27)

The avowal here to follow Virgil "as I can" is like the "yif I kan" tag from *House of Fame.* As Rita Copeland observes, the phrase "produces an awkward uncertainty, suggesting . . . another kind of betrayal [other than Aeneas's betrayal of Dido], that of a translator whose inadequacy or tentativeness will betray his source."[47] In the *Legend of Good Women,* the narrator announces the type of betrayal he has in mind: He will not bother with the text of the *Aeneid* so much as he will take just the main point from it, augmented by Virgil's temperamental opposite, Ovid:

> In thyn Eneyde and Naso wol I take
> The tenor, and grete effectes make.
> (928–29)

Finally, the narrator admits, the *Aeneid* is just too tiresome to be faithful to:

I could folwe, word for word, Virgile,
But it wolde lasten al to longe while.
(1002–3)

Spurning Virgil, and turning away from the promise to be true to him, Chaucer's narrator enacts the literary equivalent of Aeneas's betrayal of Dido. Like Aeneas's, however, this act of betrayal is foundational. It "becomes the bridge into the narrator-translator's statement of his *materia* and *modus agendi*," as well as a statement of liberation from the constraints of his source.[48]

One of Chaucer's readers, Gavin Douglas, a Middle Scots poet who died in 1522, condemns what he saw as Chaucer's overly free use of Virgil, and in the process, he replicates Chaucer's "crime." Douglas begins his own vernacular translation of the *Aeneid* with a discussion of proper translation practices. He allows room for the exigencies of language and the difficulties inherent in moving between tongues:

Sum word I pronunce as nyghtbouris doys:
Lyke as in Latyn beyn Grew termys sum,
So me behufyt quhilum or than be dum
Sum bastard Latyn, French or Inglys oys
Quhar scant was Scottis—I had nane other choys.
. . . .
Sum tyme I follow the text als neir I may,
Sum tyme I am constrenyt ane other way.[49]

Despite these generous allowances for his own textual deviance, Douglas cannot condone what the English poet did with his source: "And netheles into sum place, quha kend it, / My mastir Chauser gretly Virgill offendit" (409–10).

Chaucer's offence is explained by his weakness for women. His predecessor, Douglas notes, "was evir (God wait) all womanis frend" (449). This famous excuse for Chaucer's corruption of the text allows a certain uneasy truce to be established and enables Douglas to praise his "mastir." Such praise can be lavish, as when Douglas compares the voice of "venerabill Chauser" to a

Hevynly trumpat, orlege and reguler,
In eloquens balmy, cundyt and dyall,

> Mylky fontane, cleir strand and roys ryall,
> Of fresch endyte, throu Albion iland braid.
> (340–43)

Retroactively attributing to Chaucer a love for women, Douglas frees himself to admire the English poet and to place his own version of the *Aeneid* in the line of noble literary descent from the old Troy to the new.

Just where in the world the new Troy is located—and through which geographical regions its validating precedent should flow—is the underlying core issue of Douglas's translation project. If we see the "Scottis" *Aeneid* as an instance of cultural self-definition as well as one of literary appropriation, Douglas's vexed relationship with Chaucer becomes more clear. For Chaucer was not only a predecessor, whose chronological priority conquers Douglas's text as belated; he was also a poet belonging to what Douglas considered the conquering imperialism of "Albion iland." Written "under the spell of a righteous patriotism at a time when the military and political threat from England was rapidly increasing,"[50] Douglas's Scottish text takes issue with Chaucer's English version as a matter of nationalistic cultural significance. As A. M. Kinghorn notes, one hundred years later (Douglas finished his poem in 1513) there would no longer be a recognizable "Scottis" as a vehicle for literature, subsumed as it was under the English language and British culture.[51]

We see several similar attempts on the part of Middle Scots writers to claim for Scotland an independent right to appropriate Trojan precedent. John Barbour's *Bruce* (1375), for example, recounts the story of Robert the Bruce, king of Scots, and his fight against Edward I of England. In this version, Edward is described as a traitor and the Bruce as a tenth worthy, and the situation in Scotland is likened to the treasons that undermined Troy, Alexander, Julius Caesar, and King Arthur.[52] Equating rather than differentiating Trojan and Arthurian precedent, Barbour claims for Scotland's hero the same right to the past as any English king enjoys and—in this case—asserts the Bruce's historical position in the place where the English are wont to be. Similarly turning to legendary history for nationalistic purposes, John of Fordun's *Chronicle of the Scottish Nation* (1385) substitutes a Scottish Gawain in the place of the English heroic figure. The text insists that Arthur was not the rightful heir to Uther. Rather, it claims, Uther's sister, Anna, wife of Loth, and her sons, Galwanus (Gawain) and Modred, should have had the throne instead of the illegitimate Arthur.[53] Barbour and John of Fordun resist English claims to sovereignty through claiming their own Scottish version of Trojan and Arthurian precedent. Like Douglas, they assert a right to a literary home for Scotland.

Chaucer's *House of Fame* constructs a home for English letters. It is a place imagined to have a past in Troy and a present, now, in new Troy. The *Gawain*-Poet, on the other hand, shows a place contaminated by the past and destined to self-destruct in the future. Chaucer's noted sympathy for Dido, the very aspect that so upset Douglas, serves as a contrast to the *Gawain*-Poet's "legend of bad women," the antifeminist outburst spoken by Gawain at his moment of humiliation, and highlights this difference as a kind of territorial divide between literary homes. As Ingledew points out, responses to the (always deviant) sexuality of Dido function as a kind of moral map that identifies one's proper place of residence, or belonging, in the historical-ethical sphere:

> In the *Confessions* Augustine repudiates the tears he had once shed for Dido and associates Dido's story with the false enchantments of the historical field represented by the fall of Troy and the wanderings of Aeneas. To indulge sexual passion or to weep at its frustration is a mark of the merely historical subject; it betrays membership in the wrong city, or an erroneous definition of home.[54]

Chaucer and the *Gawain*-Poet explore in their variously peevish and despairing responses to the past the seductiveness of the misrecognition of home, but they also translate themselves and their moment of literary history into the present and the future. In doing so, they help articulate the beginnings of a self-conscious empire of English letters in the late fourteenth century.

WHAT IS YOUR NAME?

Chaucer spoofs the notion of a famous, canonical afterlife for authors when he has Geffrey fantasize about his own sure death. Soaring to great heights in the claws of the eagle, Geffrey worries that he will be dropped:

"O God," thoughte I, "that madest kynde,
Shal I noon other weyes dye?
Wher Joves wol me stellyfye,
Or what thing this may sygnifye?
I neyther am Ennok, ne Elye,
Ne Romulus, ne Ganymede,
That was ybore up, as men rede,
To hevene with daun Jupiter,
And mad the goddys botiller."
Loo, this was thoo my fantasye.

(584–93)

Geffrey's morbid fear of being made a star contributes to what Derek Pearsall calls the poem's "embarrassed giggle" at the prospect of fame.[55] Misrecognizing himself as one worthy to be stellified, Geffrey is quickly disabused of his fantasy by the eagle:

Thow demest of thyself amys,
For Joves ys not theraboute—
I dar wel putte the out of doute—
To make of the as yet a sterre.

(596–99)

The humor evident in this passage is refigured more seriously later in the poem when Geffrey denies the charge that he is seeking fame. A bystander in Fame's castle, who later will lead him to the wicker house of tidings, asks his name and whether he is "come hider to han fame" (1872). Geffrey's answer is unequivocal:

"Nay, for sothe, frend," quod y;
"I cam noght hyder, graunt mercy,
For no such cause, by my hed!
Sufficeth me, as I were ded,
That no wight have my name in honde.
I wot myself best how y stonde."

(1873–78)

But these protests, stiffly asserting interpretive autonomy over one's own textual products, are as doomed as those with which the narrator began the account of his dream. As with *Sir Gawain and the Green Knight, House of Fame* demonstrates the horrible necessity of losing control over one's own name if the translation into the future is to proceed.

As Douglas knew, translation is never simply a matter of being accurate to the past. Rather, *translatio,* whether of empire or of letters, is the movement of a culture from one location in space or in time to another. Issues of conquest, submission, theft, and usurpation surround the process of translation.[56] Rather than wondering whether a translation is accurate, we might instead ask, with Sherry Simon, what translations do, how they circulate in the world, and how they elicit response.[57] Or, to put it another way, the process of translation underscores not so much the discrete boundary between things as the way that boundary "becomes the place from which something begins its presencing."[58] The "presencing" of Chaucer as a voice in 1380s London poetry begins here in *House of Fame* through his translation of the Dido episode, and it is finished—that is, his reputation is sealed—through the responses to this work, including his own.

The case of the *Gawain*-Poet follows a similar logic with very different consequences: The Arthurian strand of legendary history is that of the Other Britain, the one that is western or northern or both but that is in all cases marginalized in relation to London. And Arthurian literary culture, as Caxton's late-fifteenth-century remark that it is more popular elsewhere than in England testifies, is likewise perceived as marginal to the translation of the main narrative: that of the Trojans to new Troy. Richard II—as I shall argue in more detail in chapters 3 and 4—increasingly excluded from London and its political and literary milieux, turned to this Other Britain with eventually disastrous consequences for himself. The choice of an Arthurian, rather than Trojan, topic in the late fourteenth century likewise may have contributed to the marginalization of the nameless *Gawain*-Poet in literary history.

Despite this apparent difference in the valuation of Arthurianism and Trojanness, it must nevertheless be noted that the line separating the two becomes fixed only in response to certain specific social and political circumstances. That is, sometimes Arthurianism is viewed as a native tradition, one that supports the notion of a home-grown British hero, whereas Trojanness, by contrast, takes on the flavor of the foreign, exotic, decadent Other. But just as easily, Arthurianism may be glossed as a bit rough—uncivilized and "out-there"—compared to the fashionableness and sophistication of Troy and its European offspring. This fluidity will be crucial for understanding Richard II's political reputation. As we shall see, he was blamed for choosing Cheshire instead of London for patronage, and for choosing Scotland and Ireland instead of France for war. On the other hand, when Richard apparently imagined himself and his court as inheritors of Trojan glory, this also was wrong. And when he finally, in the late 1390s, tried to claim an imperial title for himself, he met with derision. The territorial boundary between Arthurian and Trojan traditions is sometimes fixed—attached genealogically through Brutus—and sometimes broken or symbolically separated.

The sober ending of *Sir Gawain and the Green Knight,* with its return to the trauma of the destruction of civilizations, bespeaks both a spiritual and a political sadness as it expresses the terrible fluidity of historical association. In keeping with the poet's other works, the conclusion here articulates his regret at man's perpetual pride, as well as the knowledge that pride will continue, despite lessons learned. In this case, the folly of the Trojans is reiterated in that of the Arthurian court.[59] The cataclysmic destruction of Troy—and the end of civilization that it represents—is doomed to be repeated in any post-Trojan civilization that looks to Troy as a model. Gawain is cast out of the protected environment of the court, out of his secure identity as a Christian knight, and even though he returns to the former, the latter is forever gone as a result of his experience.

Arthurianism as well seems to have been cast out of the Galdfridian structure of meaning that had asserted its legendary (which is to say, exemplary) status. Despite the *Gawain*-Poet's apparent delight in describing the fine things and people of the court, he certainly does not portray Arthur as a model of chivalric practice, moral virtue, or even political good sense. He is instead presented as a young, petulant king who is unaware of impending disaster and who thus can be seen, in hindsight, as contributing to it.

While the *Gawain*-Poet trades primarily in the discourse of man's spiritual aspirations and inevitable descent into sin, his choice of the Trojan background and Arthurian setting historicizes this discourse and locates its terms of rise, fall, conquest, humiliation, and reputation in the realm of secular chronology. The fall of Arthur that the poem necessarily looks forward to is a prediction of the failure of any king who descends from him. The crisis of the past is necessarily the crisis of the future.

Just which future the poem at least implicitly warns of is a matter of some debate, a debate centering on its date of composition. The earliest estimate, of the 1360s, would situate the poem in the moment of Edward III's demise, and the latest, very close to the 1400 dating of the manuscript, would point to the demise of Richard II. Dates in between these estimates would implicate Richard at various moments of political irrelevance and reemergence. It is tempting to associate Richard II's visits to the northwest of England with instances of the imagined composition or presentation of the poem, but direct assertions of contemporary significance are impossible in the absence of a more precise date.[60] I prefer instead to argue for the historical relevance of *Sir Gawain and the Green Knight* not in terms of a specific response to political events but, rather, in terms of its reception in a literary future the poet may have imagined (and certainly believed in) but could not control.

Michael J. Bennett's review of Richard II's movements during the final decade of his reign notes the king's "growing disaffection" with London and the Home Counties, coupled with an apparent interest in the wider realm. The 1394–95 campaign in Ireland, for example, may testify to "a new phase of royalist assertion" for Richard.[61] The regionalism of Richard's politics, Bennett argues, was "a reaction against London." The king "claimed not to be safe" in the southern part of the country and recruited a retinue of loyal Cheshire men to protect him. But there may also have been a more "positive side" to this regionalism, Bennett continues, "an embracing of his kingdom's larger British identity, incorporating both its Anglo-Saxon and its Celtic past."[62] I would suggest that these movements away from London and toward the northwest part of England (and also toward Ireland) were an attempt to consolidate political power regionally through an embracing of an alternative identity. Richard tried to translate his empire to a part of the kingdom he hoped would protect him against his southern enemies. The fate and fame of the region's letters can be seen to follow the king here, as they did in London as well.

Noting the favoritism shown by Richard II to Cheshire, at the perceived expense of other regions, John Bowers observes that "a *translatio imperii* from one part of the country to another would have been facilitated by a *translatio studii*."[63] But the problem, for both Richard and the *Gawain*-Poet, was that the "choice" of Cheshire constituted a declaration of amity with the Other Britain, the wrong place for either political or literary triumph. As Richard "chose" Scotland and Ireland for his military exploits, instead of the more aristocratic (and popular) enemy, France, so also did he choose for patronage a part of England that was marginal to the emerging understanding of its national identity. This is not to say that the region of Cheshire, or the temperament of the *Gawain*-Poet for that matter, was devoid of aristocratic sensibility. Rather, I am suggesting that the place was strange to Londoners and that the poet may take such delight in describing the wild terrain of Wales and the oddities found therein because of a sense of its pure strangeness to mainstream English culture. But as Bennett notes, the king's surprising presence in the northwest did not only underscore the region's difference from London; it also tamed it in a sense. As more opportunities and wealth came to the region, Cheshire and its environs were drawn more into the national mainstream:

> The paradox is that the conditions for cultural production in the region became more favourable at the time when its regional culture was most under threat. Sir Robert Grosvenor's entanglement with the court of chivalry is symbolic: the local community of honour was being integrated in, and subordinated to, a national one.[64]

The reference to Robert Grosvenor's troubles is especially apt for demonstrating here not only the split between different geographical regions of the country but also Chaucer's position in the translation of English culture from the past to the present and back to the future.

According to testimony given in October 1386 in the court of chivalry, Chaucer wandered by a London inn one day and saw what he thought was the sign of Sir Richard Scrope's arms hanging outside. Scrope was a Yorkshire knight, but he was very much a man about the country and a familiar presence in London. As it turned out, however, the arms were said (by a stranger Chaucer hailed on the street) to belong to a Sir Robert Grosvenor, a knight of Cheshire. Chaucer testified that he was surprised to discover this and that he had never heard of Grosvenor. Ultimately Grosvenor was fined and made to apologize for unlawfully bearing Scrope's arms.

The Scrope-Grosvenor controversy speaks to a number of issues regarding aristocratic identity politics, as chapter 3 will discuss in some detail. But for now it is enough to note that Chaucer serves in this case as an arbiter of more than just "good taste." The identity of Scrope had been assumed by an imposter and his reputation thus put at risk. Chaucer's testimony helped decide which of the two men would have good fame and which would have disgrace. He is, in short, an authoritative voice in his community at this time.[65]

As early as the middle to late 1370s, *House of Fame* points to Chaucer's emergence as a public figure in terms strikingly similar to these.[66] The "unfinished" poem predicts, as its own unstated conclusion, Chaucer's arrival as a literary authority. It further predicts—and even provokes—*Troilus and Criseyde*. Whereas the end of *Sir Gawain and the Green Knight* returns to the burnt "askes" of ancient Troy, the end of *House of Fame* turns from old stories to new ones and from the classical world to the contemporary one. The wicker house is an image from late-fourteenth-century London. It contains and fails to contain the hustle and noise of a public place, within which discourse is generated and repeated and from which it is disseminated. Here, units of discourse are imagined as taking on a life of their own as tidings fly up to the window, compete for dominance, and then agree to be allies, for better or for worse (as when "soth" and "fals" join together). Tidings are exaggerated and distorted as they are repeated. In this happenstance and often illegitimate way, history is made, as is literary fame. Geffrey is represented as a spectator, even a voyeur, in this marketplace of tidings, but at the same time he contributes to the din of rumor and gossip himself. He says that as he ran about,

a tydynge for to here,
That I had herd of som contre
That shal not now be told for me—
For hit no nede is, redely;
Folk kan synge hit bet than I;
For al mot out, other late or rathe,
Alle the sheves in the lathe—

I herde a gret noyse withalle
In a corner of the halle,
Ther men of love-tydynges tolde.
(2134–43)

Embedded in this parenthetical passage is a series of tidings: the rumor he wants to hear; the one he heard and is not revealing, since other people can tell it better than he can; and the news that the great noise, a big story, has begun. The series, however, may be collapsed into one rumor. In its several guises, the tiding is a prognostication of Chaucer's own fame, and particularly his fame as a love poet.

Toward the love-tidings corner of the hall, the people run and shout and fight for a desirable vantage position. The narrator himself squeezes in for a view:

Atte laste y saugh a man,
Which that y nevene nat ne kan;
But he semed for to be
A man of gret auctorite.
(2155–58)

The identity of this "man" is as elusive as the rumor that Geffrey earlier refused to divulge.[67] It is, for that matter, the same rumor, the one that everyone knows even though Chaucer is too modest to say it. The non-revelation in both instances prompts us to ask, "[N]ost not thou / That ys betyd, lo, late or now?" (2047–48). The rhetorical question includes the audience of the poem in the hurly-burly of the London gossip syndicate, as members of the same discursive community. Chaucer's audience, as Strohm and others have argued, was probably composed of a fairly circumscribed group of men who, like him, were part of the king's affinity, and Chaucer's understanding of the term "audience" would be "close to its etymological sense of 'those within hearing.'"[68] The poem's assumption of a knowing group of listeners as its audience makes this conclusion quite the inside joke: His friends can laugh with him at the absurdity of his positing himself as a "man of gret auctorite."

And yet all jokes contain within them their unfunny core, which is to say their truth. The humor of *House of Fame* is of the nervously self-effacing sort, a type of mockery that suggests the presence of something significant enough to be mocked in the first place. For all its imagined humorous effect with his circle of friends, Chaucer's poem nevertheless depicts his arrival on the London literary scene. Worried that he may be judged harshly or misinterpreted altogether, Chaucer is aware of his becoming "Chaucer" and of his fame being produced as he speaks. As easily as any other worthy or unworthy candidate, he will emerge out of the competing voices and trampling discourses of contemporary London as an authoritative figure. His foreseen arrival as such is met with embarrassment and some degree of defensiveness, both of which will be replayed in *Troilus and Criseyde*. Ultimately, the conclusion to *House of Fame* witnesses Chaucer sending himself, via his narrating "Geffrey," as a tiding to the future.

3

Chaucer's Troy Book

Troilus and Criseyde revisits the matter of Troy as it was explored in *House of Fame,* through a meditation on the failure of sexual love. But whereas the earlier poem embeds the Dido episode within a series of disorienting descriptive frames and hallucinatory loci—the dream, the temple, the eagle's discourse, the castle, and the wicker house—here the focus is fixed on the "Criseyde episode" throughout. The physical setting of *Troilus* likewise is fixed, situated almost entirely within the walls of wartime Troy. Despite this setting, which might provoke in the reader expectations of historiography, the narrator maintains that the topic of his poem is the "sorwe of Troilus . . . / In lovynge."[1] He briefly recounts what he says everyone already knows—"how that the Grekes stronge / In armes with a thousand shippes wente to Troiewardes" (I, 58–59)—only then to move away from the Trojan history of Dares and Dictys to treat his "woful vers" (I, 7) in other terms.

Rather than locating history in a purely linear, diachronic narrative, *Troilus and Criseyde* considers how individuals and empires might be able to move around in, or even transcend, the apparent fixity of the past. Within an etiological cultural enterprise that assumes Trojan origins for Britain, Chaucer's text wonders about teleology: whether and then why the future must be what it was foredoomed to be. Troilus becomes knotted up with this problem in Book IV, as he attempts to explain to himself the paradox of historical necessity:

> For although that for thyng shal come, ywys,
> Therfore is it purveyed, certeynly—
> Nat that it comth for it purveyed is—

> Yet natheles, bihoveth it nedfully
> That thing to come be purveyd, trewely.
> (IV, 1051–55)

A foreseen historical event, in other words, does not occur simply *because* it was foreseen, but nevertheless, an event that happens must necessarily have been foreseen. Chaucer's poem worries over and sets in motion the multiple interpretive chronologies belonging to historical necessity. The text on the one hand returns to the past, the matter of Troy, and retells what had to happen; but it also imagines the city before its fall and considers what may have happened in a different future.

Troilus and Criseyde is concerned especially with how the past interacts with the future. The future was at this moment new, in several respects. First, the word "future" itself was introduced into the English language by Chaucer in his *Boece,* where he felt it necessary to explain its meaning: "For alle thing that lyveth in tyme, it is present and procedith fro preteritz into futures (that is to seyn, fro tyme passed into tyme comynge)."[2] By the time of *Troilus,* "future" goes unglossed in Criseyde's discussion of her awareness of the necessity of her ill fate:

> On tyme ypassed wel remembred me,
> And present tyme ek koud ich wel ise,
> But future tyme, er I was in the snare,
> Koude I nat sen . . .
> (V, 746–49)

That Criseyde should literally speak the "future" is particularly apt, since as we shall see it is through this character that Chaucer develops and expresses his understanding of the tragedy of foreknowledge. But the poem simultaneously engages the tragic future of Richard II and of Britain in its depiction of Troy. Old Troy is pretendedly present in the poem; it is not yet fallen. Likewise, the new Troy of the 1380s is not yet gone. The "yet," however, is in both instances the important term. Chaucer's poem, completed by 1386 or early 1387, speaks to the history of London and of his and Richard II's place in it during a moment of national self-definition. In this moment, Troy, new and old, serves as a crucial mediating term in the contemporary issues of conquest and submission and of foreignness and nativism that make up the matter of Britain in the late fourteenth century.

The Time and Place of New Troy

Although Chaucer did not provide his testimony in the case until 15 October 1386, the aforementioned dispute between Scrope and Grosvenor actually began on 14 August 1385, when the two men, serving in the king's Scottish campaign, bumped into each other in northern England unhappily wearing the same insignia (the *azure* with *bend'or,* a blue shield with a rising gold diagonal bar). As it happens, this was not the first time Scrope had been challenged for his exclusive right to bear these specific arms: In 1373 a Cornish knight named Thomas Carminowe wore the *azure* with *bend'or,* prompting Scrope to protest. In this earlier dispute, Scrope swore that his family's right to the arms went as far back as the Conquest, while Carminowe claimed that they had been granted to his lineage by King Arthur.[3] As in the later challenge from Grosvenor, a Cheshire knight, Scrope's identity here is challenged by an outsider, in this case by a knight from the country's southwest periphery, Cornwall.[4] Both Scrope and Carminowe claimed ancient precedent to support their rights to the arms. But despite Carminowe's invocation of Arthur, Scrope prevailed with the less ancient precedent of the Conquest. These competing claims do not simply refer to two episodes, one earlier and the other later, on a continuous timeline of history. Rather, they set in opposition to one another two prominent understandings of the definition of English identity in the late fourteenth century. Like the collapsing of chronology—and, with it, the distinction between old and new Troys—at the end of *Troilus and Criseyde,* here also simultaneity of time and multireferentiality of place make "straight" historical narrative (as well as claims to certain specific histories) impossible.

Arthurianism belongs specifically to the Celtic past, and in some respects it is located specifically in the British Isles (Wales and Cornwall in particular). And yet, like its Trojan predecessor, the Arthurian myth was an unstable chronotopic phenomenon, one that could be claimed by multiple parties and often at cross-purposes. The legend of Arthur could, for instance, serve the English in the limited and local function of justifying their many attempts at subduing the Welsh and the Scots, since it was Merlin's prophecy that Britain would one day, after Arthur, be again a "united kingdom."[5] When Edward I was called upon to explain "the right and dominion that belong to us in the realm of Scotland," he did so by appealing to his superior right as the descendent of Locrine, the eldest son of Brutus of Troy.[6] The Scots, for their part, were equally willing to claim historical and pseudo-historical evidence with which to counter Edward's. Making their case to Boniface VIII at Rome, the leaders of the Scottish resistance argued that the three sons of Brutus had shared Britain as equals.[7] Closer to our period, Edward III's well-known cultivation of Arthurianism helped him define and celebrate English conquest on a wider world stage. His institution in 1348 of the Order of the Garter followed his triumphant victories in 1346 at Crécy and 1347 at Calais and served to collect in a "Society, Fellowship and College" the best knights of the realm. Edward's Arthurianism, however, was as politically strategic as it was ceremonial. The king's widely advertised visits to the supposed tomb of Arthur in Glastonbury were paid as part of a deliberate program of asserting a national Christianity.[8] As Juliet Vale observes, "the Garter was an integral part of Edward's Norman campaign from its inception, not merely a retrospective commemoration of its success."[9]

Like Arthurianism, Trojanness also was deployed on the world stage as well as in the local contexts of English politics. As Patterson reminds us, England's Trojan history was uneasily shared with other realms: Guido delle Colonne, for example, designates as Trojan foundations not only Britain but also France, Venice, Sicily, Tuscany, Naples, and Calabria; among other claimants, the Danes, Saxons, and Normans were linked to Troy, as were Turkey, Belgium, the German emperors, and the Capetians.[10] And since the claim to Troy was a cultural as well as political indicator, literary evidence may also be brought to bear in this global competition for the right to the best history: The dukes of Burgundy were "avid collectors" of Trojan texts (Philippe le Bon owned seventeen Troy manuscripts and founded the Order of the Golden Fleece), and the Visconti library contained four copies of Guido's work along with six other "Troy books."[11]

For England, the most significant of these alternative claimants to the precedent of Troy was the French enemy. Hatred of and cultural competition with France was particularly acute in the mid-1380s, coinciding with a series of humiliating military defeats for the English on the Continent.[12] At several points during the war with France, reference was made by both parties to the Trojan War. In the summer of 1386, for example, the French gathered a huge invasion fleet at Sluys that was compared to the Greek fleet that invaded Troy.[13] Patterson also notes that in the 1350s Richard of Bury invoked the idea of *translatio imperii* to predict an English victory in the war, while Jean de Roquetaillade was simultaneously claiming that the Trojan *imperium* inevitably would pass to France.[14] Toward the end of the war, in the fifteenth-century *Debat des Herauts de France et d'Angleterre,* representatives of the competing nations argued over which was the true descendant of Troy and so entitled to the future.[15] At stake in these skirmishes was not only the identification of the premier European nation but the position of its inhabitants as the standard-bearers of aristocratic civilization. When Scrope claimed the Norman conquest as the date for his family's investment with the arms of *azure* with *bend'or,* he claimed an aristocratic French heritage for an English knight.[16] This claim underscores the particular difficulty for English identity during the Hundred Years' War, insofar as the imperative to conquer and humiliate the enemy, the French, was at odds with the fact that the English house of Plantagenet was, itself, French.[17] What, then, was Englishness during this period, and how could it be defined and invoked when the nation needed an identity with which to oppose the French, on the one hand, and to assert their right to France, on the other?

The continuum of Trojan, Roman, and Arthurian precedent offered a range of possible martial, political, and cultural subject positions for the English. The difference between the supposedly native imperialism invoked by the specter of King Arthur and the competing, or threatening, "foreign" imperialism of Troy or France is an ill-defined territorial boundary. Both the Celtic past and the Norman past could define the English present, and they could do so in unpredictable ways. When Richard II negotiated a truce with France in the 1390s, for example, and sought instead to conquer Ireland, he was seen as choosing a definition of regnal identity rooted in an inappropriate place.[18] His armies were largely drawn from retinues of his Cheshire supporters, who were regarded as irregular wildmen, whereas by contrast, the future Henry IV was gaining his reputation as a knight through the more customary avenue of crusading on the Continent.[19] This is not to suggest that Richard did not have designs of empire that focused on Europe—he did, as chapter 4 will discuss—but his neglect and eventual abuse of London and his failure to engage the French enemy abroad colored his reign as one that deviated from what was considered England's proper national identity and destiny.

Of course, the knowledge of Richard's failure is through hindsight, largely produced by the consciously propagandistic efforts of Lancastrian chroniclers. The record shows that Richard failed to achieve a secure power for himself and his circle: He is noted in most chronicle sources as a king who brought upon himself deposition, the ultimate expression of the failure of rule. Justification for this failure is found in chronicles written after the revolution, in narratives that emphasize that Richard surrounded himself with the wrong sort of person: Instead of consorting with accomplished English warriors, as his grandfather had, the king "pleased himself" with the company of his young friends and favorites and with foreigners.[20] He was noted for his lively court, which featured frequent games, feasts, and musical and literary entertainments, and he was notorious for partying. The Monk of Evesham wrote that the king was "prodigious with gifts, extravagant in dress, faint-hearted in war, and often spent half the night up carousing with his friends and indulging himself in other unmentionable ways."[21]

The record of Richard II, "the most beautiful of kings" and "flower of youths" ("flos puerorum"), as Gower called him,[22] includes entries noting his taste in fine clothes and a fondness for self-display. The king's interest in ritualized displays of knighthood is evident in his sponsoring of large-scale tournaments, such as the one held at Smithfield in 1390, when he welcomed its participants to "la neuf Troie,"[23] and in his interest in the Order of the Garter. But unlike Edward III, whose nominations to the order "read like a roll call of honour, echoing across the fields of France,"[24] Richard II installed his young friends in positions of inappropriate chivalric grandeur.[25] Most detested, according to contemporary commentators, was Richard's close friend, Robert de Vere, who was elevated to the order and also made duke of Ireland.[26] These awards of status were so inappropriate, in Walsingham's eyes, that they proved that de Vere must have resorted to black magic to gain power over the king and also that the two shared obscene intimacies ("familiaritatis obscoenae").[27] In addition to such charges, it further was said that the royal household spent too much on hospitality and entertained too many foreigners. Indeed, just four years into the reign, the king's chancellor was dismissed as part of a commons reform package in response to the financial abuses perpetrated by the royal household.[28]

The charges that Richard's court was extravagant are unfair, particularly when Richard's expenses are compared to similar expenses for the court of Edward III. And similarly, on the topic of military failure, it is important to note that Richard inherited many of his difficulties.[29] And yet the history of the reign of Richard II is such that it is impossible to read even his early, untainted years without imposing on them our knowledge of what was to come. Historians have cautioned against letting this retrospective knowledge pollute our analyses of the record and have urged us not to postdate our views of Richard to accord with what we know came after him.[30] But how can we read the past without reference to its already enacted future? What sorts of possibilities exist for reentering and reimagining a historical event already achieved? The textual strategies of *Troilus and Criseyde* address these questions in ways that mimic the practice of a historian belatedly seeking the cause and consequence of the past from the knowing vantage point of the future. It is a literally forward-looking version of history that seeks to justify the events of the past in light of what comes later—the kind of history that, although already knowing the future, pretends not to in order to make it so.

Chaucer's poem offers a vision of a prelapsarian old Troy that coincides with a moment of prelapsarian but foredoomed new Troy, before the fall of Richard II and its inevitable entry into the chronicles. In this vision, we catch a glimpse of London and of the court that is impossibly untainted, and we can also trace the kinds of reading practices that make our own visions of history possible. The text is not a roman à clef, with purposeful and specific reference to its context; rather, it demonstrates the kind of accidental clairvoyance that characterizes this genre of history. As Pearsall suggests, the poem's narrated progress of Troy follows the fate of the aristocratic world in which it was produced:

> The brilliance and joyousness of Books II and III of the poem may have to do with a time when Richard and Anne's court was, in the early 1380s, specially a place of youth and festival, and the old idea of London as "the New Troy" could have a momentary flourishing.[31]

The joyousness of the poem's early phases certainly does match the mood of Richard's court in the 1380s, but so do the cynicism, despair, and ultimate resignation of Books IV and V capture the mood of what was soon to follow. The Trojan court of the poem is one of misplaced chivalric exuberance, insofar as its failure is the historically necessary consequence of its grandeur: Troy simply must fall. New Troy also must fall, and with it its king and its principal poet. Through the seductive figure of Criseyde, the poem speaks to the seductive impossibility of historical revisionism, and in the process, it manufactures nostalgia for Ricardian and Chaucerian glory in advance of their disappearance.

In *Troilus and Criseyde*, the narrator's relationship to his historical material is characterized by the paradoxical impulse to remain true to an authoritative account of the story while simultaneously regretting and resisting that authoritative precedent. Most readers would agree with Barbara Nolan that in between resisting the historical and submitting to it, "Chaucer's narrating 'I' opens out alternatives to the inevitable conclusion of his ancient tragic history." Such alternatives have been discussed structurally, as when Strohm observes that history is only one of several genres invoked in the poem. The narrative coordinates, he writes, shift "from tragedy to history to romance and back to tragedy again." Scholars have also focused on the narrator's portrayal of human character as a means of avoiding his historical material: Nolan suggests that it is through his detailed psychological representations of the lovers that the narrator "develops several 'interim' fictions designed to evade or transcend the sad truth of mortal history"; and Patterson argues that the poem is "a meditation on history that effaces the historical," replacing it with "the meditating mind itself."[32] Offered in the place of history's absence from the poem are generic variations (tragedy, romance, fiction, subjectivity) on the theme of "not history." But even though critics have located in the narrator a desire to suppress his historical material, they have also acknowledged that this desire is at odds with his project. The narrator ends up writing history anyway.

This paradoxical relationship is best addressed by thinking of *Troilus and Criseyde* as a utopian text. Utopianism, particularly as outlined in the work of Ernst Bloch and Louis Marin, offers a conceptual framework for understanding the possibilities and limitations inherent in resisting history, and it helps explain how, in Chaucer's poem, the suppression of history is a prerequisite for its inscription. Premised on the interplay of presence and absence, utopia's ambiguity designates both something good and something simply "not": not history, not real, and ultimately not true.[33] Although Chaucer's *Troilus* "trafficks in lies,"[34] the lies are wishful as well as willful, based on a hope for an impossible future and designed to deceive the teller at least as much as the hearer. If, as Strohm writes, historical documents present us with "the paradox of the lie that might as well be true,"[35] *Troilus and Criseyde* presents us with the paradox of the utopian fiction, the lie preferred over the historical truth.

The narrator would prefer to believe that Criseyde fell in love slowly, that she guarded her honor carefully, and that even though she had to leave Troy and Troilus, she did so most unwillingly.[36] These wishful and willful revisions of Criseyde have often been discussed as symptomatic of the narrator's desire for her. As Talbot Donaldson notes, Chaucer's narrator is seduced into believing his own revised version of events because he is thoroughly charmed by its central character, Criseyde: "[I]n his love [he] pines for what is not so desperately that he almost brings it into being."[37] What the narrator almost achieves is an ideal utopian world—situated before the fall and inhabited by a beautiful, available, discreet widow—that, for the first three books, nearly succeeds in persuading him of its own viability. The narrator is almost convinced that a world that has Criseyde in it "is not only the best of all possible worlds, but the most possible."[38] The "most possible" world is a fantasy other time and other place, no time and no place, pretendedly situated outside of its negated term, history. A chronotopic alternative to history that nevertheless is tied to its objectionable truth, utopian figuration is precisely "not history," with equal emphasis on both words.

The narrative of *Troilus and Criseyde* takes place according to a utopian chronology, what Bloch calls the "not yet," in its conceit that history (the fall of Troy, Criseyde's betrayal of Troilus) has not yet happened. Unlike historiography, "which merely reproduce[s] perceptions of the past,"[39] utopia's posture is anticipatory and points, paradoxically, to a future better than the one we know is coming.[40] The utopian "not yet" is a moment of freedom from the restrictions of history, and *Troilus and Criseyde,* situated as prior to history, is "free" for the first three books to anticipate a future other than the one demanded by history. Criseyde in the pre-apocalypse Troy is represented as the pre-treachery Other of her historical identity.

But even while the poem points to a different future, one in which Criseyde perhaps will not be false and thus Troy perhaps will not fall, that possibility has already been foreclosed. Before proceeding with his account, the narrator announces that Criseyde "forsook" Troilus (I, 56) and that "Troie moste ben fordo" (I, 74). Knowledge of this tragic future is asserted throughout the poem in the form of the narrator's many asides to the reader. He frequently interrupts with reminders, however veiled, that Troilus's joy cannot last. As Morton Bloomfield has noted, "it is just this knowledge that Chaucer the commentator-historian gives us as he reconstructs the past. Hence we are forced into an awareness of the inevitability of the tragedy and get our future and our present at the same time." The simultaneity of chronological markers in the text (the past is colored with knowledge of the future) makes the narrator's utopian desires ultimately hopeless, since, as Bloomfield continues, "there is no escape from the past if one chooses to reconstruct... [it] from the vantage ground of the present."[41]

The limited ability to resist history by means of a chronologically prior posture is voiced in the poem by Pandarus, who acknowledges that the end of any narrative is its point:

> How so it be that som men hem delite
> With subtyl art hire tales for to endite,
> Yet for al that, in hire entencioun
> Hire tale is al for som conclusioun.
> (II, 256–59)

Pandarus says what the narrator knows is true but cannot stand, that "th'ende is every tales strengthe" (II, 260). Whatever alternatives may be produced in utopian "not history" necessarily are temporary and incomplete. Historical knowledge cannot be held at bay forever, and neither can it be entirely repressed.

But to write "not history" is different from simply not writing history. It is to write history anyway, under the conceit that one is not doing so. Like the mechanics of negation as outlined in Freudian psychoanalysis, utopian figures stand in for what has been repressed and replace the objectionable truth with something that is at once less distasteful but also thoroughly transparent in its motivation. Occupying a liminal space between complete repression and full consciousness, utopian figuration anticipates the truth and provides "a way of taking cognizance of what is repressed" without having to acknowledge it fully.[42]

Bloch's understanding of the utopian "not yet" is similarly based on a theory of preconsciousness. The utopian impulse anticipates a future not yet possible in the present. In this way, utopia is pure potential—both hopeful and hopeless.[43] Repressive and liberating at the same time, utopian figuration is poised on the boundary between revising the past and anticipating the future, between masking the objectionable and constructing the desirable, and between lying and dreaming.

Like the Freudian subconscious, utopia works on the matter of the past, translating it into different but readily familiar terms. But this process, as relentlessly textual as history writing itself, is also as subject to the same vagaries as the "old" history it was meant to replace. The term "history," in this context, thus carries with it two competing senses of signification. One, the more familiar and supposedly more oppressive, is the sense of history as an authoritative record of the thing done: The *res gesta*—always already inscripted, occupying pride of chronological place and thus seeming to foreclose alternatives—transmits its own presence as a transparent, monolithic entity at least as much as it transmits its record of the past. Posing as (and received as) that which is merely handed down, abstracted from all mediation, this is the sort of history associated with those Trojan War texts dismissed by the narrator at the beginning of his project.

But, as many (including the narrator) are tempted to forget, history is only ever a textual product: Textually mediated and textually constructed, the *auctoritee* of history is generated by its writers and, in turn, granted by its readers. The insistent textuality of history precludes the possibility of simply or passively rerecording (whether merely repeating or even consciously revising) an account of the past. "To return" in writing is a fictive pose, a disguise for "to create." The narrator's recuperative effort on behalf of Criseyde, his return to narratives of ancient Troy, is more accurately seen as a projection of himself into the past. Psychoanalysis again provides a useful model: The subject goes back in time to her or his "prior self," not so much to change or erase the past but rather to (re)construct it. As Slavoj Žižek writes,

> The subject is confronted with a scene from the past that he wants to change, to meddle with, to intervene in; he takes a journey into the past, intervenes in the scene, and it is not that he "cannot change anything"—quite the contrary, only through

> his intervention does the scene from the past become what it always was: his intervention was from the beginning comprised, included.[44]

Chaucer's narrator's journey back to ancient Troy, before the fall of the city and before Criseyde's betrayal of Troilus, is similarly doomed as a recuperative expedition. His intervention into the historical scene of the love affair, his "meddling" with previous renditions, is scripted to become exactly what he seeks to change *because* he seeks to change it.

The depiction of Criseyde, the fruit of the narrator's illusions of intervention into the past, both resists and confirms—in some ways, even creates—her historical status as a symbol of treacherous feminine duplicity. Criseyde is linked genealogically to the past despite the narrator's attempts to negate her ties to history and, in a Žižekian sense, precisely because of these attempts. *Troilus and Criseyde* postpones and negates the past and thereby anticipates a powerfully seductive alternative future that is nevertheless hopelessly illusory. Ultimately, it is impossible to write "not history," and this is why, despite Karl Mannheim's claims to the contrary, utopias always fail.[45] Perversely, utopia becomes history, its Other, during the process of figuration.

The first extended description of Criseyde indicates the narrator's desire to separate her from her past. She is depicted as so angelic in her native beauty that "lik a thing inmortal sęmed she, / As doth an hevenyssh perfit creature, / That down were sent in scornynge of nature" (I, 103–5). Although she has already been mentioned briefly in relation to her father, Calkas, this breathless description emphasizes her disconnectedness from the world and from other people in it. Instead of being defined in terms of her history, she is portrayed as an ethereally beautiful lady of romance, and her origins are said to be literally nebulous.

It is in Criseyde's interest to be dissociated from her past, especially from her treasonous father. Because of Calkas's defection to the Greeks, popular opinion in Troy held that "he *and al his kyn* at-ones / Ben worthi for to brennen, fel and bones" (I, 90–91, emphasis added). When Criseyde appeals to Hector for protection from the violent mob, she is also asking for protection from her father's reputation and, in effect, to be excused from association with her own familial history. Hector is moved to help her primarily because she was "sorwfully bigon" (I, 114)—a phrase that, although glossed idiomatically in the *Riverside* note as "in a sorrowful situation," more literally refers to her already being consigned to a state of sorrow: Her sorrowful origins, or beginnings, as the daughter of Calkas predetermine her future. When Hector grants her all the honor she used to have before Calkas's shameful disappearance and decrees that her "body shal men save" (I, 120–22), he replaces her father in Troy, becoming the guarantor of both her good name and her physical safety.

Hector's act of surrogacy replaces not only Calkas the man but also what the man, a "lord of gret auctorite" (I, 65), means: the history of Troy that is "not" going to be told in this poem. Calkas is a gifted prophet. Like history, he asserts foreknowledge of all conclusions. Like the historiographers who are banned from *Troilus* at its outset, he spends most of his time in exile from the poem. Finally, Calkas is a traitor who abandons his daughter and leaves her alone to contend with his crime. In a similar way, the written, authoritative history of Troy had also disowned Criseyde by depicting her simply as the treacherous vixen who destroyed the noble Troilus. When Hector tells Criseyde to "Lat youre fadres treson gon" (I, 117), he attempts to erase all this bad history, declaring it out of bounds in his vision of a perfect civic realm.

Simultaneous with Hector's erasure of the past, however, is a glimpse into the inevitably tragic future. Calkas's crime, which is here called upon in order to be dismissed, is the same one that Criseyde eventually will commit: faith-breaking.[46] By trying to negate the past, Hector's words have brought the future into consciousness, as objectionable as it still may be. Hector's negation of Criseyde's history is thus similar to the narrator's own practice: While Hector is trying to allow Criseyde freedom from Calkas's notoriety, the narrator is trying to grant her a reprieve from her own notoriety. Hector protects her within the community of Troy by virtue of his political authority. The narrator sets out to salvage her reputation within the community of letters, using his position as a literary *auctor*. The poem thus enacts Hector's order of forgiveness, creating a time and a space in which Criseyde can be something other than the traitorous daughter of a traitor.

Criseyde's alternative identity is as "joie," both for Troy and for Troilus. It often has been noted that Troilus's name means "little Troy" and that his death was considered a prerequisite for the fall of the city.[47] But Criseyde is the one responsible for the death of Troilus and, by extension, for the death of the city as well.[48] Serving as a marker for this connection between the woman and the fate of the city, "joie" is what

Troy and Troilus have when Criseyde is present, and it is what they lose when she leaves. The narrator explicitly equates Criseyde with joy when he exclaims at her departure, "But Troilus, now far-wel al thi joie, / For shaltow nevere sen hire eft in Troie!" (V, 27–28). From the moment Hector first makes Criseyde part of the community—"ye youreself in joie / Dwelleth with us, while yow good list, in Troie" (I, 118–19)—until she is taken out of the city and traded for Antenor, when Fortune "gan pulle awey the fetheres brighte of Troie / Fro day to day, til they ben bare of joie" (V, 1546–47), joy in and for the city hinges upon Criseyde's presence in it. When Troilus loses his joy, he dies, as do Troy's hopes for civic survival.[49]

To allow for a time of utopian joy, much of what we know about the city and about Criseyde must be withheld from the poem. The erasure of Calkas, along with Dares and Dictys, the two historians with the best reputation for accuracy in the Middle Ages, creates the illusion of an untroubled Trojan space—a place that has been emptied of its traitorous enemies, collectively known as history.[50] One early signal that history (the kind characterized by irrefutable knowledge of the past) has been removed from Troy is the extended allusion to springtime that introduces the historical city with an oddly ahistorical conventionality:

> And so bifel, whan comen was the tyme
> Of Aperil, whan clothed is the mede
> With newe grene, of lusty Veer the pryme,
> And swote smellen floures, white and rede,
> In sondry wises shewed, as I rede,
> The folk of Troie hire observaunces olde,
> Palladiones feste for to holde.
>
> (I, 155–61)

This is not Troy under siege, "for it were a long digression / Fro my matere" (I, 143–44). This is not life during wartime. Instead, "Palladiones feste" is as cyclical and predictable as April itself, the usualness of the event asserted by the conspicuously casual narrative process marker "and so bifel." By not mentioning the Greeks, or the war, or even which April it is, the narrator is free to move on to populate the temple with the timeless and placeless figures of "many a lusty knyght" and "many a lady fressh and mayden bright" (I, 165, 166).

This emptied-out good place/no place, however, is full of associations with what has been repressed in its construction. For one thing, as Patterson has noted, the theft of the "relik, heet Palladion" (I, 153), was understood to be one of the preconditions for Troy's ruin.[51] Furthermore, the physical description of Criseyde here among the fresh ladies and bright maidens at the feast noticeably sets her apart from the idyllic world of Troy during "not wartime." Everybody else in the temple is "ful wel arayed, both meeste, mene, and leste, / Ye, bothe for the seson and the feste" (I, 167–68). But Criseyde is dressed "in widewes habit blak" (I, 170), marking her separateness from the rest of the happy company. It is not just that she is wearing black clothes. Rather, her clothes announce that she has a history. Criseyde is placed along a chronological continuum at this very moment of otherwise highly conventional timelessness. The particular kind of history that her widow's garb announces, moreover, is a former affiliation with a man. The black habit is an allusion to her sexual past that inevitably looks forward to her sexual future, when Troilus, too, will be her former man. Indeed, when the moment that she must leave Troilus comes, Criseyde vows to wear her widow's habit again: "And, Troilus, my clothes everychon / Shul blake ben in tokenyng, herte swete, / That I am as out of this world agon" (IV, 778–80). Unlike the other, uncomplicated Trojan ladies in the company, whose beauty is apparent (fresh and bright), Criseyde is described as occluded, wearing dark clothing, standing back in a corner, her beauty a bright star under a black cloud. Right from the very beginning of her new figuration as "joie," the narrator's Criseyde is marked as belonging to history.

The many narratorial comments to the reader throughout the poem similarly assert historical knowledge in the midst of "not history." The repressed returns the way the repressed always does: in the form of seemingly inexplicable symptomatic eruptions in discourse. The famous allusion to "myn auctour called Lollius" (I, 394) is one such outburst that offers itself as a productive enigma, simultaneously masking and suggesting its own logic. As an embodiment of the utopian fiction—the kind of lie that reveals its truth in the process of trying to hide it—Lollius's presence here points loudly and silently at Chaucer's real *auctor,* Boccaccio.[52] The authority for the story of the disastrous love affair of Troilus and Criseyde, whether residing in supposedly historical treatments like Guido's or in literary treatments like Boccaccio's, is framed as an obstacle in Chaucer's version. These objectionable authorities, the "fathers" of the story, have to be removed and replaced by more congenial authorities. Just as Hector replaces Calkas as Criseyde's paternal protector, so does Lollius replace Boccaccio as Chaucer's paternal source. Lollius is a fantasy stand-in for history, a surrogate authority that, in the process of replacing an objectionable source, calls attention to its own fabricated status.

The avoidance of Boccaccio and the corresponding preference for Lollius suggest that the inevitability of the literary source provides an occasion for resistance that is, like the resistance to historical determinism, both hopeful and hopeless. The utopian possibility for poetic originality is foreclosed by the determinism of Boccaccio's prior text, which—like Dares, Dictys, and Calkas—must be removed to allow for a temporary alternative narrative. But the authority of *Il filostrato,* whose status as source imposes its rule upon the freedom of *Troilus and Criseyde,* nevertheless is an authority granted by the narrator: on the one hand, the passive, belated reader of Boccaccio as a limiting source, and on the other hand, the writer of Boccaccio as the definitive source. The narrator completes the circuit of the transmission of Boccaccio's "prior" authority by insistently refusing to name him.

Knowledge of what the future will bring, despite and because of the narrator's efforts to deny it, keeps bringing the repressed historical material back into the poem. The repressed thus returns from the future in *Troilus.* As in analysis, where the story of the past is told to someone presumed to know its consequences, here the narrator's comments on his story of the past allude to a future that we are presumed already to know.[53] For example, when Criseyde is thinking about loving Troilus, casting his "excellent prowesse" (II, 660) around in her mind, the narrator breaks in to describe what he imagines to be his readers' response:

> Now myghte som envious jangle thus:
> "This was a sodeyn love; how myght it be
> That she so lightly loved Troilus
> Right for the firste syghte, ye, parde?"
> (II, 666–69)

This comment, presumably designed to deny our knowledge of the future, when Criseyde will forsake her easy-come, easy-go love, actually achieves the opposite result: It reminds us that Criseyde is famous for taking Troilus too lightly and that this unsavory future is very much a part of the present matter. These kinds of narratorial intrusions can be read as the symptomatic traces of the historical unconscious that (although repressed) necessarily attends the narrator's utopia. Whether or not we already knew the tragic conclusion, the narrator's denial of it functions as an announcement of the inevitable end of the affair. He creates our knowledge of Criseyde's betrayal in the process of disavowing it. The phenomenon of negation, whereby that which is repressed is allowed expression as long as it is denied, serves to explain to the reader that the opposite is probably true: "For I sey *nought* that she so sodeynly / Yaf hym hire love" (II, 673–74, emphasis added).

The narrator's stumbling refusal to say that Criseyde yielded herself "sodeynly" is suggestive of Chaucer's own reluctance to follow Boccaccio's rendition of the sexual union of the lovers. Chaucer's "lengthiest and most ambitious departure from the *Filostrato*" occurs in the first half of Book III, when arrangements are being made to bring the lovers together to consummate their affair.[54] Instead of moving directly from the conversation between Pandarus and Troilus about the need for discretion to a climactic bedroom scene, as Boccaccio did, Chaucer adds an initial bedroom scene at Deiphoebus's house, greatly expands the conversation on discretion, details Pandarus's careful maneuverings to get the lovers together, and even describes a dinner party at Pandarus's house before literally pushing Troilus into bed with Criseyde.[55] This overly wrought strategy of protraction and delay is present even within the confines of the lovers' meeting at Deiphoebus's house, where the possibilities for a sexual union are already foreclosed by the sheer preposterousness of the arrangement. The scene is interrupted by the Prologue to Book III just as Troilus is in the height of anxious anticipation of Criseyde's arrival at his "sickbed": "O myghty God, what shal he seye?" (II, 1757). Stopping the action completely to praise Venus and call on Calliope for help with writing about Troilus's gladness, the narrator stretches the moment of anticipation over the seam between two books of the poem. When we finally return to Troilus's bed, the narrator acknowledges the hiatus by almost jokingly reminding us of where we were before the interruption: "Lay al this mene while Troilus" (III, 50).

Reiterating the delay achieved through the structure of the poem, the lovers themselves participate in extending the amount of time they spend in a condition of unrequited desire. Even once they are within reach of fulfillment, they resist the end. When Pandarus has seen to all the details of where in his house everyone is to sleep on this rainy night and has guaranteed that everything is going to plan, he sits down next to Troilus and, "shortly to the point right for to gon" (III, 701), tells him his time has come: "Make the redy right anon, / For thow shalt into hevene blisse wende" (III, 703–4). Troilus, instead of leaping up and going to Criseyde immediately, calls on the gods for help for three stanzas before Pandarus impatiently grabs him by the "lappe" (III, 742) and brings him through the trap door.[56]

These departures from Boccaccio's text have the effect of delaying consummation and have generally been understood as part of Chaucer's "courtly" impulse: He slows down the unseemly speed with which Boccaccio's lovers come together in an attempt to emphasize Criseyde's virtue.[57] This interpretation is surely correct insofar as it examines the discrepancy between Chaucer's text and the source outside it. But even within the poem, according to its own internal logic, the postponement of sex serves a telling function. Delaying the consummation of Troilus and Criseyde's affair protects the lie in which the lovers are participating, that which asserts that their liaison is based on something more exalted than mercantile sexuality. Elements of pandering and prostitution that necessarily focus on the sexual end, or point, of relationships are revised in the poem into elements of courtly love, friendship, and pity—forms of relationship that encourage desire but discourage sexual gratification. Pandarus is the orchestrator of this translation of terms, but both Troilus and Criseyde come to accept his master-glossing.

Pandarus negotiates between crass sexuality and exalted courtly love and comes up with the perfect gloss for both: euphemism. Troilus, who needs to be brought out of his chivalric paralysis if he is to join the community of men who have sex with women, is seduced by Pandarus's innuendo. "To good port hastow rowed," Pandarus says upon learning the identity of Troilus's love, since Criseyde, he hints, will be relatively easy to bring around for Troilus's sexual pleasure: "It sit hire naught to ben celestial / As yet" (I, 969, 983–84). The blasphemous tableau in which Pandarus makes Troilus "confess" his sins and pledge his faith to Love is filled with sexual puns, including one that looks forward to the General Prologue of the *Canterbury Tales* (214): "[T]how shalt ben the beste post, I leve, / Of al his lay" (I, 1000–1001). Troilus must be made to understand what Pandarus is getting for him, but he must also be convinced that this sort of ignoble arrangement is perfectly acceptable. Pandarus initiates Troilus into the community of lovers by offering him forms of codified, crafted behavior to follow: ride by her window just so, write her a letter, and wink at bawdy jokes, for these are the things that lovers do.

Pandarus's seduction of Criseyde similarly relies on euphemism both to express and to mask what is being said: She must be made to understand what she is being asked to do, but she must also be made willing to do it. When Criseyde suddenly interrupts a conversation of small talk with her uncle to ask if Troilus can "wel speke of love" (II, 503), Pandarus understands that, at this request for romantic fantasy, the crass deed is done: "Tho Pandarus a litel gan to smyle" (II, 505). After telling Criseyde an elaborately embellished account of Troilus's first expressions of love for her (II, 507–74), Pandarus slides his narrative coyly back to its point when he concludes with a vulgar suggestion:

> Wel in the ryng than is the ruby set.
> Ther were nevere two so wel ymet
> Whan ye ben his al hool as he is youre
> There myghty God graunte us see that houre!
> (II, 585–88)

Criseyde's response—"Nay, therof spak I nought, ha ha! . . . / As helpe me God, ye shenden every deel!" (II, 589–90)—indicates her playful resistance. She understands the distinction between love fantasies and pragmatic sexuality, but she requires the fantasy.

Pandarus has constructed a love affair based on delusion and, as he acknowledges, "fantasie" (III, 275). His pragmatic maneuvering between the lovers is willingly glossed over by both Troilus and Criseyde because the truth is something they would prefer to repress. In between delusion and knowledge, a utopian fiction requires a "state of mind in which one knows and does not know a thing at the same time."[58] Troilus and Criseyde are situated in between "knowing and yet not knowing" to such a degree that they, like the narrator, almost fully believe their own lie. Troilus, for one, becomes such an expert liar that he seems even to convince himself. Although he pretends to be sick at Deiphoebus's house, "his brother and his suster for to blende" (III, 207), by the time he is pretending to be sick with jealousy at Pandarus's house, he plays the role so well that he faints and has to be undressed and tossed onto the bed. Criseyde asks the right question at this moment when she wonders, "Is this a mannes game? / What, Troilus, wol ye do thus for shame?" (III, 1126–27).

For Troilus has indeed been playing a "mannes game," Pandarus's game of pretending that the lovers' relationship is courtly. A remarkable exchange between the two men shows to what lengths Troilus is willing to go to preserve this fiction. Pandarus, who is never a believer in any of the lies he propagates, explicitly tells the truth to Troilus and admits that his own role as a go-between is shabby and corrupt:

> For shame it is to seye:
> For the have I bigonne a gamen pleye
> . . . .
> That is to seye, for the am I bicomen,
> Bitwixen game and ernest, swich a meene
> As maken wommen unto men to comen;
> Al sey I nought, thow wost wel what I meene.
> (III, 249–50, 253–56)

He is trying to make clear to Troilus just what has happened, what kind of contract has been agreed upon: "Thow woost ek what thi lady graunted the, / And day is set the chartres up to make" (III, 339–40). Despite Pandarus's rare honesty and frank talk, Troilus refuses to believe that his lady has been procured for him. He willfully revises pandering into an exalted form of friendship:

> Me thoughte by thi speche
> That this which thow me dost for compaignie,
> I sholde wene it were a bauderye
> . . . .
> It is nought so, that woot I wel, parde!
> . . . .
> And this that thow doost, calle it gentilesse,
> Compassioun, and felawship, and trist.
> (III, 395–97, 399, 402–03)

Moreover, to prove just how acceptable Pandarus's behavior really is, Troilus makes an offer to him in kind:

And that thow knowe I thynke nought ne wene
That this servise a shame be or jape,
I have my faire suster Polixene,
Cassandre, Eleyne, or any of the frape—
Be she nevere so fair or wel yshape,
Tel me which thow wilt of everychone,
To han for thyn, and lat me thanne allone.
(III, 407–13)

Troilus's imitation of Pandarus's "bauderye," stunningly articulated by the representation of Troilus's noble kinswomen as so many members of a "frape," performs a kind of contract of its own between the two men. It is a demonstration that they both understand the same euphemistic language, even in the face of the naked truth, and that they agree on mutual complicity: "Thus held hym ech of other wel apayed" (III, 421). Troilus has been brought fully into Pandarus's system of gloss and euphemism and has found that it suits him, "so wel dissimilen he koude" (III, 434).

The prolongation of desire, whether achieved by the temporal delay of sexual gratification or by a discursive practice of willful euphemism, is the means by which Troilus and Criseyde's relationship is made to "feel like" a courtly romance. Similarly, desire has been driving the narrator's utopian fiction, making it feel like something other than history. Troilus and Criseyde and the narrator prefer to dwell in a state of hopeful desire, a condition that seems to postpone the end even while it moves toward fulfillment. The lovers' lingering *alba* (dawn song) signifies not just their reluctance to part in the morning but also their regret at no longer dwelling in a state of perpetual desire, since, after the climax, only the end is still to come.[59] Troilus goes back to his usual pursuits of jousting, feasting, hawking, hunting, and fighting Greeks: "In suffisaunce, in blisse, and in singynges, / This Troilus gan al his lif to lede" (III, 1716–17). And the narrator goes back to his task of telling of the double sorrow of Troilus in loving; he "returns" to the tragedy demanded by history. In this way, the lovers' *alba* speaks for the narrator's own trauma at now having to turn to the end of his matter. The suspension of time achieved through the utopian dilation of "joie" is over when everything we knew was coming finally does: daylight, the lovers, and history.[60]

The coming of history requires the return of Criseyde to her legendary status as the deviant woman who brought down Troilus and Troy. Before and after Chaucer, Criseyde was a famous figure whose name was synonymous with feminine duplicity: Hers was not just the usual kind of sexual infidelity, where one man gets burned, but the political kind insofar as, by betraying Troilus, she betrayed Troy, and the city burned.[61] The word "Criseyde" was not so much a term used to describe a certain woman as it was a term indicating a legend, which, as Linda Charnes writes, is

> a cultural product which depends on the naturalizing or "forgetting" of its own history as a manufactured thing. Always read as a paradigm for some authoritative reality, the legendary elides the space that originally existed between its constructedness and that "reality" to which it refers.[62]

"Criseyde" was a word used to designate natural feminine treachery. As Charnes observes, the infamy of such a name is produced in and replicated by "historical" narratives that invest characters with meanings that exceed the boundaries of their originary loci.[63]

Chaucer's narrator, by treating the legendary Criseyde in terms other than a historiographer's, calls attention to the ideologically suppressed space between the infamous name and its particular origin, and it is in this limited sense that his utopia might be said to succeed. As Marin's discussion suggests, utopian figuration resists the historical by "playing with" its available terms of signification. Existing in the "operative space or crevice" between history and its representation, utopian figuration calls attention to and plays with the dichotomy between the two. At some moments describing Criseyde and her innermost feelings and thoughts in such a way that critics have confessed themselves seduced by her, and at other moments bursting into the narrative with intimations of her infamy, the narrator plays multiple fields of Criseydan representation against each other. Despite its ultimate failure to achieve real change, the narrator's utopia "liberates a plural voice" and calls into question the historiographical system that produced Criseyde as a legend.[64]

But Chaucer's narrator's attempts to re-create the legendary Criseyde in "not history" are similar to Hector's attempts to protect her: They cannot be sustained against overwhelming necessity. When Hector objects to trading Criseyde for Antenor with the argument "We usen here no wommen for to selle" (IV, 182), he is met with a flood of opposition and advised to get over his idealism: "O Ector, lat tho fantasies be!" (IV, 193).[65] The utopian world in which Criseyde would be protected from the Trojan throng ends when Hector's call to adhere to a noble cause is drowned out by popular demand. The "noyse of peple," representative of the clamorous voice of predestined history, requires this future, and Hector's political authority—as well as the narrator's literary authority—is impotent in the face of it.

History requires both the fall of Troy and the inscription of Criseyde's reputation as an embodiment of feminine treachery, and as the poem moves along in time this future looms all the larger in its inevitability. The "fast-forwarding" of narrative time (it is announced at the start of Book V that the affair had been going on for three years) makes the already tenuous distinction between history and "not history" all the more difficult to maintain. The teasing promise that perhaps Criseyde and Troilus would not part is converted here into an inevitable fate, the one in which Criseyde will forsake her lover, Troilus will die, and Troy will fall. The alternative future that was once anticipated hopefully has become the same old future, the one to be dreaded and resisted.

This recasting of the nature of the future changes the nature of Criseyde as a utopian figure. Chaucer's poem has, in a sense, entered the present tense in Book V, and Criseyde is confronted with her historical identity while she is still in the remains of the utopian "not yet." With the conflation of past, present, and future, the difference between history and "not history" collapses, and Criseyde becomes what Charnes calls "a legend in her own time." Recognizing herself in the most unflattering of mirrors, the one held up for her by authoritative history, Criseyde witnesses her own transformation into a "notorious identity":[66]

> Allas, of me, unto the worldes ende,
> Shal neyther ben ywriten nor ysonge
> No good word, for thise bokes wol me shende.
> O, rolled shal I ben on many a tonge!
> Thorughout the world my belle shal be ronge!
>
> (V, 1058–62)

Criseyde's lament at what she has become is at the same time an acknowledgment of what she has always been. She returns to her familiar history when she returns to her father, Calkas.

Troilus, too, in his excursus on predestination, recognizes what he has always known but what his "conversion" to Pandarus's system had made him almost forget: "Thus to ben lorn, it is my destinee" (IV, 959). This is not haphazard Fortune, as cruel as that may be, but worse: Troilus's misery has been predicted. His recognition of "necessite," like Criseyde's sudden recognition of the truth of the future, comes as no surprise to him:

> And in this manere this necessite
> Retorneth in his part contrarie agayn.
> For nedfully byhoveth it nat to bee
> That thilke thynges fallen in certayn
> That ben purveyed; but nedly, as they sayn,
> Byhoveth it that thynges whiche that falle,
> That they in certayn ben purveyed alle.
> (IV, 1002–8)

Troilus's grief in the face of the horror of necessity, although certainly genuine, is nevertheless a return to his rightful position. His participation in the community of Love's servants was based on a lie, and his true identity was always located outside that community of lovers. Troilus's removal to the eighth sphere, where he finally achieves his predestined status as the ultimate outsider and laughs, suggests the appropriateness of his present torture. But even before he dies, Troilus anticipates his tragic end with a lovingly detailed fantasy of himself as a pathetic figure:

> And of hymself ymagened he ofte
> To ben defet, and pale, and waxen lesse
> Than he was wont, and that men seyden softe,
> "What may it be? Who kan the sothe gesse
> Whi Troilus hath al this hevynesse?"
> And al this nas but his malencolie,
> That he hadde of hymself swich fantasie.
> (V, 617–23)

Troilus's return to his familiar misery is so agreeable (not in the sense of producing happiness but, rather, as "fitting") to him that he participates imaginatively in his own destruction. As is the case with the narrator, he writes his own demise.

Like Criseyde's specifically literary nightmare of herself (she laments that her notoriety will be recorded in books), Troilus expresses his position in textual terms when he declares his woe in love so dramatic that "men myght a book make of it, lik a storie" (V, 585). But the character whose self-inscripted "fantasie" is the most damaging is that of Chaucer's own narrator, who finds himself writing the very thing he had sought to avoid: "[H]ow Criseyde Troilus forsook— / Or at the leeste, how that she was unkynde" (IV, 15–16). More importantly, however, Criseyde's forsaking of Troilus spells the end of Troy, the city that fell so that new Troy could rise. The alternative offered by the narrator's utopia, the one in which Criseyde does not forsake her lover and consequently Troy does not fall, is a future without the place founded by Aeneas's descendant Brutus. The text thus projects into the future the history and even the very existence of Britain.

But the poem is far from joyful at the prospect of the rise of new Troy. Instead, the impending fall of old Troy seems here to figure the fall of Britain, not its rise. The text asserts a simultaneity, or equation in both time and space, between old and new Troy rather than a chronologically sequential order to them as separate places.[67] Whereas in the *Aeneid*, as Jerome E. Singerman observes, "there seems always to be hovering over the Carthage of the poem the impossible possibility that it and the new Troy might have been one,"[68] *Troilus and Criseyde* imagines (impossibly) that Troy and London must be one. This "confusion" is expressed by the narrator and by Chaucer, as well as represented by them, when these two supposedly distinct figures meld, like old and new Troy, into one traumatized site in the final stages of the poem.

Peace between the Trojans and Greeks, however much "joie" it may have brought to Troilus and to Troy, is not a viable future. That the prospect of peace is doomed is clear when Criseyde initially uses it as one of her excuses not to run off with Troilus—"Ye sen that every day ek, more and more, / Men trete of pees" (IV, 1345–46)—but then just as quickly admits, twice, that such a peace is improbable: "And though so be that pees ther may be non, / Yet hider, though ther nevere pees ne were, / I moste come" (IV, 1359–61). Criseyde's prophecy, brutal as it is, demands that the utopian alternatives to the fall of Troy fail. Her notoriety, the death of Troilus, the destruction of Troy, the founding of Britain—in short, history—"moste come." The end of the court of Richard II, seen as necessary to the "progress" of the future, is implicated in this predestined history, as is the demise of Chaucer in his own time.

THE RICARDIAN SCENE OF *TROILUS AND CRISEYDE*

The court of Richard II in the early to middle 1380s was a place of splendor and elegance, but it was also one that lacked any real political power. Richard and Anne were young and beautiful, and the king's mother, Joan of Kent, was "la plus belle de tout la roiaulme d'Engleterre et la plus amoureuse" ("the most beautiful woman of the whole realm of England and also the most amorous"), but governmental policy was controlled by a group of powerful magnates—most notably the king's uncles, the dukes of Lancaster and Gloucester.[69] Gervase Mathew writes that by the spring of 1384, when Richard and Anne were both seventeen, "there was already very clearly a court, and a court party with its programme to assert and to extend the royal prerogative," but the king's party did not yet have the means or the power to do so.[70] It was in some respects a court waiting to happen and in others a court waiting to fail.

In 1385, when the war with France was going particularly badly for the English, Richard II went to Scotland.[71] The purpose of this campaign (during which Scrope and Grosvenor met) was to harass the Scots, who, as allies of the French but just as often acting of their own volition, were continually invading the north of England. But the campaign was equally important as a kind of chivalric debut for Richard. As Patterson writes, its purpose was "to provide the eighteen-year-old king with an opportunity to come into his own not only as monarch but as the leader of the chivalry of England."[72] The memorable victories of his grandfather having been overshadowed by numerous losses, Richard's Scottish campaign was to serve as an announcement of his capability as a military leader. The campaign, however, was a disaster, provoking John of Gaunt (whose Lancastrian faction "cosponsored" the assault) to quit in disgust and make for better chances in Castile. The excursion to Scotland "did nothing to dispel the sense of chivalric impotence" that pervaded the national mood.[73] This early misstep can be seen in retrospect to prefigure

Richard's later problems with his chivalric identity when instead of pursuing the French in war, he sought peace, and instead of cultivating attachments in London, he lavished patronage on the northwest. But even here in the early to middle 1380s, before his troubles truly began, the factional alignments and military blunders that were to contribute to his alienation and final demise already were in place.[74]

Discontent over Richard's failure in Scotland coincided with more general rumblings about English foreign policy. The pursuit of peace with the French was especially unpopular, and professional soldiers began to murmur about the "national disgrace" of any surrender of towns or territory to France.[75] At the same time, criticism of the king's unheroic friends and favorites was growing more vociferous. Those who supported Richard's attempts to extend his royal prerogative included the chancellor, Michael de la Pole; the chief justice, Robert Tresilian; and a group of London victuallers led by Nicholas Brembre. But they were no match for the hostile magnates who were incensed by the young king's attempts to wrest power away from them and into what they saw as unworthy hands: Richard's own and those of his associates. Particularly vexing, and a point of repeated complaint for many years, was the king's invention of the title of "marquis" for Robert de Vere in December 1385. The *Westminster*-Chronicler notes this invention and explains its symbolic consequences: "A marquis is superior to an earl and less than a duke; so that the king caused him to be seated in parliament above the earls" ("Marchio enim est major comite et minor duce; unde rex in parliamento supra comites fecit eum sedere").[76]

Having disappointed potential supporters by failing to engage in time-honored military pursuits and having antagonized many others by raising Robert de Vere to an unheard-of rank, Richard's attempts to gain control of his own rule went from bad to worse, culminating in the crisis of 1387–88. Although many literary historians have discussed this crisis of rule in Ricardian politics, few have fully pointed out just how destabilizing and dangerous the episode really was—perhaps in light of the comparatively more dramatic events of the deposition. But not least in its implications for Chaucer's life, the magnates' seizure of power from the king competes for importance with the deposition of 1399. Too often, the term "factionalism"—or even "fierce factionalism"—tends to make the whole problem sound like a mere political embarrassment for Richard II. It is more accurate to see the king not only as humiliated in the late 1380s but, for all practical purposes, as deposed.[77] The conflict centered on how and where power was to be defined in the realm. Significantly, Richard recruited in the northwest, while the magnates sought support in London.

In the October 1386 Parliament, at which Chaucer represented the king's party as MP for Kent, the opposition impeached the chancellor and imprisoned him. They further appointed a commission of magnates to reform the royal household and specifically to investigate corruption by officials appointed by Richard.[78] In response to this so-called Wonderful Parliament, the king set about to create a political stronghold in the western parts of his realm. As part of his ten-month "gyration" around the Midlands and the northwest, he made his first march through north Wales, drumming up support and soldiers for his cause. In August 1387 he induced five justices to give judgment in favor of the royal prerogative; and in September he appointed de Vere justice of Chester.[79] The opposing magnates, meanwhile, won over more support for themselves by spreading rumors to the effect that the king's inner circle, led by de Vere, had convinced him to sell his overseas possessions to the French.[80]

The accusations of treason against de Vere and other members of the king's party came late in November 1387, and it was agreed that no action would be taken in the matter until the Parliament set for 3 February 1388. But Richard, realizing the imminent threat to his friends and even his crown, immediately sent for the mayor and aldermen of London to ask for military support should he need it. Already, however, the city of London was against him. The mayor replied that the inhabitants of the city were just craftsmen and merchants, with no great military experience, and thus it was not possible for them to devote themselves to warfare.[81]

In November, Thomas of Woodstock (duke of Gloucester) and Thomas Beauchamp (earl of Warwick) marched an army on London. Near Highgate, they were joined by Richard Fitzalan (earl of Arundel), and together with Henry of Bolingbroke and Thomas Mowbray, they seized control of the city. De Vere, meanwhile, who had raised a small army in north Wales and Cheshire, marched southeast in December in an effort to join the besieged king in London. The Lords Appellant, as they came to be called, intercepted him in Oxfordshire, and de Vere was defeated on 20 December at Radcot Bridge.[82] Finally, on 27 December, the Appellants entered the Tower and took possession of the person of the king. It is possible that Richard II was actually deposed over a period of three days when he was thus trapped in the Tower.[83] Although de Vere escaped to exile, several of the king's friends and favorites—including his boyhood tutor Simon Burley, the former mayor Nicolas Brembre, and the writer Thomas Usk—were executed by order of the Merciless Parliament of 1388.

Richard was trounced, perhaps even lucky to have escaped with his crown: The Appellants' march on London was an invasion and occupation of the proper site of royal power. More significantly, the Ricardian claim to new Troy and any aspirations Richard may have had for a glorious court there were dashed.[84] Gower's 1400 *Cronica tripertita* describes the phases of the destruction of the relationship between the king and the city during this period, underscoring first their interdependence and then their ultimate alienation from one another:

> The shadowy one who bore the sun did not see the light, for during Troy's extremities he took vengeance upon the assembled peoples. It was first because of Troy that his sun sank to the depths: the people grew pale with fear at his eclipse, for he showed them no favor.[85]

Following the disaster of 1388, Richard moved ever further away from London and from the model of Troy: Not only did he repeatedly antagonize the citizens of the capital, as we saw in the example of the quarrel discussed in chapter 1, but he increasingly held court in remote, "Arthurian" parts of the country.

At the end of the composition period for *Troilus,* the failure of Richard II's new Trojan moment was imminent. The event was not foreseen literally by a clairvoyant Chaucer, but—according to the dreadful logic of Trojanness explored so fully in his poem—this future, once it happened, nevertheless must have been foreseen. The concluding movements of *Troilus and Criseyde* become, in retrospect, part of the record of the disintegration of Ricardianism. Attending this destruction is the transformation of Chaucer's identity as a poet of the Ricardian court.[86]

In response to the knowledge that he must tell the inevitable, Chaucer's narrator breaks down in Books IV and V of *Troilus and Criseyde* in expressions of deep regret and despair, denying responsibility for the text he has produced. In Book IV, for example, we find these lines: "And after this the storie telleth us" (IV, 1037), "I fynde ek in stories elleswhere" (IV, 1044), and "But trewely, the storie telleth us" (IV, 1051)—within fifteen lines of each other. When the "ancient history" of Troy's past collides with the necessity of its new Trojan consequences, Chaucer's narrator insists that the story is not his. He relinquishes his temporary benevolent paternity (as did Hector) and takes on a different form of paternalism.

The paternal figure most associated with history in the text is Calkas, the traitor who set the tragedy in motion and then disappeared. Here at the end of the poem, however, Calkas is resurrected in a telling comparison. In the Prologue to Book IV, the narrator reports that his own heart "right now gynneth blede, / And now my penne, allas, with which I write, / Quaketh for drede of that I moste endite" (IV, 12–14). Calkas, who has not been treated with any degree of sympathy in the poem so far, is then described in a way that echoes the narrator's own emotional distress:

> Tellyng his tale alwey, this olde greye,
> Humble in his speche and in his lokyng eke,
> The salte teris from his eyen tweye
> Ful faste ronnen down by either cheke.
> (IV, 127–30)

This association of the narrator with Calkas represents a major shift in the poem. Throughout the first three books, the narrator shared an affinity with Hector, a benevolent authority who uses his position to help a widow. But when Hector loses his ability to protect Criseyde from Calkas's demands, so, too, must the narrator relinquish his protective surrogacy and hand his utopia over to history. But unlike Hector, the narrator cannot simply fade out of the poem; by continuing to tell his tale to its end, he assumes as much responsibility for the tragedy as does Calkas himself. Finding himself Calkas's double, demanding Criseyde's return from a utopian time of joy, the narrator recognizes himself as a historiographer. During and because of the process of writing "not history," he has become exactly what he had sought to avoid. In a sense, he has become himself.

This imaginary reluctant writer of history both is and is not Chaucer. Of course, it is not Chaucer in an easy or obvious identification of the narrating voice with the historical person. It is more precisely a version of Chaucer, one that is mediated by the text and located in the "elsewhere" of discourse,

> the "space not visible in the frame but inferable from what the frame makes visible." This space is not so much beyond or external to the text as within the text, constituted as the text's own tacit admission of inability to control its own terms.[87]

The apparent lack of control evident at the end of *Troilus and Criseyde* has been the subject of some critical comment. Alternatingly scandalized and jaded, urgent and flippant, the tone is distinctly one of distress—"But God it wot, er fully monthes two, / She was ful fer fro that entencioun!" (V, 766–67)—and one of cynicism as well:

> But Troilus, thow maist now, est or west,
> Pipe in an ivy lef, if that the lest!
> Thus goth the world. God shild us fro meschaunce,
> And every wight that meneth trouthe avaunce!
> (V, 1432–35)

The narrator poses defensively in one stanza, sending readers back to their history books to corroborate his story (V, 1086–90), while in the next he articulates his helpless position:

> Ne me ne list this sely womman chyde
> Forther than the storye wol devyse.
> Hire name, allas, is publysshed so wide
> That for hire gilt it oughte ynough suffise.
> And if I myghte excuse hire any wise,
> For she so sory was for hire untrouthe,
> Iwis, I wolde excuse hire yet for routhe.
> (V, 1093–99)

The historical unconscious has become undeniable, impossible to negate, and the poem has become as complicit as any other Ricardian text in the perpetuation of false history as true.

Characters become historical identities at the end of the poem. Criseyde and Troilus, who formerly lived and breathed and wept, are transformed in Book V into literary pastiches: impoverished versions of themselves and of Chaucer's descriptive art. "Criseyde mene was of hire stature" (V, 806) and famously, "slydynge of corage" (V, 825). "And Troilus wel woxen was in highte" (V, 827), "yong, fressh, strong, and hardy as lyoun" (V, 830). The highly conventional language with which they are reintroduced here is a signal of the end: As the narrator disengages from the story, he separates himself, and his readers, from the former humanity of his characters, whom he must now forsake to the future.[88]

Like the lovers, already dead before they die, Chaucer is over as a court poet before he is finished with *Troilus and Criseyde*. The character of the narrator becomes the historical Chaucer in Book V, a point emphasized not only by a change in tone but also by an announcement of contemporary place and time:

> O moral Gower, this book I directe
> To the and to the, philosophical Strode,
> To vouchen sauf, ther nede is, to correcte,
> Of youre benignites and zeles goode.
> (V, 1856–59)

With this passage, we are in 1380s London, the new Troy, witnessing Chaucer's dedication of his Trojan text to his fellow poet, John Gower, and his lawyer friend, Ralph Strode. Old Troy has become new, as it must, and the embarrassed Geffrey of *House of Fame* has become the Chaucer of *Troilus and Criseyde,* a voice of some authority. But these translations, the necessary marches of empire, are far from joyful. They are here, at the end of this most imperial, canonical text, narratives of almost unbearable loss as the fantasy of a brilliant and youthful court gives way to the history of its fall.

As the poem writes its predetermined end, and "not history" becomes history, the narrator (insistently "not Chaucer" to medievalists) must himself arrive as a poet worried about the reception of his text, about its transmission into the future, and ultimately, about his own place in the canon of "poesye." As the utopian voice becomes what it always was, that of a reluctant historiographer, so also Chaucer the poet of possibility becomes Chaucer the mere glossator upon his all-determining source. Knowing his place, and the derivative place of his Trojan poem, Chaucer warns his text to be impossibly true to its predecessors:

> But litel book, no makyng thow n'envie,
> But subgit be to alle poesye;
> And kis the steppes where as thow seest pace
> Virgile, Ovide, Omer, Lucan, and Stace.
>
> (V, 1789–92)

This projected vision of the future of his poem is restricted to a kind of place for poems in the sky; it is the afterlife of literature. But *Troilus* also necessarily looks forward to life in the mundane world, a place as unstable and precarious as the literary house of fame imagined here. And the watchword for behavior in London is to be as careful and as obsequious (even while making one's reputation) as the "litel book" should be in its future. As Pearsall notes, the closing lines of Chaucer's poem support the idea that "it is, quite self-consciously and deliberately, his masterpiece."[89] Chaucer is indeed conscious of his own status as a poet of *auctoritee,* but he is deeply anxious about what is to come.

Although Chaucer was probably never in any real danger himself, he nevertheless was worrisomely close to the court party and to several of the victims of the Merciless Parliament. Burley and Brembre had worked alongside him as associates at the customs, and Usk had praised him in *Testament of Love.*[90] It is unclear whether or to what extent Chaucer himself felt threatened by what was happening, but the events of 1386–88 certainly affected his situation: He left both his royal appointment at the customs and the rent-free apartments that came with the job within a fortnight of the adjournment of the Wonderful Parliament, on 4 December 1386.[91]

Although eventually brought back to Richard II's employment, as clerk of the works, Chaucer did not regain his position as a member of the court literati: There was no longer any such thing. By 1387, the latest date for the composition of *Troilus and Criseyde,* the moment of the poem's completion is also the moment at which Chaucer himself began to fall. Occurring at the height of his literary powers, his meditation on the "moral" and "philosophical" crisis of the fall of Troy is provoked by an awareness of the necessity of history and is accompanied by an understanding of his own position in that history. His full arrival on the literary scene as the authoritative poetic voice of the 1380s necessarily anticipates the compromising of that voice, as he seems to acknowledge in his address to his "book":

And for ther is so gret diversite
In Englissh and in writyng of oure tonge,
So prey I God that non myswrite the.
(V, 1793–95)

As it happens, someone did miswrite *Troilus:* Lydgate's *Troy Book* returns to the matter of new Troy and helps define for posterity Chaucer's place in it. Just as Troilus is translated to the empire of the heavens and sees his experience from a new perspective, so also is Chaucer translated to and in another place and time, from which he will have a different identity. Richard II and Chaucer go down in history as witnesses to the destruction of new Troy in their era, but in both cases their Trojanness will be resurrected by Lancastrian writers.[92]

4

Chaucer and Richard II in Lancastrian London

The period of transition from Ricardian to Lancastrian rule proves an especially rich environment for a concluding examination of the extraordinary signifying power of Troy. This transitional phase, however, encompasses more than the occasion of the actual deposition itself and extends well beyond the handful of years on either side of 1399. The shift from Ricardian to Lancastrian rule was always already happening from the earliest parts of Richard's reign, and furthermore, it was not accomplished until after the triumph of Henry V over France (when the Lancastrian moment began to fade). The assertion of the Lancastrian royal prerogative was a long time in coming, in other words, as was the destruction of Ricardian rule.[1] These two "events" find themselves variously expecting and repeating each other, and often overlapping, in historical narratives written between 1389 and 1422. As this chapter will show, the Lancastrian future not only depends upon but also often coexists with the Ricardian past.

Gower's *Confessio amantis* and Lydgate's *Troy Book* associate the reigns of Richard II, Henry IV, and Henry V with Trojan precedent. Invoking the matter of Troy variously to praise and blame their actual or imaginary patrons, Gower and Lydgate shape figures of these monarchs in the images of Hector and Aeneas. The two poets share many rhetorical strategies and political perspectives despite their chronological distance (that is, despite the fact that Gower looks forward to the fall of Richard II whereas Lydgate looks back at it). Both texts work hard to dissociate the glory of Troy from its Ricardian locus, and to reattach the benefit of the ancient city to the Lancastrians, as they process "memories" of Troy in the service of specific political goals. Gower's *Confessio amantis* and Lydgate's *Troy Book* offer visions and revisions of that old new Troy inhabited by Richard II and by Chaucer while they attempt to make legitimate history in the new (Lancastrian) new Troy for a king who has only pretendedly inherited, Henry IV. As such, they participate in what Benedict Anderson calls "ghostly national imaginings"—the textual construction and cultural definition of the nation in advance of its literal manifestation.[2]

Writing in English, and for specifically identified royal patrons, Gower and Lydgate assume a notion of the past that has direct relevance to their present circumstances. That is, they are not subtle in their association of Trojan traitors and heroes with Richard and Henry, respectively. Unlike Chaucer, they speak directly to contemporary affairs and public persons. In this regard, Gower and Lydgate self-consciously write for the betterment of the body politic. Theirs is a public poetry for their own time and place.[3] Both poems assert clearly that the past contains lessons for the present, and both imply, moreover, that the past can serve as a metaphor for the present. Chronology in *Confessio amantis* and *Troy Book* is thus not as straightforwardly serial as it may appear. Rather, it is understood as a set of near-simultaneous truths: The morality of times past informs the morality of times present, which threatens to become that of the future if the audience is not careful.[4]

As important as this understanding of time, and closely linked to it, is the understanding of place developed by Gower and Lydgate. To speak of "the nation" in the late fourteenth or early fifteenth centuries is something of an anachronism, for the word is generally understood as part of the modern political definition of the state. Until the very late fifteenth century, as Guenée observes, *status* (or "state") meant nothing more than condition or situation. There was no concept of the state as we understand it. Although marriage alliances often bound realms together, "lines of succession were unable to create or sustain any state." Edward III, for instance, despite his convincing legal arguments and military dominance, was not allowed to become king after the death of Charles IV because "he was a stranger in France."[5] Ethnic identity and political identity, although intertwined and mutually dependent, were nevertheless maintained as separate conceptual categories when the matter of nationhood was at stake.

As the recent work of several scholars suggests, however, the use of English rather than French or Latin in the period following the death of Edward III was itself a political development.[6] John H. Fisher connects the rise of English as a literary language with the fanning of nationalist sentiment: The two together constituted a conscious propagandistic program on the part of the Lancastrians. Immediately after 1400, Fisher writes, we see a "sudden burst of production in English," which was encouraged by Henry IV and even more so by Henry V, "as a deliberate policy intended to engage the support of Parliament and the English citizenry for a questionable usurpation of the throne."[7] But the use of the English vernacular, particularly by Gower and Lydgate, does more than support Lancastrian policy. It also calls England as a nation into being.

If we consider, with Homi K. Bhabha, that "the language of culture and community is poised on the fissures of the present becoming the rhetorical figures of a national past,"[8] we can better see how Gower and Lydgate create a past for the Lancastrians in order to legitimate the faction's present and future. This creation of the past is simultaneously the creation of the future Lancastrian state. It is not that the concept of the nation *emerges* in the Middle Ages, as if slowly and inevitably moving toward modernity, but rather that the "complex time of the national narrative" operates, like Freud's understanding of the uncanny, in

> a liminal, uncertain state of cultural belief when the archaic emerges in the midst of margins of modernity as a result of some psychic ambivalence or intellectual uncertainty. The "double" is the figure most frequently associated with this uncanny process of "the doubling, dividing and interchanging of the self."[9]

The late-medieval English nation is a "national timespace,"[10] composed of a series of simultaneous and contesting definitions not only of what and who the English are but of when they are. This national timespace, the "doubling, dividing" self of Englishness, competes with the notion of a chronological trajectory—that which claims movement *from* Richard II *to* Henry IV, from Ricardian deviance to Lancastrian exemplarity, from old Troy to new—and asserts instead a model for historical figuration that is composite, made of mutually implicating instantiations. Lancastrian texts do not just see the truth of the future after the fact. They often, like Chaucer's texts, imagine themselves both coming and going in a Ricardian world.

Richard II's deviance, which is necessary to the Lancastrian revolution, will be considered here as a phenomenon created by that revolution rather than as one that preexisted it. The Lancastrians are thus more "Ricardian" in their production of deviance than Richard himself. Those terms usually launched as proof of the necessity of the deposition ("tyranny," for instance, or "bad foreign policy") become Ricardian signifiers in the Lancastrian era and in many ways become the Lancastrians.

Žižek has written eloquently on this topic of doubling in historical figuration. Speaking of the "transition" from Julius Caesar to Augustus, he notes that, to those who believed in the Republic,

> Caesar's amassing of personal power—which was, of course, contrary to the spirit of the Republic—appeared an arbitrary act, an expression of contingent individual self-will: the conclusion was that if this individual (Caesar) were to be removed, the Republic would regain its full splendour. But it was precisely the conspirators against Caesar (Brutus, Cassius, and the others) who . . . attested the Truth (that is, the historical necessity) of Caesar: the final result, the outcome of Caesar's murder, was the reign of Augustus, the first *caesar*.[11]

The problem of repetition, or of doubleness in history, is illustrated here insofar as "the murder of Caesar—historical personality—provoked, as its final result, the installation of caesarism."[12]

It is important to note, however, that the collective satisfaction at the movement from Caesar to caesarism (or from Richard II to Ricardianism) is not to be understood as a matter of objective necessity (finally) breaking through the previously unready consciousness of the people. Instead, the symbolic status of the event is itself changed:

> [S]o-called historical necessity . . . is constituted through misrecognition, through the initial failure of "opinion" to recognize its true character. . . . [W]hen it erupts for the first time it is experienced as a contingent trauma, as an intrusion of a certain non-symbolized Real; only through repetition is this event recognized in its symbolic necessity—it finds its place in the symbolic network; it is realized in the symbolic order.[13]

The truth of history thus arises from failure that, in being repeated, becomes legitimate.

The above example of Caesar is particularly apt for the present purpose. In the murder of a ruler perceived as tyrannical, in the political movement toward empire, and in the crisis of illegitimacy becoming legitimacy's triumph, we have a cluster of terms that trace the fate of Ricardianism in the Lancastrian era. Even more interesting is the way these terms also help illustrate what happened to the idea of Chaucerian poetry between the late 1380s and the early 1420s.

The curious absence of Chaucer in the fifteenth century has been noted. For example, Stephen Partridge observes "the frequent failure to attribute Chaucer's works to him" in the surviving manuscripts of his poetry—all of which date from the early decades of the century—including the Morgan *Troilus* owned by Henry V when he was still Prince of Wales.[14] But how can Chaucer be considered erased at the very moment that established his reputation? For of course, it is also well known that it was in the early fifteenth century, rather than in his own day, that Chaucer's imitators flourished and that he was identified as a major figure in English poetry. But these two interpretations of Chaucer's fifteenth-century status are less opposed to one another than we may think, insofar as the silencing, or even murder, of one type of reputation is the prerequisite for the emergence of another. With Chaucer and with Richard II, an erasure and subsequent substitution was necessary for and productive of the ascent of the Chaucerian school and the definition of the English nation—not just respectively, but simultaneously and interdependently. The two men are intertwined as historical figures, rising and falling together (and dying within a year of each other); their interlinked fates, moreover, are predicted and remembered in similar *de casibus* narratives at the turn of the century.

As they make and unmake Richard in new Troy, so do Gower and Lydgate make and unmake the reputation of Chaucer, new Trojan poet par excellence. Wallace's observation with regard to Adam of Usk's *Chronicle* applies equally to Gower's *Confessio amantis:* In both texts, "the fall of Richard II . . . is written before it happens."[15] Similarly, the reputation of Chaucer (his rise and fall) is written before it happens. In some respects, as we have seen in the conclusion of *Troilus and Criseyde,* this reputation is written by Chaucer himself.[16] But the case is not so much that Chaucer sees the future of himself or of the king as that, thanks to Chaucer, the future writes the reign of Richard II as a version of the fall of Troy. History, in this way, asserts the story of the king as a literary narrative while Chaucer writes himself into the literary history that will come to be known as Ricardian.

The terms that designate the regnal periods of this era (and thus those that designate corresponding literary periods)—Edwardian, Ricardian, and Lancastrian—are as mutually complicit as they are distinct from one another. Such regnal signifiers operate like the terms "Arthurian" and "Trojan": They are fluid rather than fixed categories, and the claim of affiliation (or the avoidance of affiliation) with any one of them is always a motivated act rather than a simple accident of historical time. These terms are of crucial significance for the identity politics of the English nation, and they were constructed—or filled with content—based on contingent and competing definitions of the cultural location of the true empire or of the best history.

Especially fascinating in this context is how, during the "transition" from Richard II to Henry IV and Henry V, at a moment when the definition of the term "Trojan" was as crucially at stake as that of the terms "Ricardian" and "Lancastrian," a combined literary and political effort was at work to create the term "Chaucerian." Gower and Lydgate create affiliations with and for Chaucer. They variously pull on and push against him, aligning themselves in the process variously as friends, advisers, and correctors of Chaucer—but always as poets who are not only under his influence but subordinate to his precedent as well. Chaucer's reputation is made in ways terribly similar to those that govern the fashioning of kings and of nations in the later medieval period.

RICHARD II'S "TRAGEDY"

That Chaucer was politically astute—aware of which way the wind was blowing and clever enough to protect himself when the situation became dangerous—is the consensus among many critics these days. One of the strongest pieces of evidence for this view is Chaucer's *Complaint to His Purse*. The last poem known to have come from Chaucer's own hand, written after the usurpation in October 1399, *Purse* includes an envoy addressed to the new king. Henry's right to "Brutes Albyon," the island founded by Brutus, is emphasized:

> O conquerour of Brutes Albyon,
> Which that by lyne and free eleccion
> Been verray kyng, this song to yow I sende,
> And ye, that mowen alle oure harmes amende,
> Have mynde upon my supplicacion.
>
> (22–26)

Strohm notes that to refer to the usurpation in terms of a conquest is a "starker formulation" than the more usual and less blunt contemporary references to Henry's "recovery" of the throne. But, Strohm continues, Chaucer then "mitigates any severity by displacing the conquest to the legendary Britain of the chronicles."[17] Chaucer's three-part argument (justifying Henry's right by conquest, by royal blood, and by free election)[18] continues in language that straddles the divide between reinforcing Henry's own interpretation of his acquisition of the throne and criticizing it. To position Brutus in relation to Henry IV is to displace the man Henry really conquered, Richard II, and to predate the conquest out of its dangerously contemporary context. But although Chaucer's strategy may have been as obvious to his readers then as it is to us now (the displacement announcing what it pretends to hide), it nevertheless "worked": He got his annuity, Henry got his association with England's mythic Trojan history, and Richard joined the ranks of the disappeared.[19] Even before this late poem, however, from *Troilus and Criseyde* onward, the site of new Troy was being cleared of its Ricardian inhabitants in anticipation of a Lancastrian occupancy.

Following the crisis of the late 1380s, Richard II regained power from the magnates when he officially claimed his majority in May 1389 and assumed his rule.[20] What happened next is a matter of opinion, for the commentators on events in the decade leading up to the deposition fall into two main camps: the Lancastrians and the French. English historians have, tellingly, until the twentieth century largely accepted the former. Alternatives to the "official" (i.e., Lancastrian) view include Creton's *Histoire du roy d'Angleterre Richard* and the anonymous *Chronique de la traison et mort de Richard II*,[21] as well as several Cistercian chronicles, most notably those from the Yorkshire abbeys of Kirkstall and Dieulacres.[22] One of the Creton manuscripts (out of nine known surviving) contains a set of sixteen miniatures that vividly detail the travails of Richard II. This manuscript, which dates from the early fifteenth century, was owned by Charles of Anjou, count of Maine, and includes realistically styled images of Richard's army revictualling in Ireland, Archbishop Arundel inciting the people against the king, and Henry leading Richard back to London for his final humiliation.[23]

Despite Creton's and the other narratives in favor of the king, the prevailing view for five centuries was that Richard became increasingly more tyrannical in the later years of his reign, thus deserving the ultimate penalty of deposition. In some ways, this account is correct: Richard did assert his power in uncustomary and politically suicidal ways, and he did retaliate against his enemies (particularly Gloucester) with terrible precision.[24] But the hostility to Richard in the Lancastrian chronicles cannot be explained completely by these actions. Many rulers can be said to have behaved rashly, stupidly, and illegally, whether justified or not. And the answer is somewhat more complicated than the observation that the Lancastrians hated Richard for being legitimate in the face of their own illegitimacy, for coming before them, and for *making them,* as it were, depose him. More particularly, Lancastrian chroniclers and later historians blame Richard II for losing France—for losing face and undermining the English nation.[25] That this set of accusations about Richard's foreign policy is unfair has been made clear in the light of more recent research.[26] More interesting, however, is the way the accusations do cultural work for Henry IV, and later, Henry V—both of whom set about the business of building a nation, and their reputations, on the myth of Richard's failure in France. As J. J. N. Palmer observes, Richard II's foreign policy, though widely unpopular, was viewed favorably by at least one person: "[H]is supplanter paid him the compliment of imitating it down to the smallest details."[27]

The main problem with Richard II, according to his detractors, is that he failed to pursue the goal—established and then elaborated by his grandfather—of subjecting the French to English rule. Lancaster, Gloucester, and Arundel were among the most vocal critics of the policy of rapprochement with France in 1386. The war had been profitable, not only for the barons themselves but for the lowlier soldiers as well: As Gloucester reminded Richard, his peace policy was a hardship for knights, squires, and archers "whose comforts and stations in society depended upon war."[28] By mid-1387, with the end of John of Gaunt's war in Castile, the king finally had his uncle's support for his peace initiative, although the truce was delayed by the domestic political crisis of 1386–88 and not established until after Richard had regained control of the government. The 1389 truce of Leulingham, which coincided with Richard's resumption of power, was extended in 1392 and again in 1393, over the objections of Parliament, while negotiators on both sides continued to treat for a permanent peace.[29] Finally, however, Parliament's opposition prevailed: During the session on 29 January 1394, the king asked for an account of the peace negotiations drafted thus far to be read out. Upon hearing it, many were dissatisfied, and the Lords and the Commons refused to consent despite the influence of Gaunt. The truce of Leulingham was extended one last time, to 29 September 1398, "and no more."[30]

Advised by Gaunt to pursue a truce and by Parliament to pursue a war, Richard was in the meantime exhorted by Philippe de Mézières, a friend and adviser of Charles VI, not only to marry the French princess but to join France in a crusade.[31] Unlike Gaunt's son, Richard never went on crusade, although there is some suggestion that he considered doing so at this point. The 1396 crusade at Nicopolis, however, which was a disaster for the English, was even more so in that the party was considered a vanguard of the eventual Anglo-French expedition encouraged by Philippe. In language meant to appeal to the legendary precedents of each realm, Philippe's 1395 *Letter to King Richard II* had suggested that the kings of France and of England take on the roles, respectively, of

> le tres vaillant et tres preux Charlemaine, et . . . le tres excellent et tres preux roy Artus, c'est assavoir contre les anemis de la foy, contre les scismatiques et hereges.
>
> the very courageous and very worthy Charlemagne and . . . the very excellent and very worthy King Arthur, namely, against the enemies of the faith, against the schismatics and heretics.

Richard did not join Philippe's Order of the Passion, described in the letter as "une nouvelle chevalerie du crucefix qui doit estre mandee oultremer" ("a new knighthood of the cross to be sent overseas").[32] Instead, the order counted as its associates Richard's uncles of Lancaster, York, and Gloucester, providing yet another opportunity for the Lancastrians to gloss themselves as inheritors of chivalric duty in contrast with the king's impropriety.[33]

Rather than joining the order and going on crusade, Richard married the young Princess Isabel, who made her state entry in November 1396 and thus sealed the peace agreement between England and France. And rather than fighting the French, Richard received from them, with their princess, a promise to "aid and sustain him with all their power against any of his subjects."[34] Richard's "maneuvers for security and power" centered on attempts to subjugate his enemies in England instead of the French.[35] Not only, as May McKisack notes, was the king "out of touch with the passions and prejudices of his own people,"[36] he actually was prepared to move against them. His first step was to compel all men of property to pledge their goods and their bodies in defense of the statutes of his "revenge" Parliament of 1397. In addition to these enforced oaths, he further alienated a large number of his subjects when he excluded from general pardon everyone who had gone against him back in 1387: the exclusion covered anyone residing in the seventeen counties, around and including the "county" of London, that had supported his enemies. As Maude V. Clarke aptly observes, "more than half the population of England was thus proscribed merely for failure to show 'constant good affection' to the king."[37] Surviving among the records of the deposition is a servile petition to the king from London and the counties of southeastern England. In it, the petitioners acknowledge the misdeeds and evil imaginings of certain of their number, admit that they deserve cruel punishment, and promise to do whatever the king imposes on them. The price they paid for "*le Plesaunce,*" or the king's pleasure, was 1,000 pounds for each shire.[38] The situation had so deteriorated that by June 1398, Richard was complaining—for good reason but also largely due to his own actions—that he was afraid to travel in the seventeen counties because of the sympathy there for his enemies. He spent nearly all his time that year in the Midlands and the west.[39]

At the same time that Richard was punishing London and the southeast, he was lavishing gifts and favors on Chester and the northwest. Notable manifestations of this affection were the king's elevation of the county of Cheshire to the status of a principality in September 1397 and his replacement of the hated Arundel's lordships with key officers of Chester.[40] This fondness for Chester is reflected in the record of the

Kenilworth-Chronicler, who describes the relationship between Richard and his men as one of great affection. Richard found not only supporters but even perhaps friends among the men in the west when he went recruiting there for his armed guard. The men were said to watch over the king while he slept, to address him in the "*materna lingua,*" and even to joke with him in intimate fashion:

> Dycun, slep sicury quile we wake, and dreed nouzt quile we lyve sestow: ffor zif thow haddest weddet Perkyn douzter of Lye thow mun well halde a love day with any man in Chester schire in ffaith.[41]

The guardsmen's apparent assumption of close affinity, or even familial identity, with Richard was used by the Lancastrians—and their many modern historian heirs—as evidence in support, or at least in explanation, of the deposition. Even the sympathetic *Dieulacres*-Chronicler blames the king's lack of popularity in part on the activities of these Cheshire archers, who were said to "plead their cases with points of sword."[42] And as R. R. Davies asserts, Richard's "infatuation with Chester and its men lost him his kingdom."[43]

But this passage from the *Kenilworth*-Chronicler stands out not only for its tone of familiarity between the Cheshiremen and the king but also for its representation of the dialectical vernacular. The peculiar sounds of English as spoken in Chester surprise the Latin narrative, just as—in their support for Richard—the men of the west constitute a surprising pocket of royalist sympathy in a country dominated, in Richard's view, by his enemies. There is some indication that this "inner citadel" of Richard's kingdom was meant as a secure base of operations against his southern enemies, and rumors raged that he planned to rule from Wales (which shares a border with the then principality of Chester) or from Ireland and might never return to England at all.[44]

Wales and Ireland, both of which have Arthurian associations and both of which were viewed as wild, uncivilized, and inhospitable places, must be seen also as particularly Ricardian places. Robin Frame notes that Richard II, like Edward II, held the principality of Wales in his own hand, "so bringing about a closer connection between Crown and Welsh leaders than was usual; his abrupt removal thus left a vacuum of control" into which Owain Glyn Dŵr (who had served on Richard's Scottish campaign in 1385 and perhaps also on the king's second Irish campaign of 1399) stepped and then proceeded to harass the Lancastrians.[45]

Richard II's Celtic affiliations may also be glimpsed in his treatment of the native inhabitants of Ireland during his two campaigns there. The infamous Statutes of Kilkenny, established in 1366 under Edward III, had distinguished only two groups of people, the English and the Irish, and had declared the latter the enemy, even those "at peace" with the settlers. But for Richard II, by contrast, loyalty rather than racial origin was the test of fidelity. As Dorothy Johnston writes,

> although it was by this time normal for the Anglo-Irish chancery, in commenting upon local hostilities, to refer to *Hibernicos inimicos,* often aided by *Anglicos rebelles,* Richard and the English chancery in the 1390s consistently described disturbers of the peace simply as *rebelles,* contrasting them with the *fideles ligeos* of the king.[46]

As long as they admitted their previous faults and swore to future loyalty, Richard II accepted the Irish chieftains as his liegemen. His famous tripartite division of the population works against the simple moral-ethnic axis asserted by Kilkenny and suggests his willingness to claim the "wild Irish" as his own loyal subjects.[47]

But these western and Celtic associations have a broader implication for the reign of Richard II. As Bennett suggests, the submissions of the Gaelic chiefs and Richard's knighting of them might be seen as evidence that the king viewed his domains "as British rather than narrowly English." The chiefs' submissions in 1394–95 and their deference to his "most exalted Crown," Bennett writes, "implied a model of high-kingship or king-emperorship" rather than testifying to the predominantly Celtic quality of Richard's support.[48] Despite the foreignness of the places to which he was attached,

> his kingship obstinately transcended place.... In this sense... Richard was the last of the Plantagenets. Like them, he saw the English Crown as the core of a grander and more glorious "British" imperium.[49]

Richard II's friendly relations with Cheshire and France, along with the apparent sympathies of the Celtic fringe, create a space and an identity for the Ricardian era that is Other to the language used—and hence the history created—by the Lancastrians. In other words, the French, Cheshire, Irish, and Welsh support for Richard comes to define the Ricardian past as anomalous or unacceptably different, whereas the London English invoked in support for Henry—including the poetry of Gower and Lydgate—comes to define the Lancastrians as proper inheritors of the nation. The Lancastrian royal party set about defining their history and that of their Lancastrian nation in relation to the not-spectral-enough Ricardian past: Henry IV and Henry V sought to differentiate themselves from Richard II even while, both of necessity and of desire, they replicated the most significant aspects of his rule. As early as 1390, however, before the Ricardian future was finished, Gower participates in this uncanny doubling of monarchical signifiers with his *Confessio amantis,* "a bok for king Richardes sake."

Gower's (Pre-)Lancastrianism

As if compensating for his decision to compose a full-length poem in English, Gower opens his 1390 recension of *Confessio amantis* with a set of Latin verses. Acknowledging his incapacity as a versifier and warning "the evil tongue to keep far away," he claims his English to be "that tongue of Hengist in which the island of Brut sings" ("Qua tamen Engisti lingua canit Insula Bruti"). After an excursus on his theory of the historical and educational value of literature and an acknowledgment that sometimes learned material is too dull, Gower announces the terms for his own current undertaking:

> I wolde go the middel weie
> And wryte a bok betwen the tweie,
> Somewhat of lust, somewhat of lore,
> That of the lasse or of the more
> Som man mai lyke of that I wryte:
> And for that fewe men endite
> In oure englissh, I thenke make
> A bok for king Richardes sake,
> To whom belongeth my ligeance
> With al myn hertes obeissance

In al that evere a liege man
Unto his king may doon or can.[50]

The middle way, composed of a bit of both pleasure and learning, is considered best for his royal patron, Richard II, for whom Gower expressly writes in English.

In a passage that has provoked some critical controversy, the poet claims to have bumped into the king one day while rowing on the Thames:

As it bifel upon a tyde,
As thing which scholde tho betyde,—
Under the toun of newe Troye,
Which tok of Brut his ferste joye,
In Temse whan it was flowende
As I be bote cam rowende,
So as fortune hir tyme sette,
My liege lord par chaunce I mette;
And so befel, as I cam nyh,
Out of my bot, whan he me syh,
He bad me come in to his barge.
And whan I was with him at large,
Amonges othre thinges seid
He hath this charge upon me leid,
And bad me doo my besynesse
That to his hihe worthinesse
Som newe thing I scholde boke,
That he himself it mihte loke
After the forme of my writynge.
(35–53)

In this image of Ricardian London, new Troy is the sort of place where king and poet, rowing separately, can happen to meet and hold a conversation about literature. Although the issue of Richard II's literary tastes is still unresolved,[51] the scene as depicted by Gower clearly shows the king to be an active patron of vernacular literature. Gower further declares his allegiance to his king, framing his understanding of himself as a poet as one who has the double responsibility of pleasing and instructing his lord.

How Gower's text imagines itself in the context of royal patronage suggests the ways Gower may have viewed himself as a public figure. In this respect, the passage from *Confessio amantis* (including its later revision) is not unlike an important passage in Chaucer's Prologue to *Legend of Good Women,* which also was revised to fit changed political circumstances. Gower and Chaucer both imagine themselves first as poets for a royal audience and then, for different reasons, as poets for a wider, though anonymous, public.

In the F-Prologue to *Legend of Good Women,* the narrator is instructed to write something nice about women for a change, as penance for the wickedness he portrayed in *Troilus and Criseyde*. The God of Love further tells him that his audience is Anne of Bohemia:

> Goo now thy wey, this penaunce ys but lyte.
> And whan this book ys maad, yive it the quene,
> On my byhalf, at Eltham or at Sheene.
>
> (495–97)

This passage was then omitted from the G-Prologue, prompting scholars to suspect that the *Legend* may have been intended for a royal presentation that never occurred.[52] Whether or not the poem was actually meant for and then later withdrawn from presentation to Queen Anne is less significant than the fact that the text represents this as the case. Chaucer here imagines himself initially as in the circle of royal patronage and then as out of it. This is also the scenario suggested in the last stanza of *L'Envoy de Chaucer a Scogan:*

> Scogan, that knelest at the stremes hed
> Of grace, of alle honour and worthynesse,
> In th'ende of which strem I am dul as ded
> Forgete in solytarie wildernesse—
> Yet, Scogan, thenke on Tullius kyndenesse;
> Mynne thy frend, there it may fructyfye.
>
> (42–47)

Because the surviving manuscripts contain marginal notes glossing "stremes hed" as Windsor, and "th'ende of which strem" as Greenwich, where Chaucer lived in the 1390s, these lines have often been taken as an expression of Chaucer's awareness of his own forgotten, marginalized status vis-à-vis the court. In this interpretation, Chaucer asks his friend in the final two lines to do him a favor—perhaps even to put in a good word for him at the court to which he has become a stranger.[53]

If Chaucer considered himself lost in the 1390s, as is suggested by the revisions to *Legend of Good Women* and by *L'Envoy de Chaucer a Scogan,* we may well wonder when he was discovered, and by whom. Scattergood summarizes recent research on Chaucer's audience when he notes that his poetry

> appears to have been written, on occasions, with an aristocratic courtly audience in mind; but its more significant readers appear to have been career diplomats, civil servants, officials and administrators who were attached to the court and the government.[54]

Because of the wide and variously powerful and influential circle of his readership, "Chaucer's failure to publish, or the loss of all his presentation manuscripts, is one the greatest mysteries of early English literary culture."[55] Although John Fisher provocatively asserts that what may be called "the Chaucer problem" stems from a combination of Chaucer's own diffidence and "the lack of prestige of English as a cultivated language,"[56] we may further consider whether there was something else in the way. This other thing, blocking the way to Chaucer's realization of his reputation during his lifetime, is the future of Richard II himself. The eventual eclipse of Richard's reputation is hoped for in Gower's poem while, at the same time, the reputation of Gower as a "friend of Chaucer" is enshrined.

In the 1390 version of *Confessio amantis,* Gower ends the poem with an Epilogue including praise for Richard II, the king for whom he wrote in English, followed by a dedication in Latin to Henry earl of Derby: "Derbeie comiti, recolunt quem laude periti, / Vade liber purus sub eo requiesce futurus."[57] Although Macaulay understands this as "a double dedication, the compliment being divided between the king and his brilliant cousin,"[58] the subsequent history of the poem's alteration provides a record of Gower's growing dissatisfaction with his royal patron. This ambivalence regarding true patronage is mirrored in the text's reliance on plural dedications in multiple languages: The London English that was soon to be the Lancastrian standard is here, in the early 1390s, still a rather risqué Ricardian tongue.

Gower's revision program was very specific and pointed. Rather than undertaking changes on a holistic level, throughout the poem, he concentrated on overhauling a limited number of objectionable passages. His selective rewriting does not suggest a concern with style or with fine-tuning nuances of meaning. Instead, it indicates a sharp change of mind about his subject. In two phases of revision, he first excised those sections of text that described Richard II's commissioning of the poem, and then further eliminated the closing verses of praise for the king. In a 1391 version, the Epilogue was changed to cancel the praise of Richard. And by no later than June 1393, the earlier Latin dedication to Henry "Derbeie comiti," which had originally appeared at the end of the poem, is introduced into the Prologue as a dedication, in English, to Henry of Lancaster:

> Bot for my wittes ben to smale
> To tellen every man his tale,
> This bok, upon amendment
> To stond at his commandement,
> With whom myn herte is of accord,
> I sende unto myn oghne lord,
> Which of Lancastre is Henri named:
> The hyhe god him hath proclamed
> Ful of knyhthode and alle grace.
> (Prologue, 81–89)[59]

And where lines 22–24 in the original version had read

> And for that fewe men endite
> In oure englissh, I thenke make
> *A bok for king Richardes sake* [emphasis added],

the revised version substitutes

> And for that fewe men endite
> In oure englissh, I thenke make
> *A bok for Engelondes sake* [emphasis added].

In these few lines, Gower articulates a changed idea of public poetry. Rather than writing for a king, he writes for the nation. England here replaces Richard in the poem's beginning, as Henry replaces Richard in the Epilogue. These two stages of the poem's alteration are a clear indication of a shift in Gower's allegiance, from the king in new Troy to a new, hoped-for state of England.

But this replacement also speaks to the equivalence of the terms. That is, if England can replace Richard, Richard and England are interchangeable. The ability to substitute one term for another on a rhetorical level yields an interpretive association between them. Richard and England are bound together through the very act that seeks to separate them.[60]

This process of displacement and resultant (surprising) association is in keeping with what we have seen elsewhere in Gower's poetic. Like the revisions made to *Vox clamantis,* those made here to *Confessio amantis* contribute to what Frank Grady calls Gower's "fugitive art, constantly fleeing from the contradictions it is incessantly uncovering."[61] Gower's flight from the recognition of what he cannot help but disclose is indicative not only of his own political preferences but of the problem of the usurpation itself, even for a Lancastrian sympathizer and even before 1399. As Grady notes, Henry's route to power, "if it is not to be ignored, must be legitimized."[62] Gower here is torn between his duty, in the form of his allegiance to the rightful king, and his passion. His preference for another is the illegitimate secret that the poem must "confess." The position of the poet in the guise of *amans,* the lover, is—as I elaborate below—doubly encoded as a form of both political and sexual love.

Along with Richard II, the reference to new Troy also disappears from Gower's text. The city is replaced with a description of the dual moral purpose of the literature of the past. Worthy poets back then, according to Gower, magnified the fame of worthy princes, on the one hand, and exposed the faults of the unworthy, on the other:

And tho that deden thanne amis
Thurgh tirannie and crualte,
Right as thei stoden in degre,
So was the wrytinge of here werk.
(48–51)

Just as writers of the past criticized unjust rulers, so Gower claims he will proceed:

> And in this wyse I thenke trete
> Towardes hem that now be grete,
> Betwen the vertu and the vice
> Which longeth unto this office.
> (77–80)

Although clearly, given the changes in dedication, these lines are designed to implicate Richard II as a ruler whose vices need correction, the poem's competing if unintentional logic of substitution and replacement juxtaposes the original target of Richard with the new subject of Henry.

Of course Gower did not mean to suggest that his lord, Henry of Lancaster, is one of "hem that now be grete" (78) and thus in need of the exposure and correction of his wrongs. Henry, in 1393, has not yet done any wrong in Gower's view or in almost anyone else's. Even Richard II himself may not have blamed Henry for his role as an Appellant in 1387: His cousin was not one of the leaders of the actions against the royal prerogative, only joining Gloucester and Arundel late in the crisis, and his was furthermore one of the (unheeded) voices of reason that argued against the execution of Simon Burley, the king's boyhood tutor. But although Gower could not have foreseen the eventuality of Henry becoming king in Richard's place, his text positions Lancaster as the king's supplanter all the same. Henry becomes Richard in the text before he becomes Richard's replacement on the throne. Gower's poem—the unrevised mass of it—addresses its new, revised subject before that subject comes into historical being.

Confessio amantis looks forward to the end of Richard II and the coming of the new king. But it also looks forward to the end of Chaucer and the arrival of a "newe thing" (51), a new style and purpose for the "office" of poetry. This linking of Chaucer with Richard is achieved through two means: parallel excision of both in the revised text, on the one hand, and their replacement by (in Gower's mind, more worthy) substitutes, on the other. The first recension of the poem, with the praise of Richard, also includes praise of Chaucer. And in the second recension, when the Epilogue was rewritten to exclude the king, Gower likewise excluded Chaucer. In the 1390 version, Amans is identified in Book VIII as John Gower, now an old man. Venus bids him to "nomore of love sieche" (2911), and says that he and she will not meet again. Before leaving, she claims Chaucer as her own when she instructs Gower to

> . . . gret wel Chaucer whan ye mete,
> As mi disciple and mi poete:
> For in the floures of his youthe
> In sondri wise, as he wel couthe,
> Of Ditees and of songes glade,
> The whiche he for mi sake made,
> The lond fulfild is overal:
> Wherof to him in special
> Above alle othre I am most holde.
> For this now in hise daies olde
> Thow schalt him telle this message,
> That he upon his latere age,
> To sette an ende of alle his werk,
> As he which is myn owne clerk,
> Do make his testament of love,
> As thou hast do thi schrifte above,
> So that mi Court it mai recorde.
>
> (2941–57)

The insistence on affiliations in this passage is remarkable, as Venus claims Chaucer as "*mi* disciple and *mi* poete" and as "*myn owne* clerk." The relationship imagined by Gower between Chaucer and Venus, however, is one that was formerly strong. It is based on the kind of poems he used to make, when he was young. Venus admires his "ditees" and "songes glade." But now, Gower suggests, Chaucer is old and, like himself, near enough to death to consider making shrift, foreswearing love and its literature in favor of a different literary form. Chaucer is advised to "sette an ende of alle his werk" by making a testament of love for Venus's court record. As was the case with the imagined scenario between himself and Richard II, Gower here places poet and audience in a political context. In this case, Gower attempts to redirect the course of Chaucerian style before, he intimates, it is too late.

Gower's own "schrifte" is his admission that he is too old to do love's work, as well as an admission that he is not suited to write love poetry. In advising Chaucer to make a similar confession, Gower (through the voice of Venus) here asks him to write a poem more like his own: a moral work of virtue and vice, addressed to the king. The imagined "testament of love" is not a love poem but, like the *Confessio* itself, a collection of exempla that illustrate the right and wrong sorts of love and that particularly illustrate the consequences of the latter. Gower is asking Chaucer to be more of a public poet, to write as a different kind of lover, and perhaps to be famous for something (and someone) else.

The reference to Chaucer in the *Confessio* is noteworthy for many reasons, and it operates on a number of levels. The fact that there is some fluidity between Gower's own voice and that of Venus is in itself problematic, if not completely improbable, for the scene depicts Venus and Gower going their separate ways. A stronger case could be made for Gower and Venus never having been bedfellows to begin with (for this we simply recall *Vox clamantis* and *Mirour de l'omme*). Venus's praise for Chaucer is thus no praise at all but, rather, a clear condemnation by Gower of the moral worth of Chaucer's art. The legal language of the passage is even more provocative, as Gower prods Chaucer to record, as a clerk, his testament of love in court. This language conjures the unfortunate figure of Thomas Usk, onetime clerk to John Northampton, whose own shrift took the form of the prose treatise *Testament of Love*.

The significance of Usk for Chaucer studies has been explored by a number of critics, who note the *Testament*'s false attribution to Chaucer and its role in providing some evidence for the dating of *Troilus and Criseyde*. And several recent studies have discussed in greater detail the literary and political relationships between the works of Usk, Chaucer, and Gower.[63] My point here is limited to the apparently confusing way Gower invokes the specter of Usk in his warning to Chaucer: On the one hand, Gower seems to be suggesting that Chaucer write more like himself, a Lancastrian. On the other hand, he suggests that Chaucer write more like Usk, who was executed in 1388 after attaching himself politically to Richard II.

At stake in this complex of political and literary affinities is more than a simple matter of Ricardian versus Lancastrian sympathies. Rather, Gower's warning serves to remind us of the vexed processes through which later readers will locate these writerly personae on the sliding scale of historical "merit." Gower's *Confessio amantis* and Usk's *Testament of Love* are both much more pointedly political texts than anything Chaucer ever wrote. Gower openly criticizes the corruption of rulers, and Usk writes to win the favor of Richard II, an association that ultimately cost him his life.[64] The two writers represent the extremes of political commitment, one Lancastrian and the other Ricardian, but both manage to implicate Chaucer as "apolitical" by contrasting his work with their own.

Gower's *Confessio* discredits Richard II and, through Venus, discredits Chaucer's art. Usk's *Testament,* by means of which he tried to curry favor with the Ricardian royal party, praises Chaucer in the voice of the Goddess of Love (who is Venus, of course, though not named as such here). It is the first recorded praise in English of Chaucer as a poet. Love instructs Usk's narrator to refer to *Troilus and Criseyde* for an elaboration of the nature of foreknowledge and predestination, and describes Chaucer as

> Myne owene trewe servaunt the noble philosophical poete in Englissh whiche evermore him besieth travayleth right sore my name to encrese . . . in a tretis that he made of my servaunt Troilus hath this mater touched and at the ful this question assoyled. . . . in the boke of Troilus, the answere to thy question mayst thou lerne.[65]

Chaucer is glossed here as a public intellectual, an authority whose philosophical work is assumed to be known widely in the sphere of London letters. Although here, as in *Confessio amantis,* Love claims him as her "owene" poet, Chaucer is specifically understood by Usk as an authority on foreknowledge. It is a particularly apt characterization.

Unlike Gower, Usk acknowledges Chaucer's moral and literary worth. But the death of this Ricardian writer also announces the death of writing associated with Richard (a death that is enacted in Gower's excision of Chaucer from the *Confessio*). The end of Ricardian letters, like that of the Ricardian era, thus occurs well in advance of the deposition and death of the king. Usk himself is erased in the sixteenth century when his text reenters literary history falsely attributed to Chaucer (in Francis Thynne's 1532 edition of *Chaucer's Works*). In Gower's *Confessio,* however, Chaucer's literary worth, as it is noted in the ultimately discredited *Testament of Love,* although not exactly killed, nevertheless suffers a devaluation. Whereas Gower changed his text to keep up with events and his own changing sympathies, leaving behind a composite of layered affiliations, Usk went down as a traitor, unable to revise either his text or his political affiliation when the winds changed.

Gower's advice for Chaucer is both political and literary, as he warns him to wise up, as it were, and write something attending to the future of his reputation. Specifically, the literary models Gower offers are those that figure the redemption of the writer and of his reputation through his exposure and criticism of the sins of the state—the very thing Usk could not do, since his *Testament* wrote him into the favor of the king. Chaucer, according to his friend Gower, is headed for the ruination of his name if he persists in his refusal to speak to the problems of their shared historical moment. The reference to the rise and fall of Thomas Usk, Ricardian fan of Chaucer, is an example in *de casibus* narrative mode for the edification of Chaucer himself.

It is tempting to look for Chaucer's response to this bit of advice in his literary production of the 1390s, the bulk of the *Canterbury Tales*. But perhaps Chaucer already had responded to it, had even preempted it, in his backhanded compliment of dedicating *Troilus and Criseyde* to "moral Gower" in the second half of the previous decade.[66] More interesting yet is the fact that Gower dropped this passage, and with it all mention of Chaucer, in the revised version of *Confessio amantis*. Like Richard II, Chaucer is a figure whose absence registers as a presence in Gower's new text. Richard and Chaucer are replaced with Henry and the state of England: Two figments with the status of premonitions (not yet king and not yet nation) substitute for two objectionable figures of the not yet past, both of whom are deserving of correction for their wicked ways. Gower's excoriation of them both in 1390 was not enough to make the future that he wanted. He thus excised them both together from his later text. But as Henry of Lancaster, inadvertently, becomes the rhetorical equivalent of Richard II, so also does the state of English letters become that which it displaced in Gower's text. Despite himself, Gower makes Chaucer the father of English poetry and subsumes his own name, in the process, under the rubric of the Chaucerian era.

Chaucerian Afterlives

By the time Gower dropped Richard II entirely from *Confessio amantis*, in 1393, Chaucer's identity as a court poet was over. And as was true with Richard's style of rule, Chaucer's style of writing took a sharp turn in the 1390s, becoming in the *Canterbury Tales* something quite different from what it had been. When early-fifteenth-century writers looked back at their predecessor, they had, in a sense, two Chaucers from which to choose: that of the courtly verses culminating quite self-consciously in *Troilus and Criseyde,* and that of the fragmented and multivalent narratives of the *Tales.* Chaucer's reputation, like that of Richard II, is thus split, with each of its primary elements separately available for Lancastrian elaboration and interpretation. Lydgate took these two Chaucers in turn, writing his *Troy Book* and then *Siege of Thebes* in response to their respective corresponding Chaucerian works.[67] Although Lydgate confesses allegiance to Prince Henry, ultimately his poetry is for Chaucer. In his apparent need to improve upon his predecessor, Lydgate betrays a desire for him.

Composed over the period between 1412 and 1420, *Troy Book* reads *Troilus and Criseyde* in terms that seek specifically to revise recent history. And *Siege of Thebes,* which was composed between 1420 and 1422, purports to be a continuation of the *Canterbury Tales. Troy Book* is extant in twenty-three manuscripts and *Siege of Thebes* in twenty-nine, most of them of the same type, that is, as Pearsall writes, "quality" texts prepared for aristocratic or upper-class patrons. In three of these manuscripts, *Siege* occurs together with *Troy Book.* The two poems are clearly associated in many ways, not least of which is the fact that "the story of Thebes existed in the medieval mind as a pendant to Troy."[68] In both poems, Lydgate tries to "out-Chaucer Chaucer" as he simultaneously revalues Trojan and Theban significance. Lydgate's choice of material in recrafting Chaucer is especially noteworthy: *Troy Book* tells the story of the Trojan War that Chaucer refused to tell in his *Troilus;* and *Siege of Thebes,* although posing as a continuation of the *Tales,* likewise takes its matter from the *translatio imperii* that Chaucer left behind. In this way, the most important fifteenth-century response to Chaucer is one that recalls his Trojanness, his Ricardianness, even as it attempts to supersede that history. Like Criseyde, Chaucer was "doomed" to become a legend, in the medieval sense of the term as something deserving to be read. More specifically, he was doomed to become a Ricardian poet, despite his repeated refusal to engage overtly with his own political moment.

Lydgate takes pains to link the new Lancastrian dynasty with the Trojan history previously attached to Richard II. Unsurprisingly, this process requires the excision of Richard from the noble line of descent that flows from Aeneas to Brutus to Arthur to Henry, but it also requires the excision of Chaucer from the line of literary authorities on the matter of Troy. Lydgate, who reveals that the patron of his *Troy Book* is Prince Henry, son of the usurping king, implicitly contrasts the deviant qualities of Richard's Trojan reign with the exemplary morality of the Lancastrian men, and he sets about revising literary history accordingly.

A good writer, Lydgate claims, preserves the knowledge of the past and makes it new, providing a "mirror only to our mind, / To see each thing truly as it was."[69] But a bad writer, a liar, will distort the truth, and by false report, he will give an undeserving man worship (Prologue, 291–92). Chaucer is significantly absent from Lydgate's catalog of truthful authors. Repeating verbatim the list to which Chaucer implicitly joined himself at the end of *Troilus* and repeating mention of Chaucer's "Lollius" (I, 394) and "Dares" and "Dictys" (I, 146), Lydgate nevertheless fails to include Chaucer himself. It is a telling omission, or rather, replacement: Instead of Chaucer, Lydgate claims his literary authority from Guido delle Colonne, one major author noticeably *not* invoked at the end of *Troilus and Criseyde*.

Buried deep within the *Troy Book* is the poem's most substantial mention of Chaucer,[70] when Lydgate refers to the separation of Troilus and Criseyde and praises Chaucer's own, earlier account. In fact, Chaucer's account is so good that Lydgate does not bother to treat the episode fully: There is no need, he says, since Chaucer has done it so well already (III, 4196–98). Lavishing praise upon his dead predecessor, Lydgate claims that Chaucer's name "shal passen in noon age, / but euer, with-oute eclipsinge, / shyne" (III, 4258–60). In this case, mention of Chaucer's name introduces Lydgate's replacement of his former authority with an alternative more suited to the Lancastrian purpose.

Despite his apologies for having to be faithful to his source, Lydgate repeats all of Guido's aphorisms on the evil of women (they speak in doubleness, they are like a serpent, they cry venomous tears, and so on). And despite his praise of Chaucer, he fails to repeat the famously sympathetic characterization of Criseyde found in *Troilus*. Instead, he notes that within the space of one day, "Crysede for-soke hir owne knyȝt" (III, 4436). In privileging Guido's treatment over Chaucer's, Lydgate has taken Criseyde back to her legendary status as the treacherous vixen who destroyed the noble Troilus. Glossing over Chaucer, Lydgate skips back a literary generation to choose Guido's treatment of the love story.

At issue here is more than a generic distinction between historiography and love poetry. That is, Lydgate is not simply "the more historical poet,"[71] accordingly turning to Guido instead of to Chaucer. *Troilus* is a historical poem, and Guido's "history" is, as we have seen, actually a Latin prose translation of a vernacular romance. Lydgate's treatment of Criseyde shows him to be a Lancastrian poet choosing and thus creating his literary history very carefully. Chaucer's version must be eclipsed not because Criseyde matters but because she mattered to Chaucer, who, despite his careful avoidance of contemporary events, is read by Lydgate as a Ricardian poet.

As Pearsall rightly observes, literary historians have been unkind to Lydgate. Rather than simply seeing him as a bad poet, we would do better to acknowledge that Lydgate's work is "an attempt to improve upon [Chaucer's] practice by doing what he did, not better but more."[72] The complex and sometimes paradoxical nature of this stance may be explained by Lydgate's concern to

> strengthen and consolidate Chaucer's stylistic achievement, an ambition that is only superficially at odds with the tone of humility he adopts towards Chaucer in his many passages of adulation.[73]

The difference, according to Lydgate, between himself and Chaucer is one of moral values. As Pearsall writes, Lydgate "approaches the matter of Troy not as a story, as Chaucer did, but as truth."[74] Guido tells the truth, in this scheme, whereas Chaucer is a liar. But many readers of Guido fail to understand that his text is as "false" as anything written by Chaucer. It is not simply that history is as false as literature but that history and literature draw on the same assumptions and foundational narratives with which to assert their conclusions. The story of Troy, after all, is not history. Instead, it is a legend—something exemplary, perhaps, but also something made, something fabricated. The belatedness of the Lancastrians and their poets, coming as they do after the "truth" of Richard II and Chaucer, encourages a form of compensatory historiography that desires as much as it regrets its precedent. Lydgate's poem, for all its reliance on Guido, is as dishonest as any version of the story of the fall of Troy.

Lydgate claims that an honest writer holds a "mirror to our mind" (*Troy Book*, Prologue, 168) in reflecting the truth. Somewhat coyly, in that he masks his source, Lydgate here borrows a phrase from Chaucer's poem. At the fateful moment when Troilus is "blinded" by love for Criseyde, "gan he make a mirour of his mynde / In which he saugh al holly hire figure" (I, 365–66). Lydgate, blinded by desire, associates his own poetic legitimacy not with his patron, Prince Henry, but with Chaucer.[75] Seeing Chaucer's figure everywhere, Lydgate concludes his *Troy Book* with

> Go, litel bok, and put þe in þe grace
> Of hym þat is most of excellence;
> And be nat hardy to apperen in no place
> With-oute support of his magnificence.
> (*Envoy*, 92–95)

Repeating not just Chaucer's words but also Chaucer's context of warning his poem to be true to its predecessors, Lydgate here conflates Chaucer with Henry as the one "most of excellence." Conscious or not, the association confuses—even as it replaces—the objectionable with an object of desire.

From the very beginning of the poem, *Troy Book* attempts to differentiate itself from its troubling predecessor. Unlike Chaucer, who opened his own "Troy book" with an appeal to Tisiphone, the "goddesse of torment" (I, 8), "sorwynge evere in peyne" (I, 9), Lydgate chooses to invoke Mars, the god of war. Although appropriate enough in a narrative of the Trojan War, Lydgate's selection of Mars is also an announcement of his poetic strategy: to combat the Ricardian monopoly on Trojanness and to assert forcefully the Lancastrian claim to that history. Mars, in Lydgate's account, is a justified warmaker. He is the "souereyn and patrown" of chivalry, and his bellicose nature is an ideal of righteous masculinity. Mars is also a usurper, since he loved Venus, "wyth whom whylom þou wer at meschef take" (Prologue, 23), adulterously: She was "Wlcanus wyf" at the time (Prologue, 22).

Like Mars, Lydgate's patron is a paragon of masculinity. Claiming that his lord

> hath desire . . .
> Of verray kny3thod to remembre ageyn
> The worthynes . . .
> And the prowesse of olde chiualrie
> (Prologue, 75–78),

Lydgate asserts that the prince commissioned the poem to learn from the noble deeds of history and to eschew the "cursyd vice of slouthe and ydelnesse" (Prologue, 83). In fact, Henry is so masculine that Lydgate can barely find the words with which to describe him:

> Thus is he bothe manful and vertuous,
> More passyngly þan I can of hym write:
> I wante connyng his hiȝe renoun tendite,
> So moche of manhood men may in hym sen.
> (Prologue, 90–93)

This surpassingly manly man, "in sothefastnesse, this no tale is" (Prologue, 101), is "callid Henry ek, the worthy prynce of Walys, / To whom schal longe by successioun / For to gouerne Brutys Albyoun" (Prologue, 102–4).

Implicitly contrasting the sexually deviant, unmanly qualities of Richard's reign with the exemplary masculinity of the Lancastrian men (the prince, Lydgate says, is just like his father), the poet sets about revising the Trojan trope accordingly. Rather than being morally questionable characters with problematic sexual appetites, the "new" (Lydgatian) Trojans are—like Prince Henry—exceptionally worthy examples of martial prowess and chivalry.

The notion that Richard II was a sexual deviant, whereas Henry IV was properly masculine, gained some currency thanks largely to Walsingham's narratives. In a celebrated passage, the chronicler characterizes the men surrounding the king at court as

> knights of Venus rather than knights of Bellona, more powerful in the bedchamber than on the field, more vigorous with words than with weapons, quick in speaking but slow to perform the acts of war. Those intimate companions of the king cared nothing about instructing themselves in that which is proper for a knight, not only the use of arms, but also those things, such as hunting and hawking, which befit noble kings during times of peace and by which royal honor increases.[76]

This complaint about the king's associates, which was in circulation by 1390, clearly draws on problematic assumptions regarding the definition of masculinity, as does the comment made by Adam of Usk that Richard II was unfit to rule because of his "sodomies" *(sodomitica)*.[77] But in light of the association of Troy with deviant sexuality, as outlined in chapter 1, we can see such comments about the king's "sodomies," or his failure to be a "proper" man, as an extension of his Trojanness: Richard is accused of mis-placing his personal affections just as he mis-recognized the proper place of the English realm in Troy (and France and Cheshire and Wales and Ireland).

Along with this representation of the king as morally unfit comes a vision of the "new" Chaucer as a morally questionable author. As does Gower before him and Henryson after him, Lydgate charges Chaucer with being an adherent of Venus. Coupled with Walsingham's remarks about the king, we can see that both Chaucer and Richard II are painted with the Venerean brush as these Lancastrian writers seek to gloss their own men as martial and masculine. Considering that the story of the fall of Troy hinges upon amorous betrayal, the gendered terms invoked here must be seen as crucial for the writing of political history. Although in some respects Lydgate specifically inserts himself as the properly masculine inheritor of Guido delle Colonne while relegating Chaucer to the closet of Richard II, it is more generally true that gendered betrayal is productive of historiography. The later author betrays the earlier one necessarily, as lovers do, for the sake of history, whether understood as the fall of Troy or the rise of Britain.[78]

The pivotal role played by literary authors in the production of history is made clear in the course of Lydgate's opening lines, where he claims that the reputation, or "fame" (Prologue, 175), of "conquerouris" (Prologue, 174) depends upon the difference between a good writer and a bad one. However, in the course of describing the exemplary qualities of these men, including

> Her hyȝe renoun, her manhood and prowes,
> Her knyȝthood eke and her worthynes,
> Her tryvmphes also and victories,
> Her famous conquest
>
> (Prologue, 199–202),

Lydgate permits some confusion as to whether he refers to kings or to writers. "From poynt to poynt rehersyng al þe trouthe" (Prologue, 203), the writers of noble deeds occupy a similar public place as the rulers who wrought those deeds. Both uphold, and both are, great men.

Although these lines about conquerors refer on one level to the Trojans and Greeks of the poem's topic[79] and on another level to Lydgate himself, they further refer to its other topic, Richard II and his Lancastrian conquerors. Calling attention to his own role as the creator of his patron's good name, Lydgate revises the reputations of the rulers of both Troy and new Troy. Paradoxically, the more he praises the Trojans (whose reputation was based at least as much on their self-destructiveness—and on the words spoken and written about them—as on their noble deeds), the more he emphasizes the constructedness of fame in general and of that of the Lancastrians in particular.

Lydgate's attempts at various historical reattachments yield a series of replacements (a string of deferrals and substitutes) occupying positions of both the desired object and the desiring subject. He substitutes his own worth as a writer for the worth of the noble deeds of his patron, replaces the lust-ridden Trojans with the exemplary masculinity of the new-Trojan Lancastrians, skips over Chaucer in favor of Guido, and finally reclaims Chaucer at the expense of Prince Henry in an act that cannot help but symbolically reclaim Richard as well. The *Troy Book* can in no way be seen as a successful or even consistent Lancastrian poem, since the signifying terms of praise and opprobrium—of the prince and his father, of the Trojans, of Guido, and of Chaucer—insistently form the parts of an "infinite chain, ineluctably multiplying the supplementary mediations that produce the sense of the very thing they defer."[80] Lydgate's attempt to appropriate the mythic history of Troy for his patron while keeping its unsavory qualities at bay allowed Trojanness to become Ricardian—and Ricardianism to define the Lancastrians—in the early fifteenth century. Lydgate also manages to cross himself out of the equation in the process, ensuring (Pearsall's admirable efforts notwithstanding) that he will be remembered primarily as the one who merely (and poorly) imitated Chaucer in the waning years of the Lancastrian ascendancy.

Following Henry V's restoration of Richard II's bones in 1413 and his triumphal return from Agincourt in 1415, the transition to Lancastrian rule could finally be said to be complete. With the decisive military victory and a number of poets on hand to articulate the triumph in English verse, the court, as Seth Lerer observes, "had reaffirmed itself as the locus of both political control and literary patronage."[81] Lydgate speaks in the second decade of the century for the arrived Lancastrians, their troubles seemingly behind them, in a poetic language "filled with possibility and promise"—a language that, in Lerer's words,

> seeks to give voice to an ideal of poetic patronage by investing in [a] fantasy of an Edenic world and furthermore, by imagining a current royal patronage along the models of an imagined Chaucerian laureateship.[82]

The imagined Chaucerian laureateship, however, is complicated and undermined by the remembered Ricardianness (which is untruthfulness from a Lancastrian perspective) of the historical Chaucer. Similarly, Lydgate's current royal patronage cannot forestall the inevitable end of the Lancastrians, an end that necessarily must follow the triumph of 1415. Within a decade (Henry V died in 1422, leaving the country with the infant Henry VI and a protectorate), as Lerer notes, Lydgate's "images of brilliance" will give way to "the rhetoric of darkness and despair."[83]

The death of the Lancastrian moment is recorded by Lydgate in one of his many willfully optimistic poems of the 1420s, the *Kings of England sithen William Conqueror.* As Linne R. Mooney has discussed, the poem has a propagandistic intent. It "seems to have been written to reassure the English people that Henry VI would be a great leader like his father... and would claim his inheritance in both England and France."[84] The opening stanza of this verse chronicle locates the birth of the nation in the Norman Conquest:

> This myghty Wylliam Duke of Normandye,
> As bokys olde make mencyon,
> By juste tytylle and hys chevalrye
> Made kynge by conqueste of Brutys Albyon,*
> Putte owte Harrolde ande toke possessyon.[85]
> [*In margin: "*id est,* Englonde"]

The foundational moment is narrated here in terms that recall the Lancastrian "founding" of 1399. As did Chaucer's *Purse,* Lydgate's poem offers a three-part justification for a usurping ruler: Whereas Henry claimed the throne by election, line, and conquest, here William claims it by title, chivalry, and conquest. Starkly, he put Harold out and put himself in. This is of course a more accurate rendition of the Lancastrian usurpation than we found in Chaucer's version. But Lydgate is not assigning this Lancastrian history to the Lancastrians. Instead, he (like Chaucer before him) is backdating the moment of rupture to the very beginning of the English nation and thus legitimizing the traumatic change in dynastic houses more than he ever could have if he had narrated it in its proper chronological place. When he does come to it in its place, Lydgate does not admit to any irregularity in the transition from Richard II to Henry IV.

The marginal gloss next to the text's reference to "Brutys Albyon," furthermore, suggests that not only is the strife between the Plantagenet and Lancastrian dynasties forgotten but one of its most stubbornly inassimilable issues has also been buried. "*Id est:* Englonde." The ancient history invoked by "Brutys Albyon," and with it the Trojanness so closely associated with Richard II and the new Trojanness linked to Henry IV and Henry V, is by the 1420s unrecognizable: The place over which English kings reign is "simply" England.

The disappearance of the past in historical narrative is of course a political strategy. In this case, the erasure of the Lancastrian disruption changes the definition of the place in which it occurred. It also changes the definition of the time in which events occur: It changes history. Albion now, Lydgate's poem seems to suggest optimistically, can be England instead of new Troy.

But the multiple purposive absences of the objectionable past in the poetry of this transitional era raise a larger question about the function of political disappearance itself. For the assertion of Lancastrian legitimacy, is the removal of Chaucer and Richard II best forgotten, denied, or justified? Ernesto Laclau and Lilian Zac note that the "several logics" regularly employed by repressive systems when confronted with an unpleasant truth about their regimes are silence, denial of responsibility, and assumption of limited responsibility (with the understanding that the repression is an "inevitable consequence" of the present triumph).[86] The result of such discursive operations is that the victims (in this context, the *desaparecidos* of many Latin American dictatorships)

> inhabit a space where they are neither dead nor alive; they can reappear, they can also be killed. Their death and their life is suspended, deferred. And by means of this operation fear is installed into that context: the *desaparecidos* point to the existence of another space, a space of suspension, which is both part of,

> and excluded from, the realm of "society," and, in this way, it becomes necessary to define its limits.[87]

The possibility of the return of the dead in cultural memory, or even the return of the undead (for their inevitable murder), creates a dread unease in the ascendant party even while these deaths have been necessary to its ascendancy. The identity of the state or regime thus is literally dependent upon a perpetual fear of its own successful strategies. As Laclau and Zac note, with reference to Lacan, insofar as "the subject appears somewhere as meaning, he is manifested elsewhere as 'fading,' as disappearance."[88] This impossibility of any stable identification is "the essential problem of politics," or conversely, "the problem of politics is not identification, but identification and its failure."[89]

I cite this discussion by Laclau and Zac to better articulate how the disappearance (and uncanny reappearance) of Richard II and of Chaucer in early-fifteenth-century texts is both necessary to and destructive of the Lancastrian program of self-legitimation or identification. Just as Chaucer necessarily must disappear in *Troy Book,* because he is a Ricardian poet, so also must he appear in it to legitimate Lydgate. Literary and historical authority create one another, each granting to the other its necessary terms for success. But so, too, do they threaten to destabilize each other and themselves through the supplementary discursive patterning discussed above. Authorial presence is granted, temporarily and incompletely, only by the dangerous strategy of absencing its others and thus exposing itself to the consequences of being made absent in turn. This paradigm applies not only to individual kings and poets or to dynasties and literary schools but also to larger political and textual systems. By way of conclusion, I shall discuss how the idea of the nation of England, created in the place of "Brutys Albyon," and that of the state (or status) of English letters veered alternately toward and away from the idea of empire between 1390 and 1415. Like the idea of nation, that of empire is a state of fantasy.[90]

An Empire of English Letters

In the late 1390s, as he adopted what was seen as an increasingly antagonistic posture toward many of his subjects and particularly as he alienated himself from the seat of royal power in London, Richard II seems to have modeled himself as a ruler of a new empire rather than as king of England. The evidence for the claim of Richard's imperial self-fashioning in this period rests on a set of changes he made to his court style, including an elaboration of existing practices of etiquette, and on a number of Lancastrian-era chronicle accounts and rumors. Among the changes in courtly practice was the adoption of the terms "Prince" and "Your Majesty" for direct address to the king. These terms had been reserved in chancery documents for references to the Holy Roman Emperor until Richard II's appropriation of them for himself in 1389–90. These changes in regnal fashion may have been influenced by Richard's apparently affectionate marriage to Anne, the emperor's daughter, and there is some evidence as well that Bohemian court style influenced that of English painting in the Ricardian era: Formal details of Richard's "coronation" portrait in Westminster Abbey, for instance, owe much to the portraits of Emperor Charles IV's ancestors in his castle at Karlstein.[91] Nigel Saul's recent discussion of these Bohemian, and thus imperial, influences on the English court, however, cautions against attributing too much significance to this pattern of evidence, and reminds us that in the 1390s the French monarchy also employed the vocabulary of imperial majesty and a heightened ceremonial style.[92]

But in the context of the later years of the decade, as Richard sought to consolidate his strength and humiliate his former enemies, the moves toward the fashions of empire are significant not despite but because of the fact that the French were doing it, too. Recall that from 1397 onward, Richard began forcefully to purge the realm of his opponents' supporters, replacing them with his own handpicked appointees. At the same time, he received from France pledges of support for himself against his own people. France was an ally not of England but of Richard against England. It is hardly surprising that in this time of looking abroad for assurances of his power, Richard behaved less like a king and more like an emperor. Indeed, when—as part of his attempt to strengthen his party—in 1396 he legitimated John of Gaunt's children by Katherine Swynford, the Beauforts, he claimed to act as "entier emperour de son roiaulme" ("complete emperor of his realm").[93]

Walsingham notes that in 1397, rumors reached the king that he was about to be elected emperor. Charles IV's son, Wenzel (Anne of Bohemia's half-brother), was deeply unpopular at this time, making plausible the notion that a new emperor was being sought.[94] In the *Annales*

Ricardi Secundi et Henrici Quarti, Walsingham describes the situation thus:

> Messengers arrived from Germany [in June 1397], including the dean of Cologne, who, knowing the rashness and ambition of the king, intimated to him that he either had been or was about to be elected emperor. The king, immediately believing this, gave the dean and his companions an extraordinary number of gifts, and sent ambassadors abroad to find out if what they had said was true.... On their return, they reported that a majority of the electors were indeed favourable to him; only two or three were withholding their consent, on the grounds that if the king could not deal with his subjects in his own country, how could he be expected to govern all his subjects throughout the length and breadth of the empire? They [the ambassadors] suggested that those who dissented ought to be bribed and won over with gifts from the king.[95]

Richard's aggressive movements in 1397 against the magnates who had caused him so much trouble a decade earlier can be seen in this context as an elaborate show to impress the German electors with his ability to control his own subjects. The financial "tyranny" that followed may in turn be seen as an attempt to raise the money he felt he needed to persuade any remaining reluctant electors.[96] But although Palmer suggests that "in offering him the imperial crown in 1397 the German princes were paying a tribute to the success of the policies he had pursued during the previous decade," we might conclude instead that it was Richard's failure of rule in the 1380s that paved the way for his imperial ambitions in the 1390s, that these imperial ambitions were matched by those of his successor, and that finally, neither monarch was actually offered the imperial crown.[97] Instead, the desire for empire, as "recorded" (that is, produced) in historical narrative, propels the figures of both Richard II and Henry IV as coincidences into the period during which England as a nation is said to have come into consciousness.

Following the start of the Great Schism in 1378, the emperor's son, Wenzel, allied himself with the Roman pope, Urban VI, who—as a reward for this show of loyalty—sent his legate to arrange the marriage of Wenzel's half-sister Anne to Richard II.[98] But as F. R. H. Du Boulay points out, this alliance ultimately caused trouble for Prague. Not only were there princely supporters in western Germany for the Avignonese pope, who of course had the French behind him, but this new diplomatic alliance among Wenzel, Rome, and England also shifted the alliance that had existed for many years between France and the house of Luxemburg. Despite this change in the political balance, Wenzel never bothered to organize an imperial coronation for himself. Such a coronation, Du Boulay suggests, might have helped him avert his eventual deposition in August 1400.[99]

Richard II's fate was also affected by schism politics. In 1396, in an effort to please his French father-in-law, Charles VI, Richard agreed to join the Franco-Florentine alliance against the duke of Milan, Giangaleazzo Visconti. He also bound himself to support the ecclesiastical policy of the French king. A joint Anglo-French embassy left in April 1397 for Avignon and Rome to try to secure the resignation of both popes (by then, Benedict XIII and Boniface IX). The embassy threatened that if both popes did not resign, the French allegiance to Benedict and the English to Boniface would be jointly renounced. Another mission set out for Germany in May of that year, hoping to win support for the scheme from Wenzel. When the news came that Benedict (predictably) had rejected the proposal, the French duly set in motion the machinery for their withdrawal of the obedience of the French church. Suddenly, however, in November 1397, Richard II turned away from his promises to France on both counts: He urged the French king to intervene to secure peace for the duke of Milan, and he failed to ask the English church to withdraw its allegiance from Boniface.

Why Richard II suddenly wanted to champion the interests of the Visconti and why he made no effort to secure from the English church a renunciation of allegiance to the Roman pope, as he had promised, are mysteries to historians of diplomacy. As D. M. Bueno de Mesquita writes,

> [O]ne of Richard's chief motives in seeking the French alliance had been the need for... support in case difficulties arose at home over the elimination of the duke of Gloucester and his faction. The refusal to follow the French lead in Italian politics shows us how soon, after the successful issue of his domestic plans, Richard was prepared to abandon the French alliance, for which he had worked so hard and had risked, only a year earlier, the alienation of his people.[100]

Richard's "fantastic hopes" of winning the imperial crown were central to this breach in English and French foreign policy.[101] While his envoys were in Germany supposedly to promote the schism plan, they were also tasked with promoting Richard's imperial cause with the German princes: Two of the electors—the archbishop of Cologne and the count palatine of the Rhine—subsequently became his vassals and liegemen in return for a pension, and four German knights took the oath of homage to him at Windsor in October.[102] Richard's reluctance to alienate Boniface also may be explained by his imperial ambitions, for not only did the Roman pope enjoy the support of the bulk of the English clergy, but he also had considerable influence among the electoral princes in Germany.[103]

An awareness of this background on the world stage of diplomacy and foreign policy is crucial to our understanding of the tone of the later years of Richard's reign. He was not simply a Francophile, a tyrant, or a pacifist. His policies did not sacrifice the political or geographical integrity of the English. That these Lancastrian charges are patently false is borne out by examining the behavior of Henry, who—while still earl of Derby and also afterward as king—implicated himself in similar ways in the same geopolitical network that Richard did. Henry, for instance, was close enough to the Milanese to have been rumored to be planning to marry Lucia Visconti (Giangaleazzo's cousin and sister-in-law) and to help the duke in his struggle against Florence.[104] Likewise, when Henry fell from royal favor at home, he found a warm welcome at the French court.[105]

The idea of empire is especially at stake in the interpretive nexus between Richard II and Henry IV, as it is in the formation of the literatures called Ricardian and Lancastrian. For Walsingham, writing after the usurpation, the rumors of Richard's imminent imperial election are not credible, and yet for him they are true enough to constitute evidence of Richard's overreaching. They confirm that the king had become a tyrant. His word in describing the rumors is *"inanes,"* or "unfounded": not inappropriate as a general category, but absurd when applied to Richard II in particular. Walsingham's language in ridiculing Richard as unfit for the emperor's throne thus manages to preserve the desirability of empire even as he attempts to make the point that any king who would be emperor deserves to be deposed.

While on the one hand, Walsingham's report helps assert the arrogant rise and justified fall of Richard II, on the other, it also invokes the model of Arthur, that other English king who would be emperor. As noted before, Arthurianism was an especially potent discourse in support of England's claims to power over its geographically contiguous neighbors, Wales and Scotland. But in addition to its local significance, the Arthurian myth also carried imperial consequences. Richard William Fehrenbacher notes that in Malory's "Tale of King Arthur and the Emperor Lucius," Arthur responds to the tyrannical emperor's demand for tribute with a counterclaim to the throne of the Roman Empire. The English king finds justification for his claim in the mythic genealogy of "cronycles":

> For this muche have I founde in the cronycles of this londe, that sir Belyne and sir Bryne, of my bloode elders that borne were in Bretayne, and they hath ocupyd the empyreship eyght score wyntyrs; and aftir Constantyne, oure kynnesman, conquerd hit, and dame Elyneys son, of Inglonde, was Emperour of Roome; and he recoverde the Crosse that Cryste dyed uppon. And thus was the Empyre kepte be my kynde elders, and thus have we evydence inowghe to the empyre of hole Rome.[106]

Arthur's claim to the imperial throne is found through a historicist impulse: The chronicles provide "evydence inowghe" for his new future as king of the Romans.

Significantly, Malory has chosen to begin his project with this episode of the Arthurian saga (in the French cycles, the episode comes last and shows Mordred's betrayal coinciding with Arthur's trip to conquer Rome). In this English version, desire for empire does not herald the end of Arthur's reign but is instead its auspicious beginning. Malory "grafts on an impossibly happy [and premature] ending," showing Arthur's conquest of Rome, crowning by the pope, and return to England and his queen.[107] The text thus permits imperial ambition to thrive, at least temporarily. For this new beginning provides only a delay of the inevitably catastrophic results of the English king's imperial designs. Malory's movement of the episode from the end to the beginning of the story inserts a long hiatus between empire and disaster and thus diminishes the causal link between them.

Richard II's movement toward empire is followed closely in historical narrative by his ultimate destruction. In Lancastrian chronicles, a clear causal relationship is drawn between the king's imperial overreaching and his deposition. The story of Richard's rise and fall is, like Malory's rendition of Arthur's fate, incomplete without its tragic consequences, as is the story of Troy. But just as Malory silently shifts the chronology of his original text, separating cause and effect from one another in time, so also do these chronicles shape the chronology of the reign of Richard II to fit a specific purpose. In doing so, they mistake not only the causes of the deposition but also its consequences. Richard's desire for the imperial throne did not destroy him, rather, his desire for it created the Lancastrians as his successors.

Richard II's heir presumptive, in the absence of an heir of the body, was Roger Mortimer, the fourth earl of March.[108] The Lancastrian chronicler Adam of Usk (himself related to the Marches) notes that Mortimer could trace his genealogy back through Brutus, Aeneas, Jupiter, Noah, Seth, and Adam.[109] Worthy to inherit the English throne, and even the empire, Mortimer was an asset to Richard II and his understanding of his regality, but he was also apparently understood as a threat, a competitor. Usk reports that shortly before his death, when the young earl appeared for a parliamentary session at Shrewesbury, in 1398,

> [h]im the people received with joy and delight, going forth to meet him to the number of twenty thousand, clad in hoods of his colours, red and white, and hoping through him, the heir presumptive, for deliverance from the grievous evil of such a king.[110]

From the point of view (paradoxically) of *both* Richard II and the Lancastrians, Mortimer's death was necessary to history.

Mortimer died in battle in Ireland in June 1398 while defending the uneasy truce that Richard's presence had established there a few years earlier. Curiously, however, the Irish chieftains who rose against Mortimer, the king's lieutenant, did so because they found him unfaithful to Richard II. One of the benefits of submitting to Richard was royal protection, not only against other chieftains but against the king's own designated heir.[111] Niall Og O'Neill, for instance, who by 1393 was calling himself "king of Ireland," made his personal submission to Richard II in March 1394 and then was knighted by him, but the problem of Mortimer remained an issue. As rumors raged that Richard was about to leave Ireland, O'Neill wrote to the king in desperation, explaining that Mortimer was sure to attack him:

> If I do not resist, in obedience to your majesty, he will make war on me *à outrance,* and all my supporters will proclaim me dastard; on the other hand, if I resist him my rivals will say that I have become rebel and traitor to your Majesty.[112]

Richard left Mortimer in Ulster and went back to England, but he wrote to O'Neill promising that he himself would mediate any disputes that arose between his Irish liege men and his own lieutenant. Mortimer's surprise attack on Armagh was thus done "apparently in defiance of the royal will."[113] But its ultimate consequence—also against the royal will—was equally necessary to historical productivity: Mortimer's death in 1398 prompted Richard's return to Ireland in June 1399. While he was away avenging the death of his supposed heir, Richard allowed Henry, his usurper (and thus his misrecognized heir), to slip into England and onto the throne.

The pressure for historical revisionism provoked by the deposition (the end of the Ricardian story) prompted revisions on the other side of the timeline as well, at the beginning of the story: Usk's account of the Mortimer episode, obviously motivated by his allegiance to the Lancastrians as well as by his own affiliation with the Marches, casts aspersions on Richard's legitimacy by moving backward in time to denigrate the king's origins. The chronicler recounts a rumor that Richard "was not born of a father of the royal line, but of a mother given to slippery ways *[lubrice vite dedita]*—to say nothing of many other things I have heard."[114] Usk's comments show an effort to discredit the king in the past, in the present, and for the future.

The problem with this strategy is that while it seeks to place Richard II outside of the boundaries of legitimate rule, it simultaneously discredits the Lancastrians' place in history. Henry IV repeated the structures and styles of his immediate predecessor to such an extent that he, rather than the earl of March, can be seen as Richard's true heir. He is a successor more than a usurper, and he inherited both the glory and the trauma of Ricardian regnal practice, including its imperial ambition.

When Henry IV wore the device of the Order of the Garter at his coronation, he perhaps meant to invoke memories of its founder, Edward III, the last king, in the Lancastrian narrative, to inhabit a fully legitimate place in history.[115] But when Henry secured the election to the order of all four of his young sons in that same year, the memory of Edward would compete with the more recent one of Richard II, whose election of Robert de Vere to the order had caused such a scandal in the early 1380s.

The precedent of Richard II returned in other ways as well, sometimes accidentally and with surprising results. In November 1399, for instance, when Henry asked the French for a princess for his eldest son, they refused to acknowledge him as king of England. War was declared in 1401. The end of the French truce brought on more trouble with the Scots, which required the king to lead an army to the Firth of Forth in the summer of 1400. He achieved nothing in Scotland and then, upon his return, had to contend with Glyn Dŵr's Welsh uprising.[116] Harried from the north and from the west as well as from across the Channel, Henry changed tactics and quickly married his daughter to the emperor's son in 1402.[117]

When Richard II sought a French princess, bungled a Scottish campaign, and moved toward empire, his actions were seen as justifying his deposition. When Henry IV did these same things, they still justified Richard's deposition. The lesson of history in this case is that anomalies, or even mistakes, from the past turn out to be legitimacy itself in the present. The destined quality of Richard's failure is acknowledged and disseminated even by one of his supporters: Froissart interrupts his narrative of Richard's deposition to recall that when the king was young, rumors had circulated that cast doubt on his lineage. The chronicler claims to have overheard some aristocratic gossip to the effect that according to a prophecy of Merlin, "neither the prince nor any of his issue would ever succeed to the throne, but that the crown would pass instead to the house of Lancaster."[118] That even a supporter records this—that he bothers to go back in time, interrupting his chronology, to disseminate as truth what he probably suspects to be false—suggests the acceptance of the overwhelming necessity of Richard II's fall.

Rather than asserting a chronologically discrete beginning and end to Richard II, we may instead think about a circuit of Ricardianness. And rather than asserting a clear demarcation between things French, Bohemian, and English, we may conceive instead of a kind of cross-pollination of political and ethnic identities during the period. Saul suggests this point when he moves away from the idea that "foreign influences" impinged upon Richard's regnal style and notes instead that

> courtly styles are likely to have been disseminated along a route broadly similar to that followed by the most beautiful symbol of regality fashioned in the late fourteenth century—the crown now in the Bavarian State Museum at Munich. Made in all probability in Paris, it found its way to Bohemia, whence it came to England—probably in the baggage train of Queen Anne—only to be taken away again, back to the Empire, by Henry IV's daughter Blanche, on the occasion of her marriage to Ludwig III of Bavaria. This record of journeyings can stand as a metaphor for the circulation of courtly fashions more generally in late medieval Europe.[119]

Aptly symbolized by the circuitous route of the imperial crown, Ricardianness, like Trojanness, comes around and goes around in the Lancastrian era.[120]

The idea of Chaucerianism is itself revived from its earlier death by Henry IV and Henry V and their spokesmen, Thomas Hoccleve and John Lydgate. The two monarchs participate through literary patronage in the restoration of the reputation of Chaucer as a poet for contemporary England and for the future. Whereas Gower had associated Chaucer back in the early 1390s with Richard II and thus with the unsavory past, the fifteenth century made him now.[121] As Fisher imagines him, at Westminster and surrounded by piles of half-finished work upon his death, Chaucer retracted all his worldly vanities. The retraction, Fisher writes, is a "puzzle" to scholars (like the "mystery" of Chaucer's "failure to publish"),[122] but it must be seen not only as the result of Chaucer's indisputable Christian faith but also as a reflection of his self-perceived failure as a public poet. Ignored and forgotten by a court that had moved on to new modes of political and cultural patronage, Chaucer suffered in his own lifetime the death of his reputation as a London voice. Just as the Trojan model of rule disappears for Richard II, London as new Troy disappears from Chaucer's poetry in the 1390s.

Chaucer is resuscitated in the early fifteenth century not as a London poet but as a poet for an England now understood (because of Chaucer) as a literary empire. Chaucer's name is invoked to create this empire, but it is also framed as a piece of evidence from the past, one that supports the idea that the empire has always existed. The Lancastrian royal party is positioned in this paradigm not so much as usurping new emperors but as legitimate heirs to Chaucerian history. Baswell discusses the Lancastrians' sponsorship of the English language as "a bearer of imperial myth" in the second decade of the fifteenth century, and he notes in particular Lydgate's support of Henry V's (and England's) imperial ambitions in the *Troy Book:* "[T]he Trojans' westward *translatio imperii* functions as a foil to Henry's fantasied eastward translation of English empire."[123] In a celebrated passage from the Prologue to the *Troy Book,* Lydgate explains Prince Henry's motivation in commissioning the translation of Guido:

> By-cause he wolde that to hyghe and lowe
> The noble story openly were knowe
> In oure tonge, aboute in eury age,
> And y-writen as wel in oure langage
> As in latyn and in frensche it is;
> That of the story the trouthe we nat mys
> No more than doth eche other nacioun:
> This was the fyn of his entencioun.
>
> (Prologue, 111–18)

As Baswell points out, this passage "shifts language distinctions from the earlier paradigm of class (aristocratic French *versus* mercantile and common English) to the paradigm of geographical nationhood."[124] The movement toward empire that justified Richard II's deposition is what defines the Lancastrians and the English nation. The Lancastrians are Ricardian doubles, repeating rather than resolving the problematics of Richard's reign.

If, as Anderson writes, "the most important thing about language is its capacity for generating imagined communities,"[125] then we might further suggest that a historical community such as the English empire can be constructed only in literary language. As Pearsall writes, the Lancastrian political sponsorship of the English language in the early fifteenth century suggests that

> it was to be, truly, the "King's English" . . . [and] to weld England into a single constituency. . . . Language was a way of creating a

> nation, for, as Henry's ambassadors were instructed to argue at the Council of Constance in 1415, "the peculiarities of language" are "the most sure and positive sign of a nation in divine and human law."[126]

The resurrection of Chaucer, like the simultaneous construction of Ricardian deviance, was crucial to this legitimizing project. Chaucer confirms the empire of English letters precisely because of his Ricardian traces.

CONCLUSION

The Historical Imagination

As I have argued throughout this study, the perpetually lost quality of Troy in the late medieval period is essential to its structuring power. Troy's absence, or lack, in other words, is precisely its strength. Writers claiming Trojan precedent do so in ways that often serve to obfuscate more than they reveal. Paradoxically, they contribute to Troy's disappearance in the process of producing its significance. Such discursive operations that simultaneously produce and conceal the idea of true Trojanness are political insofar as they serve motivated definitions of monarchy, nation, and literary history. But although it has perhaps become a truism that contingencies of history structure literary practice (including our own reading practices), these concluding comments will consider how certain specifically literary conventions are called upon in the production of historiography. The historical imagination, in this case the late-medieval English discourse of Troy, typically invokes gender as a model for structuring history and its Others. Gender also serves as a means by which authors attempt to stave off that necessary failure of authority to which their texts admit even as they assert themselves as *auctoritates*. Whereas Judith Butler asks how we can trace the way gender fables establish and circulate the misnomer of natural facts, I shall consider here how gender fables establish and circulate history.[1]

In Lacan's formulation, the category of woman belongs on the side of the Other: She is placed beyond (beyond the phallus, beyond the symbolic order) insofar as her meaning is fixed in the "elsewhere" of desire or in the "something more" than satisfaction. Lacan associates such a categorization with the Freudian concept of repetition: The recognition of woman's supposed lack provokes attempts to fill it, cover it, or compensate for it. But because these attempts are doomed to inadequacy (insofar as lack, or desire, must by definition persist in the symbolic economy that assigns it an empty value in the first place), they are never "resolved." Rather they are always repeated.[2]

Woman as a category, like the category Trojanness, operates as a guarantor of masculine historical fantasy that nevertheless fails to guarantee that fantasy. She stimulates the desire for legitimacy while seeming to alleviate it, but she likewise inspires the desire for texts. Medieval Troy stories typically position woman as "beyond" the linear narrative of the *translatio imperii* from the ancient city to Brutus's new Troy. She is designated as that which provokes *and* as that which impedes national founding legends. In this way, the category of woman can be said to both permit and frustrate histories of empire—and ultimately to provoke repeated narrations of the *translatio,* narrations that nevertheless manage to fail to satisfy. The manipulation of women characters in the Troy tradition is a phenomenon of repetition in search of and in place of a truth designated as "lost." More broadly, the alternating presence or absence of woman as an interpretive category in the *translatio imperii* is an indicator of the elusive power of historical narrative itself.

When Aeneas remembers the fall of Troy, as an entertainment for Dido, his geographical and political progress is delayed. He thus seduces (from *seductere,* "to lead away" or "to lead astray") not only Dido but himself when he strays away from his imperial mission and into the pleasures and pains of narrative. In Carthage, a remembered narrative is an impediment or an obstacle to history at the same time that it is necessary to it. This loss of narrative control necessary for the production of history is framed in medieval versions of the Troy story as both pleasurable and dangerous. Whereas Ascanius is the son of Aeneas and Creusa, and Julius is the son of Aeneas and Lavinia, the treacherous and unstable Fama is the daughter of Aeneas and Dido here in Carthage. Fama, like the goddess Fortuna, is a feminine allegorical figure born out of sin whose main attributes include willfulness and inconstancy.[3] To have fame is not necessarily desirable, since even the most illustrious of heroes end up "graven" in compromising positions as part of the process of literary canonization. But to be a part of history, on the other hand, is conceived as something worthwhile and authoritative, something edifying. The split between the two different types of renown is striking: Fame is deviant and feminine, and history is exemplary and masculine.

But however ideologically separate, fame and history are nevertheless linked in both theory and practice. Even John Hardyng, rather self-servingly trying to assert the value of historical writing in his fifteenth-century *Chronicle,* "lapses" into a description that sounds more luxurious than necessary, more pleasurable than instructive, when he claims that among all writers,

> None haue behynd theim left so greate treasure,
> Ne to their posteritee haue dooen such delite,
> As thei whiche haue taken peines to write
> Chronycles . . .

Such texts, he continues, "are matier of pleasaunce, fruite, and comforte"[4] and have a generative function as well: They produce new texts in their wake. As such, the masculinist phenomenon of history writing is not unlike the status of feminine sexuality in the production of fame: The chronicler's language captures the integral role of deviance in the construction of exemplary masculine history.

In the Troy stories examined in this book, we have seen that although Calkas, Antenor, and Aeneas are acknowledged as traitors, Helen and Criseyde take the blame for causing the destruction of Troy. Gawain and Arthur, in turn, are unworthy inheritors of Trojan precedent, but Lady Bertilak and Morgan—and in Gawain's famous antifeminist outburst, women in general—are understood as inhibiting the moral and political triumph of the Arthurian court. Women in the Troy story are thus both enablers of and obstacles to the fantasy of *translatio imperii:* They both stand in for and cause what is lost.

Dido as a sexual lure, for example, plays a foundational role in the establishment of post-Trojan empires. Her bed provides a necessary stepping-stone for Aeneas in his travels from Troy to Rome. And Lady Bertilak, too, through her "ruination" of Gawain in the bedroom, is the ignoble origin of the Order of the Garter. But the shameful behavior of Aeneas and Gawain with these women is out of place in narratives of heroic nationalism. In both cases, the seductive women are elided in the official, "historical" versions of the adventures: The Round Table knights categorically reject Gawain's sexualized shame and guilt (and symbolic castration), and Virgil—by pressing the divine imperative of his hero's quest—erases the causal function of Dido's sexuality in Aeneas's glory. That which is necessary is translated into an obstacle after the fact.

"History" is thus created through a loss of interpretive control that more broadly characterizes the writing process. As Chaucer himself lamented on many occasions, once a text is "published" and sent out to the future, anything might happen to it. This loss of control is simultaneous with the process of trying to fix, to capture, to solidify an event as history. Fama and history are bedfellows, and the authority of history is as dangerous as the supposed impediments to it. Criseyde's complaint, for instance, that "no good word" (*Troilus and Criseyde,* V, 1060) will be written or sung about her, foresees and thus calls into being her posthumous fame even as it imagines catastrophic results. Similarly, Dido's threatened revenge at the conclusion of the "Legend of Dido,"

> "But syn my name is lost thourgh yow," quod she,
> "I may wel lese on yow a word or letter,
> Al be it that I shal ben nevere the better,"[5]

speaks to an association between losing control in love, losing control over one's name, and writing Trojan stories. Seduction yields the production of texts as surely as treason makes history.

Richard II himself, as a "character" in Lancastrian history, is assigned a feminine role. His status as famous (and deviant) secures his successors' historical truth in their narrative of *translatio imperii.* In many respects, Richard is assigned a "Dido function" in the glorious establishment of Henry IV and Henry V: Ricardian passion, considered an obstacle to true governance, simultaneously produced the Lancastrian triumph. Chaucer's reputation is likewise seemingly split between his deviant Ricardian status as "woman's friend" and his role as the guarantor of the robustly masculine Lancastrian machine. But this division masks the causal function of the one term in the production of the other.

History is a narrative product more aligned with the "feminine" dangers of temptation, deviation, and loss of reputation than with the masculine processes of fixing stable meaning or with those tropes that claim to conquer uncertainty and illegitimacy. The performance of masculinity inherent in the historiographical impulse is just that: a gendered masquerade that attempts to hide absence and loss. The haunting of texts by their predecessors and the subsequent transformations of these new texts into ghosts for their descendants are driven by the "wound" of history. This wound is feminine and paradoxical—an absent space filling the record of empire and masculinity. The generative source, the feminine secret behind the public and published masculine enterprise of history making, cannot be acknowledged. It can only be glossed over in a process of absencing that in turn, incites the manufacture of ever more compensatory narratives.

The marked ambivalence of medieval Troy stories toward the very matter that sustains them calls attention to a more general difficulty embedded in historical discourse. As Hayden White writes, history—like all discourses—"moves 'to and fro' between received encodations of experience and the clutter of phenomena which refuses incorporation."[6] A dynamic rather than a static enterprise, historiography actively fashions history (as opposed to merely repeating its "truths"). As White continues, such a discourse is essentially

> a mediative enterprise. As such, it is both interpretive and preinterpretive; it is always as much about the nature of interpretation itself as it is about the subject matter which is the manifest occasion of its own elaboration.[7]

In this case, historical discourse is always as much about itself as it is about anything else.

Troy was doomed, or fated, to become new (and thus to become empire): Only after its destruction could it enable imperial fantasy as Trojan ethnic and political boundaries expanded in space and in time to conquer new imaginary territories. The gap between what Troy was and what it could be for later redactors, this "disjunctive space of temporality," suggests itself as the productive lag of signification itself. In it, "new times" are created in which emergent cultural identificatory strategies can be pursued.[8] Such an opportunity, however, is founded on an illusory premise: Like that of the utopian mode of figuration, the power of the new resides in its fantasmatic quality. As Žižek notes, in our attempts to link sign with symbol, old with new—and thus to create a coherent, unified identity—"we identify ourselves with the other precisely at a point at which he is inimitable, at the point which eludes resemblance."[9]

The ability of medieval redactors of the Troy story to create a new Trojanness in the model of the old is likewise productively flawed. These authors repeat the structures, characters, and themes already familiar in Trojan narrative, creating themselves through replication rather than remembering Troy itself. Repetition, however, is exactly what cannot happen in a successful translation of empire. The very idea of the *translatio imperii*—and its attractiveness to its later manifestations, the nations and states of Europe—rests precisely in its linearity, its assertion of movement in both time and space from the old to the new.[10]

Aeneas as a central figure in this chronotopical dynamic illustrates the point, insofar as he permits and obstructs latter-day heroes and traitors who cluster around his precedent in ways that fix their identities in surprising patterns. A mobilizing figure for the ambitions and elisions attending England's mythic history, Aeneas creates Chaucer in his image: The medieval poet becomes, after his death, the founder of an empire (of letters). He is the "father of English poetry" just as Aeneas is the father of Europe. But both foundations are based in treason, or in heroic defections from authoritative precedent, and both prompt disavowals and revisions in their wake.

The Trojan narratives of Gower, Maidstone, and the *Gawain*-Poet—like those of Chaucer and Lydgate—create Troy's invisibility through the process of authenticating themselves in the fantasmatic empire of English literary history. They make Troy neither visible nor new. Rather, they obscure the origin through claiming to find it, and in the process, they insert themselves in literary history. Thus, the validating authority of precedent is achieved only through fantastic figurations.

Unlike a dream, a fantasy is "always progressive . . . always heading for the world it only appears to have left behind."[11] Fantasies are always political, and, as Jacqueline Rose writes, they are always constitutive discourses insofar as they involve, "alongside the attempt to arrest the present, a journey through the past."[12] A claim to a particular past, such as Troy, is thus part of the ongoing dialogue of the present "creating and recreating itself, hardly a 'claim' since always in process, of necessity incomplete."[13] Fantasies of Troy in late-fourteenth- and early-fifteenth-century texts make and unmake the new Troy in various political guises, but they leave behind themselves as witnesses to the creation of an empire of English letters.

Notes

Introduction

1. "Freud to Fliess, 28 May 1899," in *The Complete Letters of Sigmund Freud to Wilhelm Fliess, 1887–1904,* 387.

2. Heinrich Schliemann, *Ilios,* 1.

3. Ibid., 3.

4. Elizabeth J. Bellamy, *Translations of Power,* 50.

5. See Susan Heuck Allen, *Finding the Walls of Troy,* 110–25, for an elaboration of how Schliemann's life story and claim to the singular discovery were fabricated by himself and repeated by his official biographer. An undistinguished student, Schliemann was excluded early in life from the pursuit of the humanities. He did, however, study Greek and Latin on his own, following the fashion for archaeology and antiquities-collecting with great, although amateur, interest. The scholar Frank Calvert shared his knowledge and theories about the location of Troy with Schliemann, who then not only used them to start the dig at Hïsarlik but also took the credit for the discovery himself (and even, it appears, backdated his diary entries to reflect the independence of "his" ideas).

In several autobiographical narratives written over a period of ten years, Schliemann created for himself an idealized identity as a Victorian gentleman-scholar. In addition to the 1880 volume *Ilios,* his evolving autobiography may be traced in the following: *Trojanische Alterhümer, Troy and Its Remains,* and finally, *Troja.* Like *Ilios,* the 1875 and 1884 volumes were published by John Murray.

6. Peter Gay, *Freud,* 172.

7. "Studies on Hysteria," in *Standard Edition of the Complete Psychological Works of Sigmund Freud,* 2:201.

8. "Freud to Fliess, 21 December 1899," in *Complete Letters,* 391–92.

9. Jacqueline Rose, introduction to Jacques Lacan's *Feminine Sexuality,* 32.

10. Brotherton Library (University of Leeds), Special Collection, MS 100 (unnumbered roll).

11. See Erich S. Gruen, *Culture and National Identity in Republican Rome,* 6–51, for a discussion of Roman uses of Trojan legend to further national identity formation, particularly in the late fourth century.

12. Marie Tanner, *The Last Descendant of Aeneas,* 69. Tanner further notes that Carolingian texts likewise developed the concept of Clovis's direct descent from Aeneas (76).

13. These portraits are now lost, but replicas are preserved in a sixteenth-century manuscript copy made for the Hapsburg emperor Maximilian II. See Tanner, *Last Descendant,* 97–98. It is commonly acknowledged that the Karlstein portraits share a visual style with Richard II's "coronation portrait" in Westminster Abbey and that this similarity may indicate Bohemian influence in the late-fourteenth-century English royal court. I discuss this influence in chapter 4.

14. Although Nennius was the first writer to claim a Trojan ancestry for the ancient Britons, Geoffrey of Monmouth embellished and ultimately came to "own" the association. See Antonia Gransden, *Historical Writing in England,* 11.

15. Geoffrey of Monmouth, *History of the Kings of Britain,* 18.

16. Ibid., 27. Geoffrey continues to note that the name "Trinovantum" was lost as a result of the political corruption of King Lud: "But afterward, Lud . . . possessed him of the helm of the kingdom, and surrounded the city with right noble walls, as well as with towers builded with marvelous art, commanding that it should be called Kaerlud, that is, City of Lud, after his own name." In an interesting precursor to Nicholas Brembre's "crime," which I discuss in chapter 1, Lud's desire to rename the city provoked dissent within London's ruling circle: "Whence afterward a contention arose betwixt him and his brother Nennius, who took it ill that he should be minded to do away the name of Troy in his own country" (27–28).

17. Francis Ingledew, "The Book of Troy and the Genealogical Construction of History," 666. In this argument, Ingledew follows Robert W. Hanning, *The Vision of History in Early Britain.*

18. For a review of the reception of Virgil in medieval England, see F. J. E. Raby, "Some Notes on Virgil, Mainly in English Authors, in the Middle Ages."

19. Ingledew, "Book of Troy," 666–67.

20. The Crusades, obviously, represent an exception to this point and could easily be seen as an attempt to form a Christian empire. On the few occasions when notorious enemies came together in a common cause, it was almost always for the purpose of a crusade. Thus, even in the midst of the Hundred Years' War, France and England could send joint armies to fight for Christendom. The Great Schism, which began in 1378, provided further opportunity for shifting alliances in the cause of Christian empire, as I discuss in chapter 4.

21. Bernard Guenée, *States and Rulers in Later Medieval Europe,* 59–60.

22. As Elizabeth Butler Cullingford, "British Romans and Irish Carthaginians," 223, observes, in the period before the British empire, Troy suited as a common ancestor to London, Rome, and Paris, but "once Britain acquired a colonial empire, descent from defeated Troy became less relevant than the analogy with imperial Rome."

23. James Simpson, "The Other Book of Troy," 397.

24. Ibid., 404.

25. See C. David Benson, *The History of Troy in Middle English Literature,* 3–34, for a discussion of how Guido's text was positioned in relation to historical truth by later medieval writers.

26. Gabrielle M. Spiegel, *The Past as Text,* xix.

27. Ibid., 20.

28. Carolyn Dinshaw, *Getting Medieval,* 35.

29. Lee Patterson, "Chaucer's Pardoner on the Couch."

30. The terms "Britain" and "England" were as politically vexed in the late fourteenth century as they are today. As I will discuss in detail, the Troy myth was often used by English writers to claim a British empire (that is, to assert England's rights to Wales, Scotland, Ireland, and beyond). Sometimes, however, "British" writers invoked Trojan precedent in support of their claim to self-sovereignty and as a rejection of English rule.

31. Michel Foucault, "Of Other Spaces," 24.

32. Ibid.

33. Kathleen Biddick, "Bede's Blush," 16; cited in Spiegel, *Past as Text,* 59. Spiegel notes that it is precisely this "dual consciousness of the Middle Ages as a place and time of non-origin (i.e., the dark, deathly period constructed in and by the Renaissance) and of origin (the origin of the modern state)" that supports medievalists' sense of their professional legitimacy.

1. Late-Fourteenth-Century London as the New Troy

1. Thomas Walsingham, *Historia Anglicana,* 2:174. Henry Knighton, *Knighton's Chronicle, 1337–1396,* 500–501, similarly records the belief that, had Brembre lived, "he would have had himself made duke of Troy by the king, for in ancient times London was called the second Troy *["Troia minor"],* and so he would have been the duke of London, the name of London being changed to Troy."

2. *Saint Erkenwald,* lines 25–26.

3. The significance of London's Trojan past is further suggested by the appearance of Troy in two late-fourteenth-century books commissioned by London citizens. Thomas Carleton, a wealthy embroiderer and one-time supporter of Brembre's rival, John Northampton, commissioned a collection of statutes relating to the government of England and the city of London. Prominent in this collection (which probably was compiled in early 1383) is a section entitled "De Londonie fama," which narrates the city's legendary history and its founding by Brutus (British Library Additional MS 38,131, fol. 83). A second book, thought to have been produced in 1395 for a London fishmonger, consists almost exclusively of ordinances related to the fishmongering trade, with a curious exception. The two paragraphs from Geoffrey of Monmouth's *Historia regum Britanniae* that recount London's foundation by Brutus and the city's legendary name, "Troia nova" (which I discuss below), are emphasized in this manuscript by marginal drawings of a finger pointing to the relevant text (British Library Egerton MS 2885, fol. 8b).

4. D. W. Robertson, *Chaucer's London,* 3.

5. Medieval redactors of the story of the Trojan War often pointed to Paris's abduction of Helen (and usually blamed Helen's lust, not Paris's) as the root cause of the trouble. Criseyde's betrayal of her lover, Troilus, similarly was seen as a direct cause of the fall of Troy, since Troilus's survival was thought necessary for the survival of the city. And a few commentators have suggested a possible incestuous, not to mention adulterous, relationship between Helen and her brother-in-law, Deiphoebus, who married after the death of Paris. These originary acts of sexual deviance were transferred to the post-Trojan world via Aeneas, who (according to Ovidian versions of the story) married Dido only to renounce her afterward. See, for example, Guido delle Colonne, *Historia destructionis Troiae*, ed. Nathaniel Edward Green, 70–74; Servius's commentary on the *Aeneid*, in *Servianorum in Vergilii carmina commentariorum*, 2:316–17 (cited in Patterson, *Chaucer and the Subject of History*, 110, n. 71); and Chaucer's *Troilus and Criseyde*, II, 1702–8, and *House of Fame*, lines 293–95, both in the *Riverside Chaucer*.

6. Walsingham, *Historia*, 2:174. Compounding the unflattering association between Brembre and Richard II, Walsingham uses this same phrase again to describe what Richard had in mind for the Londoners during his 1392 quarrel with the city, as discussed below.

7. Bellamy, *Translations of Power*, 34.

8. The problem with Brembre's alleged designs on the city's name is worsened by the prospect of his being raised to the status of duke. As chapter 3 will discuss, Richard II was seen to be in the habit of raising his friends to positions of undeserved glory. In particular, his elevation of Robert de Vere to the position of duke of Ireland was criticized in contemporary chronicles.

9. Bellamy, *Translations of Power*, 34.

10. Ned Lukacher, *Primal Scenes*, 24, writes that the primal scene is "situated in the differential space between historical memory and imaginative construction, between archival verification and interpretive free play."

11. See Andrew Prescott, "The Judicial Records of the Rising of 1381." R. B. Dobson, *The Peasants' Revolt of 1381*, provides edited and translated chronicle accounts that trace the events leading up to the revolt and record its consequences. Studies of the social composition of the rebels include Christopher Dyer, "The Social and Economic Background to the Rural Revolt of 1381"; Sylvia Federico, "The Imaginary Society"; and Andrew Prescott, "London in the Peasants' Revolt."

12. Maidstone (d. 1396) was a doctor of theology who wrote tracts against the Wycliffites and defenses of begging friars (for example, the 1380 *Protectorium pauperis*). Born in Kent and ordained in 1376, he was a member of the Carmelite house at Aylesford. See the biographical notes in the introduction to the text, *Concordia facta inter regem Riccardum II et civitatem Londonie*, 1–10.

13. See Caroline M. Barron, "The Quarrel of Richard II with London: 1392–97."

14. London's internal conflicts prompt David Wallace, "Chaucer and the Absent City," 84, to speak of the impossibility of representing the city as a unified whole. London is an "absent city" in Chaucer's poetry because "there is no idea of a city for all the inhabitants of a space called London to pay allegiance to; there are only conflicts of associational, hierarchical, and anti-associational discourses, acted out within and across the boundaries of a city wall or the fragments of a text called *The Canterbury Tales*."

15. Elizabeth Grosz, "Bodies—Cities," 242, explores the "constitutive and mutually defining relation between bodies and cities," arguing that the body and its environment "produce each other as forms of the hyperreal, as modes of simulation which have overtaken and transformed whatever reality each may have had into the image of the other: the city is made and made over into the simulacrum of the body, and the body, in its turn, is transformed, 'citified,' urbanized as a distinctively metropolitan body."

16. Lacan, *Feminine Sexuality,* 50.

17. The controllable, manageable position of "woman" as sexual difference, or lack, and the uncontrollable, unmanageable position of "woman" as *jouissance,* or excess, are impossible to keep separate. The *petit autre* inscribed as difference in the phallic order, and the Other whose mysterious *jouissance* threatens and promises to exceed the boundaries of that order, collapse together in Lacan's formulation to become the tenuous fantasy upon which man's identity is constructed.

The danger of being annihilated, however, also represents the pleasure of being released. According to Lacan, the fantasy of woman is like the fantasy of God; "she" offers the promise of an escape from the restricted and always inadequate positions of identity available in signification. In this way, the fantasy of woman's extrasymbolic position threatens, but also promises, to release man from the system of self-identification he conjured through "her." See Lacan, *Feminine Sexuality,* 138–48.

18. *The Major Latin Works of John Gower,* trans. Eric W. Stockton, 50. Subsequent quotations of *Vox clamantis* in English translation will be cited parenthetically in the text according to page numbers in Stockton's translation.

19. *The Complete Works of John Gower,* ed. G. C. Macaulay, vol. 4, book I, lines 2139–40. Subsequent quotations of Gower's Latin poem will be cited parenthetically according to book and line numbers in Macaulay's edition.

20. See John H. Fisher, *John Gower,* 170–73.

21. Here and throughout, I mean by the word "fantasy" a heavily invested alternative to reality that may or may not be consciously constructed. There is a debate in psychoanalytic discourse as to whether fantasy (or "phantasy") properly denotes a conscious desire, like daydreaming, or an aspect of the unconscious process, like the dreamwork. Freud, *Standard Edition,* 7:165, n. 2, was himself unable to distinguish between the two types, since he found that the contents of both conscious and unconscious fantasies "often coincide with one another even down to their details." What Freud *was* able to say definitively about fantasies is that they always seek to express themselves (they will out), and they always reflect a desire on the part of the subject—regardless of her or his awareness of this desire. See Jean Laplanche and Jean-Bertrande Pontalis, *The Language of Psychoanalysis,* 314–19.

22. My translation of Walsingham, *Historia,* 1:459. The Latin reads: "Nam quis unquam credidisset, non solum rusticos, sed rusticorum abjectissimos, non plures, sed singulos, audere thalamum Regis, vel matris eius, cum baculis subintrare vilissimis. . . . Et cum haec omnia facerent, et, ut diximus, plerique soli in cameras concessissent, et sedendo, jacendo, jocando, super lectum Regis insolescerent; et insuper, matrem Regis ad oscula invitarent quidam."

23. Ibid., 2:12.

24. Ibid.

25. Macaulay's note, *Complete Works*, 374, n. 545, reads: "*Coppa:* used as a familiar name for a hen in the *Speculum Stultorum*, pp. 55, 58, and evidently connected with 'Coppen' or 'Coppe,' which is the name of one of Chanticleer's daughters in the Low-German and English *Reynard*."

26. Symbols of feminine misrule were plentiful in Gower's era, and they were often linked to political misrule. Pointing out the several similarities between Chaucer's Wife of Bath and the rebels of 1381 (inferior social status, exclusion from and consequent hostility toward haute literate circles), Susan Crane, "The Writing Lesson of 1381," argues that the Wife's *Prologue* is perhaps Chaucer's most overlooked response to the rebellion. Alison "identifies herself as the voice of a maligned group" (215), and her tearing out the page of Jankyn's Book of Wicked Wives is seen by Crane as analogous to the rebels' famed violence against texts.

The Wife's *Prologue* and Gower's earlier French poem, *Mirour de l'omme*, provide a combined contribution to the relationship between unruly commons and unruly women in nearly parallel passages that describe the three evils that can beset a man. Gower writes that "[t]here are three things with a single behavior that ravage mercilessly when they get the mastery. One is flood waters. Another is wild fire. The third is the multitude of little people when they are stirred up, for they will not be stopped by reason or by discipline" (*Mirour*, 347–48). In the Wife of Bath's *Prologue*, Alison speaks for one of her three old husbands in a way that tracks, with a significant difference, Gower's three evils: "Thow seyst that droppyng houses, and eek smoke, / And chidyng wyves maken men to flee / Out of hir owene houses; a, benedictee!" (lines 278–80; unless otherwise noted, all quotations from Chaucer's works are from the *Riverside Chaucer*). Misbehaving women and rising commons are not only intolerable, they are symbolically interchangeable. See Federico, "Imaginary Society," for further discussion.

27. See Barron, "The Widow's World in Later Medieval London." The degree of economic self-sufficiency afforded to women, and especially to widows, in the late fourteenth century has been seen as evidence of a "golden age" for women during the period. See Barron, "The 'Golden Age' of Women in Medieval London."

28. Gower, *Mirour*, 246.

29. Gower's allusion here to faithless Londoners admitting the rebels into the city intersects with several other contemporary opinions regarding how the rebels gained entrance. Dobson records a group of chronicle entries that blame the poor of the city and its environs: *Letter-Book H*, the Anonimalle chronicler, and Walsingham all more or less agree that the "perfidious commoners" of London and its suburb, Southwark, demanded that the bridge be lowered for the rebels to cross into the city. See Dobson, *Peasants' Revolt*, 209, 156, 168–69. Jean Froissart dramatically adds to this consensus by claiming that poor Londoners thought to themselves, "why do we not let these good people enter into the city? they are our fellows, and that that they do is for us" (quoted in Dobson, *Peasants' Revolt*, 188).

Another grouping of records suggests that the blame lay with a more established and privileged segment of London's population but does not explicitly articulate this charge. Knighton, *Chronicle*, 210–11, says that the rebels passed over the bridge with no opposition, even though the citizens had long known that they were coming ("et tamen ut dicebatur ciues Londonienses de eorum aduentu longo ante tempore intellexerunt"). *The Westminster Chronicle, 1381–1394,* 9, similarly suggests that "the whole of London, the prey of internal confusion and, as many thought, of some degree of internal dissension, was without a clear view of what was to be done."

The rumor that several treasonous aldermen conspired to admit the rebels has been discredited because of the "unscrupulously partisan" nature of the supporting documents, the jurors' returns of 1382. These two returns, which accused certain members of the victualling party of treasonously plotting the destruction of the city, had their genesis in the strife between the mayoral factions of Brembre and Northampton. See B. Wilkinson, "The Peasants' Revolt of 1381," for a discussion and transcription of the jurors' return of 4 November 1382, and Andre Réville, *Le Soulèvement des travailleurs d'Angleterre en 1381,* 190–96, for the return of 20 November.

30. The description in *Vox clamantis* of the city opening herself up for the rebels' entrance is not unlike Gower's earlier condemnation, in *Mirour de l'omme,* of a prostitute plying her trade in Southwark: "Every day of the week, behold, Wantonness leads her life near the stews. Very basely she drags out her life there, where she is every man's companion, caring nought to what class he belongs. . . . Ah, whore, . . . thus you are common in your wantonness as the roads of the country are common, over which all men, both worthy and miserable, great and small, may go at will" (127).

31. No doubt Gower would argue that the city's deceased husband was Edward III (d. 1377), the king who was considered a paragon of chivalric masculinity before senility and Alice Perrers took their toll on him.

32. Knighton, *Chronicle,* 212–13, similarly remarks: "The knights who were to accompany [the king] foolishly allowed their ardour to cool, lamentably hiding the boldness of their spirit, and as though struck by some womanish fear *('quasi timore femineo'),* not daring to go out, stayed in the Tower."

33. Steven Justice, *Writing and Rebellion,* 212, 213.

34. Justice, in ibid., 209, makes a very similar point. The difference in my view is that Gower's strategies of self-reconstruction become visible in light of his *failure* to discredit the rebels, as opposed to his success in doing so.

35. Wallace, "Chaucer and the Absent City," 60. See also Martha Carlin, *Medieval Southwark,* for the economic, political, and social marginalization of London's major suburb.

36. That Gower's moral censure of the upper tiers of English society is akin to the rebels' own views does not mean that Gower "sympathized with" the revolt. No doubt he was horrified by what happened in June 1381—not just because of the outrageous acts of violence but also because, in his view, the lower tiers of the population had no business in governmental affairs, no right to assert themselves, and no proper voice with which to complain (even if they had a legitimate grievance). The responsibility to speak out about social and political problems is one Gower firmly reserves for himself or men like himself. The rebels' violation of their proper place in the tripartite social structure is as noxious to Gower as the corruption and treason of the knights and clerics in the upper levels of the hierarchy.

37. An indication of Gower's evolving views of Richard II might be noted in his textual emendations to his English poem, *Confessio amantis,* as I discuss in chapter 4.

38. Barron, "Quarrel," 189. For the economic and political contexts of the quarrel, see also Ruth Bird, *The Turbulent London of Richard II*, 102–9; May McKisack, *The Fourteenth Century: 1307–1399*, 467–68; and Pamela Nightingale, *A Medieval Mercantile Community*, 326–37, who suggests that the citizens may have refused the king his loan because of a widespread shortage of coin or a genuine crisis of cash availability. But it is still unclear how the Londoners had the money (or for that matter, the time) to stage an elaborately organized and expensive reconciliation ceremony on such short notice and with such limited cash.

39. Besides Maidstone's poem, the pageant is described in Knighton, *Chronicle*, 547–49; Walsingham, *Historia*, 2:207–11; and *Westminster Chronicle*, 503–9. See also "A Letter Describing Richard II's Reconciliation with the City of London, 1392" for a record of the pageant, apparently written by a member of Richard's party.

40. Maidstone, *Concordia facta inter regem Riccardum II et civitatem Londonie*, 163. All subsequent quotations of Maidstone's poem in English translation will be cited parenthetically in the text according to the page numbers in Smith's edition.

41. *Concordia*, line 55. Subsequent quotations of Maidstone's Latin text will be cited parenthetically according to the line numbers in Smith's edition.

42. Paul Strohm makes this point in *Hochon's Arrow*, 108.

43. Louise Fradenburg, *City, Marriage, Tournament*, 74.

44. The tension between these rival factions was such that, as late as 1391, a mayoral proclamation forbade mention of either Brembre or Northampton within city limits, upon pain of imprisonment. See Wallace, "Chaucer and the Absent City," 85, citing *Memorials of London and London Life in the Thirteenth, Fourteenth, and Fifteenth Centuries*, 526–27.

45. *Calendar of Letter-Book H, 1375–1399*, 348, 359, records the skirmishes during the early 1380s between the two dominant trade factions, represented most famously by the mayoralties of Brembre and Northampton. This struggle is seen to continue even as late as 1389, when the legitimacy of the mayoral election of William Venour, a grocer, was contested by the loser, goldsmith Adam Bamme, who then went on to achieve the mayor's seat in 1390 in voting clearly delineated along the established factional lines between victuallers and nonvictuallers.

Although there is some consensus that the overt conflict between these two parties died with Brembre in 1388 and that the city of London then proceeded to solidify a relatively unified and stable ruling oligarchy (see Barron, "Quarrel," 174, and Bird, *Turbulent London*, 119), perhaps the rivalry between victuallers and nonvictuallers enjoyed a fate more like Northampton's: exiled for a time, only to return when court and city politics required its usefulness. Nightingale's study, "Capitalists, Crafts, and Constitutional Change in Late Fourteenth-Century London," shows members of the two parties to be surprisingly mobile, often forming alliances across party lines when circumstances could benefit from a unified front. Even more suggestive, Nightingale traces how the political machinations of the king, John of Gaunt, and others frequently depended on the trade groups' differences and exploited these local antagonisms for their own ends. We might then see the apparent unity of the competing guildsmen in the pageant as a symbolic response to this divide-and-rule strategy: A show of allegiance would be the most threatening display possible to a king who had depended on a bitterly divided citizenry for his own political viability.

46. Fradenburg, *City*, 74.

47. Gordon Kipling, "Richard II's 'Sumptuous Pageants' and the Idea of the Civic Triumph," 97, suggests this dynamic in his discussion of the religious significance of the pageant: "[T]he king, through his willing acceptance of the Christlike role that the civic triumph thrusts upon him, must *imitate* Christ the King."

48. Equally complex in its characterization of imperial fullness is William Dunbar's praise poem, "London," read at the Christmas feast given by the lord mayor of London to the Scottish ambassadors in 1501. Dunbar invokes the city's new Trojan identity in ways that mingle the language of sexual pleasure with that of imperial domination:

> Gladdith anon thou lusty Troynovaunt,
> Citie that some tyme cleped was New Troy,
> In all the erth, imperiall as thou stant,
> Pryncesse of townes, of pleasure and of joy,
> A richer restith under no Christen roy.
> (lines 9–13)

The poem concludes with praise for the mayor, stating, "No Lord of Parys, Venyce, or Fraunce / In dignytie or honoure goeth to hym nye" (51–52).

This association of London with Troy, by a Scots poet and for an occasion supposedly honoring the Scottish, is highly ambivalent—especially as Gavin Douglas soon was to embark on an overtly propagandistic translation of the *Aeneid* in "Scottis." As chapter 2 will discuss, the appropriation of Trojan precedent served a nationalistic purpose for several European entities, as well as specific local purposes within English politics.

49. The feminine city's display of submissiveness is part of the same form of political vocabulary that Queen Anne uses to persuade her husband. The keeper of the city articulates the logic of this strategy when he prays that Anne will "soften royal severity that the king may be forebearing to his people. A woman mellows a man with love" (191) ("Fleotere regales poterit regina rigores, / Mitis ut in gentem rex velit esse suam. / Mollit amore virum mulier" [229–31]).

50. Fradenburg, *City*, 12. That this "gift of difference" is specifically feminine becomes clear in Fradenburg's discussion. Included in a system of aristocratic order, that is, when she is behaving herself, the city "may be the 'free maternal city' of plenitude; . . . repudiated, it may be Babylon, the city of earth—site of sexuality, ungovernable women, beautiful clothing, trade, crafts, and, in the end, grief" (12).

51. As Barron, "'Golden Age,'" 40, points out, married women in London "were frequently working partners in marriages between economic equals." Moreover, this equality of husband and wife may have resulted in financial advantages for both of them, in the form of "being able to shift goods, or cash, from one partner to another in times of economic pressure."

52. Ibid.

53. As Kipling, "Richard II's 'Sumptuous Pageants,'" 95, writes, "in Richard's eyes, London's refusal of a loan had constituted a breach of the city's feudal loyalty."

54. Benjamin R. McRee, "Unity or Division? The Social Meaning of Guild Ceremony in Urban Communities," 105, notes that "guild processions, however simple or elaborate their external trappings, were, at heart, public declarations of autonomy. They announced that the marchers were part of an independent body with its own goals, its own rules, and its own corporate identity. . . . They emphasized not the wholeness of the community, but its division into separate, semiautonomous subgroups."

55. Glynne Wickham, *Early English Stages, 1300–1660,* 1:64, argues a similar point and concludes that the pageant represents the king's capitulation to the merchants, who "were powerful enough through their wealth to call his bluff."

56. Strohm, *Hochon's Arrow,* 111.

57. Michael Hanrahan, "'A Straunge Succesour Sholde Take Youre Heritage': The *Clerk's Tale* and the Crisis of Ricardian Rule," discusses the political implications and cultural anxieties attending Richard II's failure to produce an heir.

58. See Barron, "Quarrel," 185–87, for evidence of how carefully Richard applied the statute of 1354, which detailed the procedures to be followed in correcting faults in London's government. But as I discuss in chapter 3, Richard's attention to legal precedents changed neither the hostile tone of his actions nor the spirit in which they were received.

59. Similarly, men needed the economic potential of women at this moment in London's history. Barron, "'Golden Age,'" 40–41, notes that the theory of conjugal unity, in which the man and the woman become one body in marriage, was eased in London in the fourteenth century to accommodate the desirable practice of having women make money. This was because women's economic potential was good for men. But as soon as their work ceased to be profitable for men, "women were pushed out of the skilled labour market" (48).

60. Strohm, "'Lad with revel to Newegate,'" 170, suggests the socially structuring power of literary representation when he writes that "the most conclusive way to gain control of an unruly but powerful symbol is by employing it in a narration, by assimilating it to an exemplary sequence of events that unfolds in time and that, preferably, ends with a determinate conclusion illustrating or vindicating one's claims."

2. Arthur's Court and Britain's House of Fame

1. The Middle English term "legende" refers to that which is noble or worthwhile (literally, deserving to be read, whether true or not), whereas "storie" is closer to our modern "history" (meaning true, either in the sense that it actually happened or that it is particularly exemplary, and thus worthy of being remembered), and "fable" refers to a falsehood. See Strohm, "Passioun, Lyf, Miracle, Legende," and "Storie, Spelle, Geste, Romaunce, Tragedie."

2. Patterson, *Negotiating the Past,* 204, notes that generic instability is one of the main symptoms of the conflicting attitudes toward secular history in the Middle Ages: "The various tensions and contradictions that inhabited medieval thinking about history . . . were registered at the level of textuality as a generic vacillation between history and romance, an instability that itself put into question not merely the authenticity of a particular narrative, or even of historiography as a whole, but the legitimacy of the historical life itself."

3. As Patterson, *Negotiating,* 160, argues, this ambivalent posture toward history is embedded in the *Aeneid* itself. In Virgil's poem, "the past is endowed with a double, contradictory value: it is at once a guilty if potent origin to be suppressed and forgotten, and a heroic precedent to be reinvoked and reenacted."

4. Christopher Baswell, *Virgil in Medieval England,* 18, articulates Aeneas's flawed character as represented by Dictys: "[The] Trojan nobility is depicted as murderous, lustful, lying, and deeply treacherous. Aeneas embodies all these sins, especially the last."

5. Michel de Certeau, *The Writing of History,* 250.

6. Ibid., 314–15.

7. Jacques Derrida, *The Post Card (from Socrates to Freud and Beyond),* 492, charts the journey to the mythical source of letters as destined to conclude in "a labyrinth of doubles without originals, of facsimiles without an authentic and indivisible letter, of forgeries without something forged."

8. Ibid., 12. Part of the joke of Derrida's discourse here is the lowercase *p* in Plato's name as it appears on the postcard in question. The trick of history is that, by attaching himself to Socrates and to his authority, "plato" becomes "Plato," the authority himself.

9. Ibid., 30. Derrida notes further that "plato has sent himself a post card, he has sent it back to himself from himself, or he has even 'sent' himself. . . . And we find ourselves on the itinerary" (30). The supplanting motive is clear in the sense that by telling Socrates what to write and by sending himself Socrates, Plato both constructs and replaces his "mentor." "Plato's dream: to make Socrates write, and to make him write what he wants, his last command, his will. *To make* him write what he wants by letting him write what he wants. Thereby becoming Socrates and his father, therefore his own grandfather, and killing him" (52).

10. Caxton, introduction to Thomas Malory's *Works,* xiii–xiv.

11. Ibid., xiv. Despite Caxton's claims, however, the story of Arthur was widely known through the English translation of the French prose *Brut.* John Taylor, "The French Prose *Brut,*" 251, notes that this translation, probably compiled between 1350 and 1380, and the continuations in English that were added to it were "enormously popular." Simon Burley, the tutor of Richard II, owned a copy, and by the fifteenth century the audience of the English *Brut* included "London merchants, literate laymen and ecclesiastics of all kinds" (253); the text "came to be regarded in time as a kind of 'national' history" (254).

12. The proposed dates of composition for *Sir Gawain and the Green Knight* range from 1360 to 1400 (the latter being the date of the single surviving manuscript, British Library, Cotton Nero A.x).

13. *Sir Gawain and the Green Knight,* ed. Malcolm Andrew and Ronald Waldron, lines 1–7. All future quotations from the poem will be cited parenthetically in the text according to the line numbers in this edition.

14. The controversy among scholars over the meaning of these lines is focused on whether the traitorous "tulk" of line three is Antenor or the same "Ennias" of line five. Alfred David, "Gawain and Aeneas," reviews the history of the different translations of this passage and concludes that Aeneas, and not Antenor, is the traitor in question. As David points out, the desire to exonerate Aeneas has led to the mistranslation of the passage in several modern editions of the poem.

15. See *The Trojan War: The Chronicles of Dictys of Crete and Dares the Phrygian.*

16. See *Trojan War,* 117–18, 167, for Dictys and Dares; and also Guido delle Colonne, *Historia destructionis Troiae,* trans. Mary Elizabeth Meek, Book XXIX, which offers a composite of these two versions.

17. David, "Gawain and Aeneas," 406.

18. In *House of Fame,* Geffrey says that he saw

> Creusa, daun Eneas wif,
> Which that he loveded as hys lyf,
> And hir yonge sone Iulo,
> And eke Askanius also.
>
> (175–78)

All future quotations from *House of Fame* will be cited parenthetically in the text according to line numbers. The explanatory note (*Riverside Chaucer,* 980, n. 177) for these lines suggests that Julius and Ascanius were the same person and that Chaucer was confused in thinking of them as two different people. But the tradition itself was confused: In addition to the familiar narrative that Aeneas and Creusa had Ascanius in Troy, Servius cites Cato's claim that in Italy, Aeneas and Lavinia had Silvius (Brutus's father). And yet other accounts, such as *The Irish* Aeneid, 201, suggest that Ascanius married Lavinia after his father's death, and that they had Julius; while, for Livy and Ovid, Silvius is the son of Ascanius and Lavinia. Such contradictions might excuse Chaucer's "mistake."

Brutus also had an extremely irregular genealogy. According to Geoffrey of Monmouth, *History,* 6, Brutus's father, Silvius (identified here as the son of Aeneas's son, Ascanius), "unknown to his father, had fallen in love with and privily taken to wife a certain niece of Lavinia, who was now about to become a mother." Ascanius asked his wizards what sex the child would be, and through their arts of magic, "they told him that the child would be a boy that should slay his father and his mother, and after much travel in many lands, should, albeit an exile, be exalted unto the highest honours."

19. See Geoffrey, *History,* 176–77.

20. Here and elsewhere, the poem engages a gendered dynamic to show the difference between those with authority and those who lack it. The knights in Arthur's court, according to the very hairy Green Knight, do not have beards: That they are not really men is the basic thrust of his taunting. This issue will become even more apparent later, in the exchange-of-winnings game at Bertilak's castle, which mobilizes the threat of sodomy. See Dinshaw, "A Kiss Is Just a Kiss," for discussion. Jeff Westover, "Arthur's End," 316, suggests that in this version of the Arthur story the king is "feminized"; he identifies with the victims of his conquests, weeps excessively, is childless, and finally suffers his mortal wound from Modred in the "felettes" (loins or genitals). Westover argues that, figuratively, the king is "castrated."

21. Dinshaw, "Kiss," 213, notes that Gawain's identity "is always in production in this poem."

22. As George Sanderlin, "Two Transfigurations," points out, the moment in which Gawain is reclothed at Bertilak's castle is reminiscent of an important scene in the *Aeneid.*

Aeneas is revealed to Dido in the Temple of Juno at Carthage in a radiance shed on him by Venus. His later incarnation, Gawain, is presented to Lady Bertilak after having been transfigured by donning the garb offered by his host ("The ver by his visage verayly hit semed / Welneghe to uche hathel, alle on hues, / Lowande and lufly alle his lymmes under" [lines 866–68]). Like Aeneas, Sanderlin notes, Gawain "is given a special beauty and brightness just before a love encounter" (256).

23. In one tale, Gawain's habit of deflowering maidens leads to his penance of having to come to the aid of all maidens, everywhere, which prevents him from joining the rest of the company of knights on martial and spiritual expeditions. See *Frederic Madden's Sir Gawayne,* which discusses Gawain's amorous adventures in *Lancelot du Lac, Mort Artus, Merlin, Jeaste of Gawayne, Tristan, Gyron, Tauree, Lancelot,* and Malory's *Morte Darthur.*

For Gawain's infamous lust, also see the very funny thirteenth-century *De coniuge non ducenda,* a popular satire in which Gawain is talked out of marriage by three angels, in *Gawain on Marriage,* and the Castle of Maidens episode in both Chrétien de Troyes's *Le Conte du Graal* and the late-twelfth-century *De ortu Waluuanii nepotis Arturi (The Rise of Gawain, Nephew of Arthur).*

24. The poem both suggests and is itself implicated in the phenomenon noted recently by Lukacher, *Primal Scenes,* 3: "[T]he subject of history is . . . the intertextual process itself."

25. See, for instance, Avril Henry, "Temptation and Hunt in *Gawain.*"

26. One of the jokes being played on Gawain here is that the lady's kisses are somehow construed as "winnings." The fact that both she and her husband coerce Gawain into kissing them shows that these "gifts" are more appropriately seen as concessions of loss.

27. Derrida, *Of Grammatology,* 36.

28. Derrida, ibid., 157, describes the phenomenon of the supplement as one that masks the absence of the origin it so stubbornly insists upon; it is "the mirage of the thing itself, of immediate presence, of originary perception."

29. See, for example, S. L. Clark and Julian N. Wasserman, "Gawain's 'Anti-Feminism' Reconsidered."

30. Derrida, *Post Card,* 453.

31. The Order of the Garter was founded by Edward III in 1348 in an attempt to associate his court with the noble precedent of King Arthur and the knights of the Round Table. Edward even commissioned a round table to be made for use in meetings. Suggesting that the poem laments the "unfulfilled Arthurian promise of Edward's reign," Walter Srebnick, "*Sir Gawain and the Green Knight* and Late Medieval Aristocratic Discourse," 15, argues that *Sir Gawain and the Green Knight* draws a contrast between the court of Edward III, the flower of chivalry, and that of Richard II, the child king. See also John M. Bowers, "*Pearl* in Its Royal Setting," for the political implications of this poet's work. For the Order of the Garter in the fourteenth century, and especially in relation to Richard II's circle of friends and advisers, see Hugh Collins, "The Order of the Garter, 1348–1461."

32. Whereas the lesson Geffrey purportedly learns from his journey is that "al mot out, other late or rathe" (2139), the poem more suggestively addresses the questions of where in the past "al" comes from and where it will go once it is out. Tidings are subject to interpretation and "mysdeming"—a choke point in the easy movement of letters that proves a consistent source of anxiety and commentary for Chaucer's narrators.

33. Derrida, *Post Card*, 485, n. 64.

34. See John Fyler, *Chaucer and Ovid*, for a discussion of the reception of Ovid in the Christian Middle Ages.

35. See Meek's introduction to Guido's *Historia*, xix, for an explanation of the misattribution.

36. Patterson, *Negotiating*, 201–2, writes, "Geoffrey's *Historia* tells of a refoundation that is accomplished only by the destruction of the very past it seeks to reenact. . . . [Troy is] a myth of origins that deconstructs the origin."

37. For Wace and Laȝamon, see Robert Huntington Fletcher, *The Arthurian Material in the Chronicles*, 125–68. Lollius appears in *Troilus and Criseyde* I, 394.

38. Baswell, *Virgil in Medieval England*, suggests this notion of the text's framing technique.

39. See Fyler, *Chaucer and Ovid*, 33–35, for the Ovidian treatment of Dido; and Marilynn Desmond, *Reading Dido*, for a broader discussion of the many uses made of Dido in the Middle Ages.

40. Sounding a bit like the philosophical eagle of the poem, Derrida, *Post Card*, 36, states its central dilemma: "In this play of representation, the point of origin becomes ungraspable. There are things like reflecting pools, and images, an infinite reference from one to the other, but no longer a source, a spring."

41. Baswell, *Virgil in Medieval England*, 246, notes that Aeneas, confronted by the images of the fall of Troy on Juno's temple at Carthage, misinterprets the goddess's depiction of his failure and turns it into a testament to Troy's former glory: "[T]he hero's tears in *Aeneid* 1 respond to images that intend to depict a triumph of Juno over her enemy, Troy; he subverts that intention and makes the pictures into a tragic revery on his lost past."

42. De Certeau, *Writing of History*, 99, 101.

43. Baswell, *Virgil in Medieval England*, 246.

44. De Certeau, *Writing of History*, 101.

45. Lisa Kiser, *Telling Classical Tales*, 115.

46. As Rita Copeland, *Rhetoric, Hermeneutics, and Translation in the Middle Ages*, 186, points out, "translation is always, in one way or another, an act of appropriation." In the case of Chaucer's *Legend of Good Women*, by locating his vernacular writings in an academic critical discourse, he "claims the status of *auctor*, thus constituting his translations as *auctoritates*."

47. Copeland, *Rhetoric*, 198.

48. Ibid., 198, 200.

49. Gavin Douglas, *Virgil's* Aeneid *Translated into Scottish Verse*, prologue, lines 114–18 and 357–58. Subsequent quotations from Douglas will be cited parenthetically in the text according to the line numbers in this edition.

50. A. M. Kinghorn, introduction to *The Middle Scots Poets*, 32.

51. Ibid., 33.

52. John Barbour, *The Bruce*, 1:21–22.

53. John of Fordun, *Chronicle of the Scottish Nation*, 2:101.

54. Ingledew, "Book of Troy," 672–73.

55. Derek Pearsall, *The Life of Geoffrey Chaucer*, 112.

56. Florence Bourgne, "Translating Saints' Lives into the Vernacular," 62, notes that "although presenting certain characteristics of the *translatio studii*, translations of saints' lives actually follow a pattern quite similar to that of the *sacra furta*" or sacred thefts of the relics or remains of lost cultures.

57. Sherry Simon, *Gender in Translation*, 5–7.

58. Ibid., 152; citing Homi K. Bhabha, *The Location of Culture*, 5.

59. As Ingledew, "Jerusalem, Babylon, Camelot: The Concept of the Court in the *Pearl* Poet," 133–34, argues, the *Gawain*-Poet views Trojan precedent as always already flawed from a Christian perspective: "The implicit presence of the figure of the Fall comments on the inadequacy of a national history that looks merely to the Fall of Troy for its founding event, and so severs national from salvation history.... Starting with the Fall of Troy... the pattern of ejection from a coherent structure supplies the poem with its meaning and form."

60. See Michael J. Bennett, "The Historical Background," for a review of the provocative links between the poem and certain aspects of Richard II's connections to the northwest, including magnificent Christmas and New Year feasts at Lichfield in 1397–98 and 1398–99.

61. Ibid., 85.

62. Ibid., 86. The use of Arthurian material for contemporary political purpose was not unheard of. According to Valerie M. Lagorio, "The Evolving Legend of St. Joseph of Glastonbury," the legendary connection between Arthur and Joseph of Arimathea was strengthened in the fourteenth century by Edward III's interest in it. He visited Glastonbury Abbey as the burial place of Arthur in 1331 and gave a royal writ in 1345 for the Abbey to be searched for Joseph's remains. The legend also may have been useful for substantiating England's claims for national autonomy during the Great Schism. As chapter 4 will discuss in greater detail, the conflict between the two popes engaged a number of nations and states competing for political advantage on the world stage.

63. Bowers, "*Pearl* in Its Royal Setting," 152.

64. Bennett, "Historical Background," 77.

65. Pearsall, *Life*, 128, notes that "between 1380 and 1386 [Chaucer] was at the height of his public career and, to some extent, at the height of his career as a poet too."

66. Ibid., 110. *House of Fame* was written after 1374, when Chaucer began his work at the customs, and probably predates his second visit to Italy in 1378, which is when he is thought to have first read Boccaccio (whose influence is not present in this poem). As Pearsall writes, *House of Fame* is probably no later than *Parliament of Fowls*, "since it would be unlikely for Chaucer to have returned to octosyllabic couplets after 'discovering' pentameter" (110).

67. Attempts to identify the man of great authority have not been satisfactory. See the explanatory note in the *Riverside Chaucer*, 990, n. 2158, for a selection of examples.

68. Strohm, *Social Chaucer*, 45.

3. Chaucer's Troy Book

1. Chaucer, *Troilus and Criseyde,* book I, lines 1–3. All future quotations from *Troilus and Criseyde* will be cited parenthetically in the text according to the book and line numbers.

2. *Boece,* V, Pr. 6, lines 17–20. Pearsall, *Life,* 169, notes this use of the word "future" as a neologism in English.

3. Patterson, *Chaucer and the Subject of History,* 181; citing *The Controversy between Sir Richard Scrope and Sir Robert Grosvenor,* 1:49–50.

4. Maurice Keen, "Chaucer's Knight, the English Aristocracy, and the Crusade," 51–53, writes of the differences between the Scrope and Grosvenor families. The Grosvenors "were a Cheshire family, not yet of any great distinction in 1386[;] . . . their military experience seems largely to have been in Gascony and in the Scottish border wars." The Scropes, by contrast, had an impressive crusading record and were known for such through wide regions of the country and abroad.

5. Thorlac Turville-Petre, *England the Nation,* 12–13. Geoffrey of Monmouth, *History,* 219–22, the source for the Merlin prophecy, also invented the story that King Arthur had conquered Ireland, another significant site for the political aspirations of Richard II.

6. R. R. Davies, *Domination and Conquest,* 4; citing *Anglo-Scottish Relations, 1174–1328,* 194–97.

7. Robin Frame, *The Political Development of the British Isles, 1100–1400,* 193. Turville-Petre, *England the Nation,* 13, notes that the Welsh also had a claim to Arthurian precedent, a claim that was thought important enough by the English to warrant its definitive rejection: When Edward I defeated Wales, he made it a point to confiscate their royal insignia, which included "Arthur's Crown," in token of their submission to English rule.

8. As Lagorio, "Evolving Legend," 220, suggests, "[T]he promotion of a legend which linked King Arthur and Joseph, and proclaimed an apostolic conversion for Britain which well antedated the founding of the Church at Rome, would bolster England's national and ecclesiastical claims to precedence and independence."

9. Juliet Vale, *Edward III and Chivalry,* 77.

10. Patterson, *Chaucer and the Subject of History,* 90–91. Heather James, *Shakespeare's Troy,* 22, writes that the Troy legend's "transmission through varied eras, nations, and vested interests radically affects the precious univocality of its authority and its singularly affirmative character in political commentary. While history deepens the tradition's authority, it also disperses it through nationalistic competition: European nations sprouted their lineal branch from the Trojans in response to the epic and chronicle accounts composed for rival nations."

11. Patterson, *Chaucer and the Subject of History,* 94; citing Eleanor Hammond, "A Burgundian Copy of Chaucer's *Troilus,*" 32; and R. A. Pratt, "Chaucer and the Visconti Libraries," 195.

12. J. J. N. Palmer, *England, France, and Christendom, 1377–99,* 67, describes the situation: "During the three years which followed de la Pole's appointment as chancellor, England suffered one reverse after another on the Continent. Flanders was lost, the Low Countries subjected to French influence, and Brittany alienated; the French made serious

36. C. S. Lewis, "What Chaucer Really Did to *Il filostrato*," observes that Chaucer generally approached *Il filostrato* from the point of view of a courtly love ideal and tailored his revisions of the Italian poem according to that ideal. For example, Chaucer's Criseyde yielded herself sexually to Troilus only "by force and deception"—an apparently more admirable handling of the situation than that of Boccaccio's Criseida, who willingly and knowingly consented to have sex with Troilo. Wallace, *Chaucer and the Early Writings of Boccaccio*, offers a more comprehensive discussion of what Chaucer really did with Boccaccio's text—an analysis on which I draw below.

37. E. Talbot Donaldson, *Speaking of Chaucer*, 90. Robertson, *A Preface to Chaucer*, 492–503, similarly noted Criseyde's seductive power, but in a much different tone than Donaldson. For Robertson, Troilus's feelings for Criseyde, although sinful, are the natural, fallen response to her disgusting sexuality. Dinshaw's brilliant discussion, *Chaucer's Sexual Poetics*, 28–39, of these two scholars' responses to Criseyde shows them reading like men. I have come to think that Donaldson and Robertson were reading more specifically like adolescents: one finding Criseyde ethereally unknowable, the other snickering over the word "queynt."

38. Donaldson, *Speaking of Chaucer*, 91.

39. Ernst Bloch, *The Utopian Function of Art and Literature*, 105.

40. John Finlayson, "Guido de Columnis' *Historia destructionis Troiae*, the *Gest Hystorial of the Destruction of Troy*, and Lydgate's *Troy Book*," 154, notes that "in Chaucer and the *Destruction* the audience knows the outcome, but the participants are permitted hope and an area in which to act, or refrain from acting—nothing is presented as a foregone conclusion."

41. Morton W. Bloomfield, "Distance and Predestination in *Troilus and Criseyde*," 22, 24.

42. Freud, "On Negation," in *Standard Edition*, 19:235. Although Freud considered negation to be a tactic belonging to neurosis, and something that had to be overcome, he nevertheless acknowledged it as a step toward consciousness as well as a useful component of analysis. Negation is a liberating mechanism, or a brand of discursive freedom, insofar as by denying the objectionable, "thinking frees itself from the restrictions of repression" (19:236). Utopia's freedom from history is similarly permitted by such a mechanics of denial; its ambivalent prefix is its "hallmark of repression," much like negation's liberating signifier, "not."

43. Bloch's discussion of the "not yet" appears in *The Principle of Hope*, 1:114–74.

44. Slavoj Žižek, *The Sublime Object of Ideology*, 57–58.

45. Karl Mannheim, *Ideology and Utopia*, 175–77. One of Mannheim's conditions for deciding if a historical event can be called utopian was whether it succeeded in "bursting the bonds" of social expectations and effecting real political change. This mode of utopian analysis was extended and sophisticated by Marin and also by Fredric Jameson, *The Political Unconscious*, 281–99, who focuses on the distinction between utopian thought and restrictive ideology and on whether or not such a distinction is sustainable.

46. Faith-breaking, of course, is also the crime committed by Antenor and Aeneas when they switch sides and help the Greeks destroy Troy. Thus, the eventual fall of the city is embedded in Hector's negation of Calkas's crime, along with the eventual "treason" of Criseyde.

47. See Patterson, *Chaucer and the Subject of History*, 110, n. 71.

48. Pandarus makes explicit Criseyde's responsibility for Troilus's life when he tells her to "lat youre daunger sucred ben a lite, / That of his deth ye be naught for to wite (II, 384–85). Troilus, too, is aware of how much he depends on Criseyde when he warns her, "Certes, if ye be unkynde, / And but ye come at day set into Troye, / Ne shal I never have hele, honour, ne joye" (IV, 1440–42).

49. This relationship between Troilus, Criseyde, and the city is expressed in the text at such moments as when, upon seeing Troilus in the street, the people of the city cry out, "Here cometh oure joye, / And, next his brother, holder up of Troye!" (II, 643–44). Then, a few stanzas later, Criseyde remarks that she is Troilus's "joye" (II, 748–49). See also V, 118–19, 426–27, 615–16, and 1380–82.

50. Despite the removal of Calkas and the historians, traitors to utopian joy continue to lurk on the margins of both the poem and the city. The Greeks are famously right outside the walls of Troy, of course, but conspirators are also still inside them. Aeneas and Antenor, the two Trojans who will eventually betray the city and help the Greeks, appear in the poem as threats to Criseyde, the figure for "joie." See II, 1464–75.

51. Patterson, *Chaucer and the Subject of History,* 110, n. 71.

52. Wallace, *Chaucer and the Early Writings of Boccaccio,* 152, suggests that Chaucer may have passed over Boccaccio in silence because the Italian poet, an outsider to the courtly world, "furthered the debasement of courtly language." Nancy M. Reale, "'Bitwixen Game and Ernest,'" suggests that Chaucer is using Boccaccio as a mediary figure between himself and Dante.

53. I am alluding here to Žižek's discussion, *Sublime Object,* 56, of the symptom as a return of the repressed. Symptoms, he suggests, are traces whose "meaning is not discovered, excavated from the hidden depth of the past, but constructed retroactively—the analysis produces the truth."

54. Wallace, *Chaucer and the Early Writings of Boccaccio,* 123.

55. The bedroom scene at Deiphoebus's house, in which Criseyde is lied to and Troilus swoons, is a prelude to the "real" bedroom scene at Pandarus's house, in which Criseyde is lied to and Troilus swoons before they finally have sex. This parallel is reinforced through the use of extremely similar language in the descriptions of how each lover responds to the other's appearance bedside. When Criseyde comes to Troilus's sickbed, he is blushingly speechless:

> This Troilus, that herde his lady preye
> Of lordshipe hym, wax neither quyk ne ded,
> Ne myghte o word for shame to it seye,
> —Although men sholde smyten of his hed.
> But Lord, so he wex sodeynliche red.
>
> (III, 78–82)

Criseyde then reacts in kind when Troilus comes to her bed at Pandarus's house:

> But Lord, so she wax sodeynliche red!
> Ne though men sholde smyten of hire hed,
> She kouthe nought a word aright out brynge.
>
> (III, 956–58)

56. At this point, we impatiently expect the sexual union of the lovers. Everything is in place, they have waited, and we have waited. But yet another obstacle threatens to destroy the carefully laid plans: the thoroughly unnecessary story concocted by Pandarus that Criseyde has made Troilus jealous. Once she hears it, Criseyde laments, professes her love, and vows to disabuse Troilus of his false belief, but not until the next day (III, 802–49)—an impulse toward postponement that Pandarus then has to spend more time correcting (III, 850–952). When the lovers are finally brought together, the false story about jealousy further threatens to extend postponement into nonevent: Criseyde hides under the sheet (III, 1056) and Troilus faints (III, 1092) before they resolve the "misunderstanding."

57. Not only does Boccaccio get to the point much faster, but once he is there, he makes Criseida a much more willing partner than Chaucer's Criseyde. Criseida has Troilo come to her own house; she is complicit in his secret arrival and coughs loudly, as prearranged, to let him know everything is going to plan. She brings a light to the room where he waits for her in darkness, and then she even casts off her shift for Troilo. See *The Story of Troilus*, 61–62.

58. Freud, "Studies on Hysteria," in *Standard Edition*, 2:117; cited in Michael S. Roth, *Psycho-Analysis as History*, 53–54.

59. Troilus continues to replicate his condition of desire even after Criseyde is gone; his painful waiting for her return from the Greek camp enacts a repetition of desire and a fantasy of postponement that is at this point completely hopeless.

60. Even within this supposed suspension of time, however, allusions to the coming of the future exist. See R. E. Kaske, "The *Aube* in Chaucer's *Troilus*," on the way Troilus is given the traditional part of the woman in Chaucer's treatment of the dawn song; Susan Schibanoff, "Criseyde's 'Impossible' *Aubes*," for the ways Criseyde's speeches prefigure her betrayal of Troilus; and Winthrop Wetherbee, "The Descent from Bliss," on the ways the "tranquility of the scene is deceptive."

61. Guido delle Colonne, *Historia destructionis Troiae*, 164–66, breaks into his account to upbraid Troilus for ever having trusted Criseyde. According to Guido, Criseyde is naturally inconstant because she is a woman and, like all women, sexually promiscuous. Robert Henryson, *Testament of Cresseid*, takes Criseyde's notoriety to new levels of condemnation. Picking up where Chaucer left off, the point at which Criseyde becomes Troilus's "dis-ease" (the phrase is borrowed from Linda Charnes), Henryson turns her into disease itself: She is leprosy personified. The disease, including its associations with sexual promiscuity, comes to mean in the place of the woman. See also Benson, *History of Troy*, 143–50, for a discussion of Henryson's treatment of Criseyde.

62. Linda Charnes, *Notorious Identity*, 2.

63. See ibid., 3–8.

64. Marin, *Utopics*, 159, 163. He further describes the difference between ideology and utopia: "Ideological discourse would hope to express historical reality by deadening and shaping it into a closed system of ideas aimed at presenting a justified and legitimated representation of it. Utopia as a figure inscribed within a fable-producing discourse puts ideological discourse and its representations into play in a double sense—implicitly but critically questioning them, and setting them apart in order to reflect upon the presuppositions of their internal systems" (195).

65. James Hoy, "Chaucer and Dictys," points out that the scene in which Hector protests against trading Criseyde for Antenor is not found in any of the possible source materials for *Troilus and Criseyde*. It does, however, appear in Dictys's *Ephemeris belli Troiani libri*. Hoy suggests that Chaucer may have had access to a Dictys manuscript at some point, perhaps during his 1378 visit to Italy.

66. As Charnes, *Notorious Identity*, 4, writes, the "subject of notorious identity becomes his or her own belated 'other': the effect of what notorious identity both produces and represses, a haunting and haunted symptom of his or her own notorious name."

67. Speaking of the profusion of "new" cities in the Americas in the sixteenth century (such as New York, Nueva Leon, and Nouvelle Orleans), Benedict Anderson, *Imagined Communities*, 187, writes that unlike earlier new establishments, where "new" and "old" are aligned diachronically, the American namings "were understood synchronically, coexisting within homogenous, empty time. Vizcaya is there *alongside* Nueva Vizcaya, New London *alongside* London: an idiom of sibling competition rather than of inheritance."

68. Jerome E. Singerman, *Under Clouds of Poesy*, 30.

69. Gervase Mathew, *The Court of Richard II*, 18; quotation at page 18, note 68; my translation.

70. Ibid., 19.

71. On his Scottish campaign, Richard led what Walsingham, *Historia*, 2:133, termed "an imperial army." See McKisack, *Fourteenth Century*, 438–39, for a discussion of the conditions leading to the king's military actions.

72. Patterson, *Chaucer and the Subject of History*, 186–87. Parliament granted money for the campaign only on condition that the king himself lead the army, noting that this was "le primer Viage nostre dit Seigneur le Roy" ("the first expedition of our said Lord the King," my translation) (*Rolls of Parliament*, 3:185). Whereas later, in the 1390s, he would adopt the disgraced Edward II and the unwarlike Edward the Confessor as his political patron saints, in this earlier period Richard was still "engaged in the process of fashioning a chivalric identity" (Patterson, *Chaucer and the Subject of History*, 187).

73. Patterson, *Chaucer and the Subject of History*, 189. The *Westminster Chronicle*, 129–31, reports that during the Scottish campaign of 1385, Lancaster entreated the king to cross the Firth of Forth and put the Scots in their place once and for all, but Richard refused. Instead, he turned on Gaunt, reminding him of his own military failures, and left for home. See McKisack, *Fourteenth Century*, 440.

74. Maude Violet Clarke, *Fourteenth-Century Studies*, 44, citing *Rolls of Parliament*, 3:149–50, notes that in 1383, the Scots had just signed a new treaty with France, prompting the chancellor, Michael de la Pole, to remind Parliament that not only Scotland but "three of the greatest kingdoms and countries of Christendom, France, Spain, and lately Flanders, with all their adherents and allies which are innumerable, [are] mortal enemies of this little realm of England." He then went on to stress the English claim to sovereignty and outline a campaign with the subjugation of the Scots as its main objective.

75. Clarke, *Fourteenth-Century Studies*, 47.

76. *Westminster Chronicle*, 144–45. In the Parliament that ended on 6 December 1385, the Commons petitioned the king to revoke grants imprudently made to others out of the possessions of the Crown (147).

77. See Judith Ferster, *Fictions of Advice,* 82, for reference to this possible deposition, which is discussed in more detail below.

78. W. M. Ormrod, "Government by Commission," 319, points out that at least until the summer of 1387, the council was in regular contact with Richard and cooperated with him on much of the business of government. The reason for the king's anger at the commissioners thus more probably lies in the council's power to vet (and to veto) royal patronage.

79. See McKisack, *Fourteenth Century,* 447.

80. *Westminster Chronicle,* 205, 251, 263. The articles of treason recorded by the *Westminster*-Chronicler mention that de Vere, de la Pole, and Alexander Neville "have caused sundry insufficient and unsuitable persons to have the guard and sovereignty of sundry lordships, castles, and theatres of war, ... as well on this side of the sea as beyond" (247).

De Vere further contributed to the rising sentiment against him by very publicly renouncing his wife, Philippa de Coucy, the granddaughter of Edward III. In 1387, he got a divorce from Rome, greatly displeasing her uncles, the powerful dukes of Lancaster, York, and Gloucester, and he then compounded the insult by marrying a Bohemian chamberwoman of the queen. Anne protested against the divorce and remarriage, and even de Vere's own mother cursed her son for bringing about the divorce (*Westminster Chronicle,* 189–91). Particularly galling must have been the fact that it was only through his marriage to Philippa in 1378 that de Vere gained entry into the royal household in the first place. See Walsingham, *Historia,* 2:160; and McKisack, *Fourteenth Century,* 425.

81. According to the *Westminster Chronicle,* 217, the mayor, himself concerned about what was developing, asked to be relieved of his office, but he failed in this request. The Londoners separately refused Richard the right to lodge his followers in their homes (225). This episode in particular underscores the notorious fickleness of the Londoners with respect to Richard II. Only a few weeks before this refusal of aid, the citizens had welcomed him back from his "gyration" in grand style. See McKisack, *Fourteenth Century,* 450.

82. The *Westminster Chronicle,* 223, reports that the duke of Ireland, with 5,000 men, raised the royal standard and that of St. George (signifying a state of war) against Arundel.

83. See Clarke, *Fourteenth-Century Studies,* 91–95. Clarke notes, "If they ever deposed him, it must have been between 28 or 29 December and New Year's Day" (93). The same evidence for the supposed deposition also suggests that Gloucester and Derby argued over to which of them the succession was due.

84. McKisack, *Fourteenth Century,* 454, notes that Richard's household was purged by the Appellants, who sent away from the king's service countless members of staff, from one hundred servants from the buttery to "courtiers of all ranks, knights, clerks, bishops, and ladies."

85. Gower, *Cronica tripertita,* in *Major Latin Works,* 292.

86. In some respects, one could argue that Chaucer's identity as a court poet had already suffered a sea change with the death of Edward III. David, "Chaucer's Edwardian Poetry," 37, for instance, suggests that *House of Fame,* with "the journey from the Temple of Venus to the Palace of Fame and its adjunct, the House of Rumor, responds to Chaucer's personal journey from court to Aldgate ... and makes a conscious break with his Edwardian poems." David argues that this "turning point" amounts to "a conscious distancing of the poet from the circle of court life and court literature, and from the ambitions engendered there" (44). The advent of Richard II thus registers in Chaucer's poetic style in a manner similar to that which I suggest applies to the moment of the king's cultural death in the late 1380s.

87. Strohm, *England's Empty Throne,* 153; citing Teresa De Lauretis, *Technologies of Gender,* 25–26.

88. The portraits of Troilus and Criseyde, coming this late in the narrative, suggest that a death of sorts has occurred. Patterson, *Chaucer and the Subject of History,* 150, n. 144; citing *Historia vitae et regni Ricardi Secundi,* 161, notes, for instance, the similar technique employed by the author of the *Historia vitae et regni Ricardi Secundi.* Here, a stylized descriptive portrait of Richard II is included just after the narrative of his death but before the end of the book. In a sense, Troilus and Criseyde, like Richard, are dead before the end of their story: All three are consigned to history even by writers sympathetic to them.

89. Pearsall, *Life,* 170.

90. For Burley and Brembre at the customs, see *Chaucer Life-Records,* 259–61; for the connection with Usk, see chapter 4, below.

91. Patterson, *Chaucer and the Subject of History,* 159, n. 162; citing *Chaucer Life-Records,* 245–46, notes that on 20 January 1388, Chaucer was asked to account for money he took in as controller of customs prior to his dismissal. As John P. McCall and George Rudisill, "The Parliament of 1386 and Chaucer's Trojan Parliament," 276, 286, argue, the "sorrow" and "cynical philosophical attitude" with which *Troilus and Criseyde* concludes is in keeping with Chaucer's own changing political fortunes.

92. Patterson, *Chaucer and the Subject of History,* 93; citing R. K. Root, *The Textual Tradition of Chaucer's* Troilus, 5, points out that along with Lydgate's *Troy Book,* the future Henry V also commissioned a personal copy of Chaucer's *Troilus.* For his part, Richard, in his self-composed epitaph, claimed that he was "lyke to Homer," who, as Patterson says, is "author of all Trojan histories" (Patterson, *Chaucer and the Subject of History,* 162; citing Stow, "Chronicles versus Records," 165).

4. CHAUCER AND RICHARD II IN LANCASTRIAN LONDON

1. David Wallace, *Chaucerian Polity,* 336, notes this narrative phenomenon at work in Adam of Usk's *Chronicle,* 30, which "records" Richard speaking his own demise through the process of narrating that of others: "'My God! a wonderful land is this . . . which hath exiled, slain, destroyed, or ruined so many kings, rulers, and great men'; and then he recounted the histories and names of sufferers from the earliest habitation of the kingdom." As Wallace suggests, "by the very act of narrating *de casibus,* Adam's Richard II convinces readers and onlookers that he is a fallen prince" (336).

2. Anderson, *Imagined Communities,* 9.

3. See Anne Middleton, "The Idea of Public Poetry in the Reign of Richard II," for a discussion of the role and meaning of public art in the late fourteenth century.

4. See, for instance, Gower's examples of deposition in Book 7 of the *Confessio*. As Macaulay remarks in his Introduction to Gower's *Complete Works*, ix, the poem clearly "was meant as an admonishment for his royal patron."

5. Guenée, *States and Rulers*, 49.

6. See Turville-Petre, *England the Nation*, for how language structures national identity in the later Middle Ages. Pearsall, "Hoccleve's *Regement of Princes*, 397–98, notes that Henry V used English specifically "to create a stronger sense of nationhood and, especially, to ensure that his subjects recognized how that sense of nationhood was uniquely embodied in his own person."

7. John H. Fisher, "A Language Policy for Lancastrian England," 1169.

8. Bhabha, *Location of Culture*, 142.

9. Ibid., 143–44; citing Freud, "The Uncanny," in *Standard Edition*, 17:234.

10. Bhabha, *Location of Culture*, 143.

11. Žižek, *Sublime Object*, 60.

12. Ibid., 60–61.

13. Ibid., 61.

14. Stephen Partridge, "Questions of Evidence," 6.

15. Wallace, *Chaucerian Polity*, 336.

16. Seth Lerer, *Chaucer and His Readers*, 3, notes that "Chaucer—as author, as 'laureate,' and as 'father' of English poetry—is a construction of his later fifteenth-century scribes, readers, and poetic imitators[;] . . . the terms of that construction—the vocabulary of literary imitation and the dynamics of reader response—are already present in his poetry."

17. Strohm, *Hochon's Arrow*, 88.

18. Gower's *Cronica tripertita*, in *Major Latin Works*, 321, likewise mentions the three ways Henry justified his taking the crown: "Note how the right to the Crown accrued to Henry IV, now our most blessed king, in three ways: first, by succession; second, by election; and third by conquest without bloodshed."

19. Interestingly, Henry also got his association with the concept of "free eleccion." Besides John Hardyng's *Chronicle*, 351, which terms Henry's usurpation a "free election," the fifteenth-century *The Brut, or The Chronicles of England*, 359, notes that "[w]hanne King Richarde was deposed, and hadde resyngned his croune and his kingdom, and hym self kept fast yn holde, than alle the lordez of the Reme, with the comyns assent, and by one accorde, chosyn this worthi lorde, Ser Henry of Bolyngbroke, Erle of Derby, Duk of Herford and Duke of Lancastre be right lyne and heritage; and for his myghtful manhode that the peple founde yn hym, before al other thei choson hym, and made hym King of Engelonde."

20. For the record of Richard's assumption of majority, see *Westminster Chronicle*, 393.

21. See Creton, *Histoire du roy d'Angleterre Richard;* and *Chronique de la traison et mort de Richard II*. Taylor, *English Historical Literature in the Fourteenth Century*, 178, discusses the relative historical value of both French chronicles and notes that the first reference to either of them occurs in the 1470s in the Lambeth *Brut* (Lambeth Palace MS 84).

22. *The Kirkstall Abbey Chronicles; Dieulacres* is printed as "The Deposition of Richard II: *Dieulacres Chronicle*." The *Dieulacres Chronicle* is in two parts: The writer of the portion covering 1337–1400 was a strong partisan of Richard II, whereas the continuator

to 1403 was an equally strong admirer of Henry IV. As Clarke, *Fourteenth-Century Studies,* 59, observes, the abbey at Dieulacres was "closely in touch with Cheshire and royalist interests, [and] also lay on the northern frontier of Lancastrian influence in Staffordshire. It is in just such a house we should expect to find both knowledge of events in Cheshire and Shropshire and clash of opinion over the rival claims of Plantagenet and Lancaster." Taylor, *English Historical Literature,* 191, speculates that we may have "a Chester chronicle, copied at Dieulacres, followed by a Dieulacres account."

23. British Library Harleian MS 1319, fols. 7b, 12, 53b. These images are cited in Mathew, *Court of Richard II,* 209–10, and reproduced there between 148 and 149. Also see the reproductions in Creton, "A French Metrical History of the Deposition of Richard II."

24. The *Westminster Chronicle,* 485–87, notes that in 1392 the temporal lords (and the ecclesiastics, too) were emphatic in their insistence that the duke of Ireland should not be restored to his former position and should on no account be allowed to return from exile to England. The king agreed and accepted that de Vere's banishment should be permanent. Richard then granted to the duke of Gloucester the keeping of Ireland for the next three years.

According to marginal notes in the inventories of lavish plate, garments, and household goods belonging to those condemned by the Merciless Parliament, the most valuable of de Vere's goods (including two of his beds, one of which was embroidered in gold with owls and fleurs-de-lis and valued at sixty-eight pounds) went to Gloucester. See Clarke, *Fourteenth-Century Studies,* 115–45.

25. As the fifteenth-century *Chronicles of London,* 34, report, the problem with Richard II was that he embarrassed the nation abroad: "[A]lmost ther was no levyng man myht have notyse off his condicioun, or myht trust in hym; But he was holde so untrewe and unstable that hit turnyd nat only to sclaundre off his owne persone, but also off the Rewme, And namely amonge straunge nacions off alle the worlde havyng knowlich theroff."

26. J. J. N. Palmer, "English Foreign Policy, 1388–99," reviews the "travesty of the facts" as they are often represented in the case of Richard II's French policies.

27. Ibid., 107.

28. McKisack, *Fourteenth Century,* 248.

29. It is often lost in discussions of these truce agreements that the Lancastrian faction, headed by John of Gaunt as the chief negotiator for England, supported them. In 1392, for example, Gaunt laid out the extensive demands made by the French (including that the king renounce his claim to the French throne and remove the *fleur-de-lis* from his arms). The Commons objected loudly, but Richard, advised and encouraged by Gaunt, decided to agree to some of the demands for the sake of peace.

30. *Westminster Chronicle,* 519.

31. See Philippe de Mézières, *Letter to King Richard II.* As Clarke, *Fourteenth-Century Studies,* 292, suggests, the Wilton Diptych represents Richard being encouraged to found a new crusading order, the Order of the Passion, which was to restore and govern the kingdom of Jerusalem: "A crusading picture with the liveries of England and France united and executed between 1396 and 1399 cannot be traced to any other origin than de Mézières' propaganda for the Order."

32. De Mézières, *Letter,* 144; both translations mine.

33. Keen, "Chaucer's Knight," 57; citing de Mézières, *Letter,* 103.

34. Mathew, *Court of Richard II,* 150.

35. See Clarke, *Fourteenth-Century Studies,* 99–114, esp. 102, for a review of these attempts.

36. McKisack, *Fourteenth Century,* 151; as McKisack further notes, "France was now the national enemy."

37. Clarke, *Fourteenth-Century Studies,* 105.

38. According to the *Chronicles of London,* 83, London paid 1,000 pounds. The *Annales Ricardi Secundi et Henrici Quarti regum Angliae, 1392–1406,* 235, reports that to placate the counties, Richard ordered these letters of submission returned before he left for Ireland.

39. Clarke, *Fourteenth-Century Studies,* 109. A third issue of consequence between Richard and his enemies at home is that of the blank charters: According to the *Eulogium historiarum,* 378, Richard decreed that all the commons in cities and towns should set their seals to blank charters, on which the king intended to write this sentence: "[B]ecause in time past we have grievously offended your majesty we give up ourselves and all our goods to your pleasure" ("ad libitum vestrae voluntatis"). Furthermore, according to the *Annales Ricardi Secundi et Henrici Quarti,* 236, it was rumored that by means of the blank charters, Richard intended to sell Calais back to France. See Clarke, *Fourteenth-Century Studies,* 107 and 107, n. 4.

40. R. H. Davies, "Richard II and the Principality of Chester, 1397–9," 262, observes that "this affection was further demonstrated in the fact that the new title of *princeps Cestrie* was henceforth proudly incorporated in the royal style in letters issued by the Chester exchequer and was equally displayed on the new seal of the principality. . . . [T]his usage was the more noteworthy because in his neighbouring principality of Wales, Richard II never deigned to use his local title prince of Wales after his accession."

41. *Kenilworth Chronicle,* British Library, Additional MS 35,295, fol. 260; cited in Clarke, *Fourteenth-Century Studies,* 98. Henry, by contrast, was not successful with the Cheshiremen, whom he tried to get to work for him in his first Parliament. In October 1399, according to the *Rolls of Parliament,* 3:439, rather than demanding that they repay to him the great sums of gold and silver given to them by Richard II, Henry said that instead, they should serve him for a certain time at their own expense. But the disturbances at Cheshire in 1400, and the exclusion from the general pardon of several prominent men from Richard's notorious guardsmen, suggest that Henry was opposed in the region. See Clarke, *Fourteenth-Century Studies,* 97.

42. See *Annales Ricardi Secundi et Henrici Quarti,* 208, for an account of the Cheshiremen's bad behavior.

43. Davies, "Richard II and the Principality of Chester," 270; citing "Deposition of Richard II: *Dieulacres Chronicle,*" 172. To speak of an "infatuation," of course, is to gloss the king's affinity as a romantic, even sexualized, relationship and to suggest further that Richard's affection was misplaced. I discuss this association of the king with sexual deviance below. See also *Richard the Redeles,* 497; Adam of Usk's *Chronicle,* 23; and *Calendar of Patent Rolls, 1396–99,* 427, for the outrages of the Cheshire guards. The *Annales Ricardi Secundi et Henrici Quarti,* 237, notes that by 1399 Richard had given himself over entirely to the men of Chester and that he and they were allies against all of England and indeed all the world: "[S]e dixerunt eum posse contra totam Angliam contutari, immo, contra totum mundum."

44. Tout, *Chapters,* 4:59; cited in Davies, "Richard II and the Principality of Chester," 272. For the rumors about Wales and Ireland, see Davies's discussion, 272–74, and *Annales Ricardi Secundi et Henrici Quarti,* 239–40. Saul, "Richard II, York, and the Evidence of the King's Itinerary," shows that for most of 1398, the king perambulated the west and north Midlands, stopping off at Bristol, Coventry, Lichfield, Nottingham, Shrewsbury, and Chester. Bennett, "Richard II and the Wider Realm," 198–99, underscores the danger of this sort of itinerary, explaining that "when the king had his treasure taken from the Tower of London to Holt castle, and took some of the regalia from Westminster abbey on his expedition to Ireland, there was widespread and justified alarm in most of England."

45. Frame, *Political Development of the British Isles,* 211–12. A former squire to Richard II, Glyn Dŵr styled himself as "Prince of Wales" from September 1400 onward and conducted diplomacy with the kings of Scotland and France and also with the Avignonese papacy. Frame notes that Glyn Dŵr took pains to present himself as heir to the British past and as "the fulfillment of the Welsh messianic tradition." Like the Bruce brothers before him, he tried to involve other Celtic peoples in his rising against Henry IV, sending letters to Ireland and reminding the aged Robert III of Scotland of their common descent from Brutus.

46. Dorothy Johnston, "Richard II and the Submissions of Gaelic Ireland," 3.

47. As Johnston reports in ibid., 6, citing E. Curtis, *Richard II [and the Submissions of the Irish Chiefs],* 267, Richard outlined the ethnic categories of Ireland thus: [E]n notre terre Dirland sont trois maneres de gentz, cestassavoir Irrois savages nos enemis Irrois rebelx et Engleis obeissantz" ("In our country of Ireland there are three types of people, which is to say the wild Irish our enemies, the rebel Irish, and the obedient English"; my translation).

48. Bennett, "Richard II and the Wider Realm," 195.

49. Ibid., 200–201.

50. *Confessio amantis,* Prologue, lines 17–28. Subsequent quotations from Gower's poem will be cited parenthetically in the text according to the line numbers in Macaulay's *Complete Works.*

51. See Edith Rickert, "King Richard II's Books," which lists a number of titles thought to have belonged to the king; and Richard Firth Green, "King Richard II's Book Revisited," which rightly cautions against assuming these titles actually were read by Richard. Bennett, "The Court of Richard II and the Promotion of Literature," provocatively outlines the evidence (and lack of evidence) for the notion that Richard actively supported the literary arts.

52. Partridge, "Questions of Evidence," 12, notes, "Lines 496–97 in the F Prologue of the *Legend* seem to provide the clearest evidence that one of Chaucer's poems was intended for a royal patron, but the lines' omission from the revised G Prologue and the incompleteness of the surviving text raise doubts that the commission was fulfilled."

53. V. J. Scattergood, "Literary Culture at the Court of Richard II," 38. Andrew Taylor, "Anne of Bohemia and the Making of Chaucer," suggests in the course of his discussion that Anne may have been Chaucer's patron at the court.

54. Scattergood, "Literary Culture," 38. Partridge, "Questions of Evidence," 12, however, emphasizes that *Troilus and Criseyde* was probably one of those poems written with an aristocratic audience in mind. Despite the references to moral Gower and philosophical Strode, the allusion in *Troilus* to Queen Anne at I, 171, plus "the poem's frequent addresses to an implied audience of 'lovers,' and the account, however fictionalized, of the poem's reception in the Prologue to *Legend of Good Women* all suggest the poem was 'presented' to an audience of rather different status and attitudes than Gower's and Strode's. The two earliest surviving manuscripts, Corpus and Morgan, likewise argue an audience of the highest class."

55. Fisher, "Language Policy," 1174.

56. Ibid.

57. Translation reads, "Go, dear book, to the Count of Derby, well considered by those versed in praise; upon him rests your future" (Fisher, *John Gower,* 123).

58. Macaulay, introduction to Gower, *Complete Works,* xxiv.

59. A. I. Doyle, "English Books in and out of Court from Edward III to Henry VII," 170, notes that the Ellesmere manuscript (Huntington EL 26.A.17) of the second version of *Confessio amantis,* dedicated to Henry Bolingbroke as earl of Derby in 1393, "was probably made for him, on the evidence of illuminated emblems, including the swan of Bohun, family of his first wife, and was presumably a presentation from the author."

60. This act of replacement might be more profitably seen as one of displacement in the Freudian sense. See Laplanche and Pontalis, *Language of Psychoanalysis,* 121–23, for a discussion of the "clearly defensive function" of displacement.

61. Frank Grady, "The Lancastrian Gower and the Limits of Exemplarity," 570.

62. Ibid., 565.

63. See David R. Carlson, "Chaucer's *Boethius* and Thomas Usk's *Testament of Love;* Hanrahan, "Teaching Textual Politics"; and Paul Strohm, "Politics and Poetics."

64. For discussions of Usk's concerted efforts to win the king's patronage, see Strohm, "Politics and Poetics"; and Hanrahan, "The Seduction of *The Testament of Love.*"

65. Thomas Usk, *Testament of Love,* Book III, chapter 5, lines 247–59.

66. Speaking of the end of *Troilus and Criseyde,* Tim William Machan, "Textual Authority and the Works of Hoccleve, Lydgate, and Henryson," 281–82, notes that although Chaucer places himself "only a step below" Virgil and the rest, "the implication is that Gower, inasmuch as Chaucer sends the book out to him, is not even on the staircase."

67. Pearsall, *John Lydgate,* 151. Pearsall, "Chaucer and Lydgate," 47, writes that "Lydgate's career, poem by poem, is a determined effort to emulate and surpass Chaucer in each of the major poetic genres that Chaucer had attempted."

68. Pearsall, *John Lydgate,* 151. Pearsall continues, arguing that this had been the case "ever since the composition of the *Roman de Thebes* in the late twelfth century as a potboiler to Benoît's *Roman de Troie*" (151).

69. *Troy Book,* ed. Henry Bergen, Prologue, lines 168–69. All subsequent quotations of Lydgate's poem will be taken from this edition and cited in the text according to book and line number.

70. Chaucer is also noted in the *Troy Book* at II, 4677 and 4712; III, 550; and V, 3521.

71. Benson, "Critic and Poet," 28, writes that "just as Chaucer had urged those who wanted to learn more about the Trojan War to read Dares and Dictys, Lydgate, the more historical poet, urges those who want to learn more about the love story to turn to Chaucer."

72. Pearsall, "Chaucer and Lydgate," 42.

73. Ibid., 43. Pearsall continues, "Lydgate's is not a servile imitation of Chaucer, but a *de luxe* version of Chaucer, obviously meant to be thought of as an improvement" (44).

74. Ibid., 44.

75. Baswell, "*Troy Book,*" 233, speaking of the "uses" Lydgate found for Chaucer, compares the two poets to the lovers in *Troilus and Criseyde* and suggests that images in the *Troy Book* "cast Lydgate and Chaucer themselves, varyingly, as Criseyde and Troilus." Baswell further observes that when, in the *Envoye* to the *Troy Book,* Lydgate says he wishes Henry "to be registred worthi as of name / In the highest place of the hous of fame" (13–14), "this locates Henry in a Chaucerian space" (237).

76. Walsingham, *Historia,* 2:156; cited and translated in Stow, "Chronicles versus Records," 160. See also Walsingham's *Ypodigma Neustriae,* 348. James L. Gillespie, "Richard II: King of Battles?," 139–40; citing Walsingham, *Historia,* 2:259, points out that although Walsingham "had unkind words for Richard's knights, he was no more impressed with the knights who surrounded the former crusader and jouster, Henry IV. He thought these Lancastrian stalwarts 'more like Dionysus than Mars, more like Laverna than Athena.'"

77. *Chronicon Adae de Usk, 1377–1421,* 29. Knighton's *Chronicle,* 404–5, in turn, characterizes Richard's circle of advisers as "seducers of the king" ("seductores regis").

78. Nicholas Watson, "Outdoing Chaucer," 97, notes the gendered dynamic at play between Chaucer and Lydgate in the *Troy Book* when Chaucer is associated with Criseyde: "[T]he effect of introducing him as Lydgate's 'maister' at the moment Criseyde enters the poem [at II, lines 4677–735, and then again at III, 4186–263] is to initiate what remains a close association between him and one of the *Troy Book*'s emblems of female falsity. Lydgate's awe of his 'maister' is tempered from the start by his contempt for Chaucer's 'mistress.'"

79. Richard William Fehrenbacher, "Blood and Virtue," 136–37, notes the difference in Lydgate's *Troy Book* between Hector and Aeneas, the former being a noble failure (as he was in Chaucer), the latter being a treacherous success (and particularly so because of his verbal dexterity). See *Troy Book* II, 244–51; III, 5361–72; IV, 4774–79 and 6441–48.

80. Derrida, *Of Grammatology,* 157.

81. Lerer, *Chaucer and His Readers,* 49.

82. Ibid.

83. Ibid., 51.

84. Linne R. Mooney, "Lydgate's *Kings of England* and Another Verse Chronicle of the Kings," 257.

85. *Kings of England sithen William Conqueror,* lines 1–5, in *The Historical Collections of a Citizen of London in the Fifteenth Century,* 49–54.

86. Ernesto Laclau and Lilian Zac, "Minding the Gap," 34–35.

87. Ibid.

88. Ibid., 34; citing Lacan, *The Four Fundamental Concepts of Psycho-Analysis,* 218.

89. Laclau and Zac, "Minding the Gap," 35; citing Philippe Lacoue-Labarthe, *Typography*, 300.

90. I borrow this phrase from the title of Jacqueline Rose's *States of Fantasy* to suggest—as she does in relation to the "states" of Israel and Palestine—that political formations such as "nation" and "empire" are discursively constructed categories (and thus open to textual deconstruction).

91. V. Dvořáková, *Gothic Mural Painting in Bohemia and Moravia, 1300–1378*, 41–65; cited in Saul, *Richard II*, 347, n. 73.

92. Saul, *Richard II*, 346–51.

93. Mathew, *Court of Richard II*, 17, my translation. Mathew notes here that the idea that he himself should become Holy Roman Emperor "had a strong appeal" to Richard. Saul, "Richard II and Westminster Abbey," 202, notes further evidence of the king's fascination with things imperial: According to an inventory of 1388, Richard gave as a gift to Westminster Abbey "three banners bearing the arms (or emblems) of St Edmund, St Edward the Confessor, and the Holy Roman Emperor, to go with the liturgical banners that the abbey already had." And in 1393, as Anthony Tuck, "Richard II and the House of Luxemburg," 220; citing *Westminster Chronicle*, 516, writes, Richard ordered masses to be said for the soul of his mother-in-law, Elizabeth of Pomerania, who died that year, and he had an "imperial shrine" of a hitherto unheard-of design constructed at St. Paul's cathedral.

94. Wenzel was actually deposed in 1400. See D. M. Bueno de Mesquita, "The Foreign Policy of Richard II in 1397."

95. *Annales Ricardi Secundi et Henrici Quarti*, 199–200; translated by Chris Given-Wilson in *Chronicles of the Revolution*, 70–71. See also Walsingham, *Historia*, 2:222–23, and *Ypodigma Neustriae*, 374, where the imperial rumors are described as "*inanes*."

96. Further evidence that Walsingham's charge is true is suggested by the fact that Richard sent an embassy (which included Janico Dartasso) to Cologne on 21 July 1397 and then granted forty pounds a year to the dean of Cologne in April 1399, after the dean had done him homage. See PRO E403/555 and *Calendar of Patent Rolls, 1396–99*, 577; both cited in *Chronicles of the Revolution*, 70, n. 1.

97. Palmer, "English Foreign Policy," 85.

98. In March 1379, a party set out for Italy with the power to arrange a marriage between Richard II and Catherine, daughter of Bernabò Visconti of Milan. But the negotiations broke down, and in June 1380, an English embassy was sent instead to Prague to settle the marriage to Anne. It was hoped that through this marriage, Wenzel could be persuaded to abandon the house of Luxemburg's traditional alignment with France. In addition to being king of Bohemia, Wenzel was by now confirmed by papal bull as king of the Romans and could expect eventually to have the imperial crown placed on his head by the pope. Oddly, he never pursued the ceremony. See Bede Jarrett, *The Emperor Charles IV*, 58–113, for discussion.

99. Among other problems, Wenzel's political activity in Italy involved a deal with Milan in which money changed hands, and its ruler, Giangaleazzo Visconti, was granted the imperial title of duke. For this, Wenzel's deposers were later able to accuse him of "dilapidating" the empire instead of enlarging it, a charge similar to the one claiming

that Richard II had diminished his kingship by sharing it with his "duke" of Ireland, Robert de Vere. F. R. H. Du Boulay, *Germany in the Later Middle Ages*, 46, suggests that the two depositions may be linked: "[I]t is not impossible, though unprovable, that the very recent deposition of Richard II of England, Wenzel's brother-in-law, may have suggested that what had proved possible and acceptable in one realm might also appear legitimate elsewhere."

100. Bueno de Mesquita, "Foreign Policy of Richard II," 631.

101. Ibid.

102. Ibid., 632; citing Thomas Rymer, *Foedera, Conventiones, Litterae, Etc*, 7:854–56, 8:2–6 and 21–24. See also Edouard Perroy, *L'Angleterre et le grand schisme d'occident*, for an account of the politics of the Great Schism.

103. Bueno de Mesquita, "Foreign Policy of Richard II," 634, suggests that "Richard had offered to sacrifice the Anglo-French understanding in return for the support of Boniface in his [Richard's] domestic struggles and in his Imperial ambitions."

104. There may be some measure of truth to the rumor: Henry had been the guest of the Visconti in Pavia five years earlier, and since that time he had frequently exchanged gifts and courtesies with them. When Henry was preparing for his duel with Norfolk, Giangaleazzo placed at his disposal the resources of his own armory and of the Milanese armorers.

105. Even though Henry was received at the French court as an exile, he was not accepted as the English king after his usurpation. Philip Morgan, "Henry IV and the Shadow of Richard II," 14, notes that the French court felt threatened by Henry's accession because it cast into doubt the truce established in 1396: "The government of Charles VI adopted a policy of opposition to Henry IV based on a refusal to recognize the new king's title. . . . Belief in the reality of the risen Richard was short-lived but French policy continued to espouse his cause and to speak in his name. Henry IV remained the *soi-disant roi* throughout his reign."

106. Malory, *Works*, 188; cited in Fehrenbacher, "Blood and Virtue," 208–9. As Fehrenbacher points out, Arthur does base his claim on lineage: "[B]ut this lineage is itself grounded not on ancient origin, but on conquest, military acumen. . . . [N]o claim is made through an appeal to the British descent from Aeneas, Rome's founder, or his grandson Brutus, founder of the British line" (209).

107. Fehrenbacher, "Blood and Virtue," 214.

108. Mortimer was the heir presumptive because by tradition if not by law, English succession went through primogeniture on the maternal line.

109. Adam of Usk, *Chronicle*, 43, claims that Mortimer was descended from a "son of Locrine, son of Brute the first king of the Britons, son of Silvius, son of Ascanius, son of Aeneas . . . son of Adam the first creature."

110. Adam of Usk, *Chronicon Adae de Usk*, 164.

111. Johnston, "Richard II and the Submissions of Gaelic Ireland," 10, writes of "the over-riding concern to secure royal protection against Roger Mortimer, the [earl of March and] absentee lord of Ulster, [who was] now intent upon recovering his diminished inheritance."

112. Ibid., 18.

113. Ibid., 20. Curiously, Mortimer died while wearing the dress and riding in the fashion of the native Irish ("Hibernicali vestitus et equitatus apparatu"; 20). This practice was specifically forbidden to Englishmen under the 1366 Statutes of Kilkenny, which state "that no Englishman who has to the value of one hundred shillings of lands or tenements or of rent by the year shall ride otherwise than on a saddle in the English fashion" on pain of prison (*Irish Historical Documents, 1172–1922,* 53).

114. Adam of Usk, *Chronicle,* 62–63. According to Froissart, *Chronicles of England, France, and Spain,* 2:696–97; cited in Bennett, *Richard II and the Revolution of 1399,* 4, Henry torments Richard in the Tower with innuendos about Joan of Kent's chastity.

115. See Collins, "Order of the Garter," 167.

116. Mathew, *Court of Richard II,* 174.

117. Walsingham, *Historia,* 2:250, notes the marriage of Henry's daughter and the emperor's son: "In this year, the king sent his daughter, with great splendor, to the land of Cologne; the emperor's son came to meet her in a style which, while befitting someone of his rank, was not well-suited for meeting such a young girl. There, however, despite her youthfulness, he took the maiden in marriage according to the customs of the land" (my translation). ("Hoc anno misit Rex filiam suam, cum grandi apparatu, ad Coloniam Agrippinam; cui occurrit filius Imperatoris in apparatu, qui, ut decuit nomen tanti fastigii, nec par erat in occursum venire tantae virgini. Ibi, tamen juvenis, duxit, more regionis, virginem in uxorem.") See also *Annales Ricardi Secundi et Henrici Quarti,* 342–43.

118. Bennett, *Richard II and the Revolution of 1399,* 4; citing Froissart, *Chronicles of England, France, and Spain,* 2:709.

119. Saul, "The Kingship of Richard II," 41.

120. By the time of Henry V, Trojanness is again considered "safe" after its earlier disastrous associations. John Strecche, a canon of the Augustinian priory of St. Mary's, Kenilworth, put together a collection of romances and historical pieces in the first quarter of the fifteenth century (British Library Additional MS 35,295). This collection includes a history of England from Brutus to the death of Henry V (fols. 228–97). The early part is derived from the *Brut,* but for Strecche's own time there is no known source. It was written shortly after the events it records took place. This "contemporary" section of the collection contains nothing but praise for Henry V, who is said to have the character of Augustus, the wisdom of Solomon, the good looks of Paris, and the loving heart of Troilus. The extract is printed, in part, in "The Chronicle of John Strecche for the Reign of Henry V."

121. The Lancastrian princes literally were raised on Chaucer by their boyhood tutor, Henry Scogan. Scogan's "Moral Balade" (printed in *Chaucerian and Other Pieces,* 237–44), which is addressed to the four sons of Henry IV, advises them on virtue by quoting Chaucer's short poem, "Gentilesse." Chaucer is noted here as "this noble poete of Bretayne" (line 126).

122. Fisher, "Language Policy," 1174.

123. Baswell, "*Troy Book,*" 215, 219.

124. Ibid., 224.

125. Anderson, *Imagined Communities,* 133.

126. Pearsall, "Hoccleve's *Regement of Princes,*" 398.

CONCLUSION

1. Judith Butler, *Gender Trouble,* xiii.

2. Lacan, *Feminine Sexuality,* 51.

3. Patterson, *Negotiating,* 167, notes that "the immediate offspring of this illegitimate conjunction [of Dido and Aeneas] is the monstrous Fama."

4. "Preface" to Hardyng's *Chronicle,* lines 3–6 and 91.

5. Chaucer, "Legend of Dido," in *Legend of Good Women,* lines 1361–63.

6. Hayden White, *Tropics of Discourse,* 4.

7. Ibid.

8. Žižek, *Sublime Object,* 109; cited in Dinshaw, *Getting Medieval,* 221, n. 66.

9. Žižek, *Sublime Object,* 109; cited in Dinshaw, *Getting Medieval,* 221, n. 66.

10. As Patterson, *Negotiating,* 169, writes, "The *Aeneid* provided the West with a definitive statement of history as progress, as a one-way development that emerges from the darkness and disaster of the East and issues in the edification and enlightenment of the West."

11. Rose, *States of Fantasy,* 3.

12. Ibid., 4–5.

13. Ibid., 23.

Bibliography

Manuscript Sources

British Library Additional MS 35,295
British Library Additional MS 38,131
British Library Egerton MS 2885
British Library Harleian MS 1319
Brotherton Library (University of Leeds), Special Collection, MS 100
Huntington Library, Ellesmere MS EL 26.A.17
Lambeth Palace Library, *Brut,* MS 84
Public Record Office, Exchequer, Issue Rolls, E403/555

Printed Sources

Adam of Usk. *The Chronicle of Adam of Usk, 1377–1421.* Ed. and trans. Chris Given-Wilson. Oxford: Clarendon Press, 1997.

———. *Chronicon Adae de Usk, 1377–1421.* Ed. and trans. Edward Maunde Thompson. London: Henry Frowde, 1904.

Anglo-Norman Letters and Petitions from All Souls MS. 182. Ed. M. D. Legge. Oxford: Clarendon Press, 1941.

Anglo-Scottish Relations 1174–1328: Some Selected Documents. Ed. E. L. G. Stones. Oxford: Oxford University Press, 1970.

Annales Ricardi Secundi et Henrici Quarti regum Angliae, 1392–1406. Ed. H. T. Riley. London, 1866.

Anonimalle Chronicle, 1333 to 1381. Ed. V. H. Galbraith. Manchester: Manchester University Press, 1927.

Barbour, John. *The Bruce.* Ed. Walter W. Skeat. 2 vols. London, 1870–89.

Benoît de Sainte-Maure. *Le Roman de Troie.* Ed. Leopold Constans. 6 vols. Société des Anciens Textes Français. Paris: Firmin Didot, 1904–12.

A Book of London English, 1384–1425. Ed. R. W. Chambers and Marjorie Daunt. Oxford: Clarendon Press, 1967.

The Brut, or The Chronicles of England. Ed. Friedrich W. D. Brie. London: Kegan Paul, 1908. New York: Kraus Reprint, 1971.

Calendar of Letter-Book H, 1375–1399. In *Calendar of Letter-Books of the City of London.* Ed. Reginald R. Sharpe. London: Corporation of London, 1907.

Calendar of Patent Rolls, 1396–99. London: Stationery Office, 1891–1916.

Calendar of Select Pleas and Memoranda Rolls of the City of London, Preserved among the Archives of the Corporation of the City of London at the Guildhall, 1381–1412. Ed. A. H. Thomas. Cambridge: Cambridge University Press, 1932.

Caxton, William. *Caxton's Eneydos.* Ed. W. T. Culley and F. J. Furnivall. London, 1890.

Chaucer, Geoffrey. *The Complete Works of Geoffrey Chaucer.* Ed. W. W. Skeat. 7 vols. Oxford, 1897.

———. *Riverside Chaucer.* Gen. ed. Larry D. Benson. Boston: Houghton Mifflin, 1987.

———. *The Works of Geoffrey Chaucer and Others.* Ed. Francis Thynne. London: H. Frowde, 1905.

Chaucer Life-Records. Ed. Martin M. Crow and Clair C. Olson. Oxford: Oxford University Press, 1966.

Chrétien de Troyes. *Le Conte du Graal.* Trans. Jacques Ribard. Paris: Champion, 1979.

"The Chronicle of John Strecche for the Reign of Henry V." Ed. Frank Taylor. *Bulletin of the John Rylands Library* 16 (1932): 137–87.

Chronicles of London. Ed. Charles Lethbridge Kingsford. Oxford: Clarendon Press, 1905.

Chronicles of the Revolution, 1397–1400: The Reign of Richard II. Ed. and trans. Chris Given-Wilson. Manchester: Manchester University Press, 1993.

Chronique de la traison et mort de Richard II. Ed. B. Williams. London, 1846.

The Controversy between Sir Richard Scrope and Sir Robert Grosvenor. Ed. Nicholas Harris Nicolas. London, 1832.

Creton, Jean. "A French Metrical History of the Deposition of Richard II." Ed. and trans. J. Webb. *Archaeologia* 20 (1814): 1–402.

———. *Histoire du roy d'Angleterre Richard.* Ed. J. A. C. Buchon. Paris, 1826.

Dares Phrygius. *De excidio Troiae historiae.* Ed. Ferdinand Meister. Leipzig, 1873.

de Mézières, Philippe. *Letter to King Richard II.* Trans. G. W. Coopland. Liverpool: Liverpool University Press, 1975.

De ortu Waluuanii nepotis Arturi (The Rise of Gawain, Nephew of Arthur). Ed. and trans. Mildred Leake Day. New York: Garland, 1984.

"The Deposition of Richard II: *Dieulacres Chronicle* (Gray's Inn MS no. 9)." Ed. Maude V. Clarke and V. H. Galbraith. *Bulletin of the John Rylands Library* 14 (1930): 125–81.

Dictys Cretensis. *Ephemeridos belli Troiani libri.* Ed. Werner Eisenhut. Leipzig: Teubner, 1973.

The Diplomatic Correspondence of Richard II. Ed. Edouard Perroy. London: Camden Society, 1933.

Douglas, Gavin. *Virgil's* Aeneid *Translated into Scottish Verse.* Ed. David F. C. Coldwell. 4 vols. Edinburgh: Scottish Texts Society, 1957–64.

Dunbar, William. *The Poems of William Dunbar.* Ed. John Small. 3 vols. Edinburgh, 1893.

An English Chronicle of the Reigns of Richard II, Henry IV, Henry V, and Henry VI. Ed. John Silvester Davies. London, 1856. London: Johnson Reprint, 1968.

Eulogium historiarum. Ed. Frank Scott Haydon. London, 1863.

Excidium Troiae. Ed. Alan Keith Bate. Frankfurt: Peter Lang, 1986.

Fordun, John of. *Chronicle of the Scottish Nation*. Ed. William F. Skene. Trans. Felix J. H. Skene. 2 vols. Edinburgh, 1872.

Frederic Madden's Sir Gawayne: A Collection of Ancient Romance Poems. New York: AMS Reprints, 1971.

Froissart, Jean. *Chronicles of England, France, and Spain by Sir John Froissart*. Ed. Thomas Johnes. 2 vols. London, 1842.

———. *Oeuvres de Froissart*. Ed. Kervyn de Lettenhove. 25 vols. Bruxelles, 1867–1877.

Gawain on Marriage. Ed. A. G. Rigg. Toronto: Pontifical Institute, 1986.

Geoffrey of Monmouth. *History of the Kings of Britain*. Trans. Sebastian Evans. Rev. Charles W. Dunn. New York: Dutton, 1958.

Gerald of Wales. *History and Topography of Ireland*. Ed. J. O'Meara. Harmondsworth, Eng.: Penguin, 1982.

The "Gest hystoriale" of the Destruction of Troy. Ed. George A. Panton and David Donaldson. 2 vols. London, 1874.

Gower, John. *The Complete Works of John Gower*. Ed. G. C. Macaulay. 4 vols. Oxford: Clarendon Press, 1901.

———. *The Major Latin Works of John Gower*. Trans. Eric W. Stockton. Seattle: University of Washington Press, 1962.

———. *Mirour de l'omme*. Trans. William Burton Wilson. East Lansing, Mich.: Colleagues, 1992.

Guido delle Colonne. *Historia destructionis Troiae*. Ed. Nathaniel Edward Green. Cambridge, Mass.: Medieval Academy of America, 1936.

———. *Historia destructionis Troiae*. Trans. Mary Elizabeth Meek. Bloomington: Indiana University Press, 1974.

Hardyng, John. *Chronicle of John Hardyng*. Ed. Henry Ellis. London, 1812.

Henryson, Robert. *The Testament of Cresseid*. Ed. Hugh Macdiarmid. London: Penguin, 1988.

Historia vitae et regni Ricardi Secundi. Ed. George B. Stow. Philadelphia: University of Pennsylvania Press, 1977.

The Historical Collections of a Citizen of London in the Fifteenth Century. Ed. James Gairdner. London, 1876.

Hoccleve, Thomas. *Regement of Princes*. Ed. Frederick J. Furnivall. Millwood, N.Y.: Kraus Reprint, 1978.

The Irish Aeneid. Ed. and trans. George Calder. Dublin: Irish Texts Society, 1907.

Irish Historical Documents, 1172–1922. Ed. Edmund Curtis and R. B. McDowell. London: Methuen, 1943.

The Kirkstall Abbey Chronicles. Ed. John Taylor. Leeds: Thoresby Society, 1952.

Knighton, Henry. *Knighton's Chronicle, 1337–1396*. Ed. and trans. G. H. Martin. Oxford: Clarendon Press, 1995.

The Laud Troy Book. Ed. Ernst Wulfing. London: Oxford University Press, 1903.

"A Letter Describing Richard II's Reconciliation with the City of London." Ed. Helen Suggett. *English Historical Review* 62 (1947): 209–13.

Lydgate, John. *Poems*. Ed. John Norton-Smith. Oxford: Clarendon Press, 1966.

———. *The Siege of Thebes*. Ed. Axel Erdmann. London: Kegan Paul, 1911.

———. *Troy Book*. Ed. Henry Bergen. 4 vols. London: Kegan Paul, 1908.

Maidstone, Richard. *Concordia facta inter regem Riccardum II et civitatem Londonie*. Ed. and trans. Charles Roger Smith. Ph.D. diss., Princeton University, 1972.

Malory, Thomas. *Works*. Ed. Eugene Vinaver. Oxford: Oxford University Press, 1971.

Memorials of London and London Life in the Thirteenth, Fourteenth, and Fifteenth Centuries. Ed. and trans. Henry Thomas Riley. London, 1868.

The Middle Scots Poets. Ed. A. M. Kinghorn. York Medieval Texts. London: Edward Arnold, 1970.

Original Letters Illustrative of English History. Ed. Henry Ellis. London, 1827.

Ovid. *Metamorphoses*. Trans. Mary M. Innes. New York: Penguin, 1955.

Proceedings and Ordinances of the Privy Council of England. Ed. N. H. Nicolas. London, 1834.

Richard of Bury. *Philobiblon*. Ed. and trans. E. C. Thomas. Oxford: Blackwell, 1970.

Richard the Redeles. Ed. W. W. Skeat. London, 1873.

Rolls of Parliament (Rotuli Parliamentorum). 6 vols. London, 1767–77.

Rymer, Thomas. *Foedera, Conventiones, Litterae, Etc*. 20 Vols. Ed. G. Holmes. London, 1704–35.

Saint Erkenwald. Ed. Ruth Morse. Cambridge: D. S. Brewer, 1975.

Servianorum in Vergilii carmina commentariorum. Ed. E. K. Rand. Lancaster, Pa.: American Philosophical Society, 1946.

Sir Gawain and the Green Knight. Ed. Malcolm Andrew and Ronald Waldron. Berkeley and Los Angeles: University of California Press, 1978.

The Story of Troilus. Ed. and trans. R. K. Gordon. Toronto: University of Toronto Press, 1978.

The Trojan War: The Chronicles of Dictys of Crete and Dares the Phrygian. Trans. R. M. Frazer. Bloomington: Indiana University Press, 1966.

Usk, Thomas. *Testament of Love*. In *Chaucerian and Other Pieces. A Supplement to the Complete Works of Geoffrey Chaucer*. Ed. Walter W. Skeat. Oxford, 1897.

Walsingham, Thomas. *Historia Anglicana*. Ed. Henry Thomas Riley. 2 vols. London, 1863.

———. *Ypodigma Neustriae*. Ed. Henry Thomas Riley. London, 1876. New York: Kraus Reprint, 1965.

The Westminster Chronicle, 1381–1394. Ed. and trans. L. C. Hector and Barbara Harvey. Oxford: Clarendon Press, 1982.

Secondary Sources

Aers, David. *Community, Gender, and Individual Identity: English Writing 1360–1430*. London: Routledge, 1988.

Allen, Susan Heuck. *Finding the Walls of Troy: Frank Calvert and Heinrich Schliemann at Hisarlik*. Berkeley and Los Angeles: University of California Press, 1999.

Allmand, Christopher. *Henry V*. London: Methuen, 1992.

Anderson, Benedict. *Imagined Communities: Reflections on the Origin and Spread of Nationalism*. London: Verso, 1983.

Aston, M. E. "Lollardy and Sedition, 1381–1431." *Past and Present* 17 (1960): 1–44.

Bann, Stephen. "Shrines, Gardens, Utopias." *New Literary History* 25 (1994): 825–37.

Barnie, John. *War in Medieval Society: Social Values and the Hundred Years' War, 1337–99.* London: Weidenfeld, 1974.

Barron, Caroline M. "The Deposition of Richard II." In *Politics and Crisis in Fourteenth-Century England,* ed. John Taylor and Wendy Childs, 132–49. London: Sutton, 1990.

———. "The 'Golden Age' of Women in Medieval London." In *Medieval Women in Southern England,* ed. Keith Bate, 35–58. Reading: University of Reading Press, 1989.

———. "The Quarrel of Richard II with London: 1392–97." In *The Reign of Richard II,* ed. F. R. H. Du Boulay and Caroline M. Barron, 173–201. London: Athlone, 1971.

———. "Richard II and London." In *Richard II: The Art of Kingship,* ed. Anthony Goodman and James Gillespie, 129–54. Oxford: Clarendon Press, 1999.

———. "The Widow's World in Later Medieval London." In *Medieval London Widows, 1300–1500,* ed. Caroline M. Barron and Anne F. Sutton, xiii–xxxiv. London: Hambledon, 1994.

Baswell, Christopher. "*Troy Book:* How Lydgate Translates Chaucer into Latin." In *Translation Theory and Practice in the Middle Ages,* ed. Jeannette Beer, 215–37. Kalamazoo, Mich.: Medieval Institute Publications, 1997.

———. *Virgil in Medieval England.* Cambridge: Cambridge University Press, 1995.

Bellamy, Elizabeth J. *Translations of Power: Narcissism and the Unconscious in Epic History.* Ithaca, N.Y.: Cornell University Press, 1992.

Bennett, J. A. W. *Chaucer's Book of Fame.* Oxford: Clarendon, 1968.

Bennett, Michael J. *Community, Class, and Careerism: Cheshire and Lancashire Society in the Age of* Sir Gawain and the Green Knight. Cambridge: Cambridge University Press, 1983.

———. "The Court of Richard II and the Promotion of Literature." In *Chaucer's England: Literature in Historical Context,* ed. Barbara Hanawalt, 3–20. Minneapolis: University of Minnesota Press, 1992.

———. "The Historical Background." In *A Companion to the* Gawain-*Poet,* ed. Derek Brewer and Jonathan Gibson, 71–90. Woodbridge, Suffolk: D. S. Brewer, 1997.

———. *Richard II and the Revolution of 1399.* Stroud, Eng.: Sutton Publishing, 1999.

———. "Richard II and the Wider Realm." In *Richard II: The Art of Kingship,* ed. Anthony Goodman and James Gillespie, 187–204. Oxford: Clarendon Press, 1999.

Benson, C. David. "Critic and Poet: What Lydgate and Henryson Did to Chaucer's *Troilus and Criseyde.*" *Modern Language Quarterly* 53 (1992): 23–40.

———. *The History of Troy in Middle English Literature: Guido delle Colonne's* Historia destructionis Troiae *in Medieval England.* Woodbridge, Suffolk: D. S. Brewer, 1980.

———. "'True Troilus and False Cresseid': The Descent from Tragedy." In *The European Tragedy of Troilus,* ed. Piero Boitani. 153–70. Oxford: Clarendon Press, 1989.

Berry, Craig A. "The King's Business: Negotiating Chivalry in *Troilus and Criseyde.*" *Chaucer Review* 26 (1992): 236–65.

Besant, Walter. *Medieval London.* London: Black, 1906.

Bhabha, Homi K. *The Location of Culture.* London: Routledge, 1994.

Biddick, Kathleen. "Bede's Blush: Postcards from Bali, Bombay, Palo Alto." In *The Past and Future of Medieval Studies,* ed. John Van Engen, 16–44. Notre Dame, Ind.: University of Notre Dame Press, 1994.

Bird, Ruth. *The Turbulent London of Richard II.* London: Longmans, 1949.

Birns, Nicholas. "The Trojan Myth: Postmodern Reverberations." *Exemplaria* 5 (1993): 45–78.

Bloch, Ernst. *The Principle of Hope.* Trans. Neville Plaice. Cambridge: Massachusetts Institute of Technology Press, 1986.

———. *The Utopian Function of Art and Literature.* Trans. Jack Zipes and Frank Mecklenburg. Cambridge: Massachusetts Institute of Technology Press, 1988.

Bloomfield, Morton W. "Distance and Predestination in *Troilus and Criseyde.*" *PMLA* 72 (1957): 33–57.

Blyth, Charles. "Thomas Hoccleve's Other Master." *Mediaevalia* 16 (1993): 349–59.

Boitani, Piero. *Chaucer and the Imaginary World of Fame.* Woodbridge, Suffolk: D. S. Brewer, 1984.

Bourdieu, Pierre. *Language and Symbolic Power.* Trans. Gino Raymond and Matthew Adamson. Cambridge, Mass.: Harvard University Press, 1991.

Bourgne, Florence. "Translating Saints' Lives into the Vernacular: *Translatio Studii* and *Furta Sacra* (Translation as Theft)." In *The Medieval Translator: Proceedings of the International Conference of Conques,* ed. Roger Ellis, 50–63. Brussels: Brepols, 1996.

Bowers, John. "*Pearl* in Its Royal Setting: Ricardian Poetry Revisited." *Studies in the Age of Chaucer* 17 (1995): 111–55.

———. "The Politics of *Pearl.*" *Exemplaria* 7 (1995): 419–41.

Buchthal, Hugo. *Historia Troiana: Studies in the History of Medieval Secular Illustration.* Studies of the Warburg Institute, 32. London: Warburg, 1971.

Bueno de Mesquita, D. M. "The Foreign Policy of Richard II in 1397: Some Italian Letters." *English Historical Review* 56 (1941): 628–37.

Burrow, Colin. "Virgil in English Translation." In *The Cambridge Companion to Virgil,* ed. Charles Martindale, 21–37. Cambridge: Cambridge University Press, 1997. 21–37.

Burrow, J. A. *Ricardian Poetry: Chaucer, Gower, Langland, and the* Gawain *Poet.* London: Routledge, 1971.

———. *Thomas Hoccleve: Authors of the Middle Ages.* Aldershot: Variorum, 1994.

Butcher, A. F. "English Urban Society and the Revolt of 1381." In *The English Rising of 1381,* ed. R. H. Hilton and T. H. Aston, 84–111. Cambridge: Cambridge University Press, 1984.

Butler, Judith. *Bodies That Matter: On the Discursive Limits of "Sex."* New York: Routledge, 1993.

———. *Gender Trouble: Feminism and the Subversion of Identity.* New York: Routledge, 1990.

Cannon, Christopher. "The Myth of Origin and the Making of Chaucer's English." *Speculum* 71 (1996): 646–75.

Carlin, Martha. *Medieval Southwark.* London: Hambledon, 1996.

Carlson, David R. "Chaucer's *Boethius* and Thomas Usk's *Testament of Love:* Politics and Love in the Chaucerian Tradition." In *The Centre and Its Compass: Studies in Medieval Literature in Honor of Professor John Leyerle,* ed. Robert A. Taylor. 29–70. Kalamazoo: University of Western Michigan Press, 1993.

Carruthers, Mary. *The Book of Memory: A Study of Memory in Medieval Culture.* Cambridge: Cambridge University Press, 1990.

Charnes, Linda. *Notorious Identity: Materializing the Subject in Shakespeare.* Cambridge, Mass.: Harvard University Press, 1993.

Clark, John. "Trinovantum: The Evolution of a Legend." *Journal of Medieval History* 7 (1981): 135–51.

Clark, S. L., and Julian N. Wasserman. "Gawain's 'Anti-Feminism' Reconsidered." *Journal of the Rocky Mountain Medieval and Renaissance Association* (1985): 57–70.

Clarke, Maude Violet. *Fourteenth-Century Studies.* Ed. L. S. Sutherland and M. McKisack. Oxford: Clarendon, 1937.

Colebrook, Claire. *New Literary Histories: New Historicism and Contemporary Criticism.* Manchester: Manchester University Press, 1997.

Coleman, Janet. *Ancient and Medieval Memories.* Cambridge: Cambridge University Press, 1992.

Collins, Hugh. "The Order of the Garter, 1348–1461: Chivalry and Politics in Later Medieval England." In *Courts, Counties, and the Capital in the Later Middle Ages,* ed. Diana E. S. Dunn, 155–80. New York: St. Martin's, 1996.

Comparetti, Domenico. *Vergil in the Middle Ages.* Trans. E. F. M. Benecke. London, 1895.

Copeland, Rita. *Rhetoric, Hermeneutics, and Translation in the Middle Ages.* Cambridge: Cambridge University Press, 1991.

Cosgrove, Art. *Late Medieval Ireland, 1370–1541.* Dublin: Helicon, 1981.

Crane, Susan. *Gender and Romance in Chaucer's* Canterbury Tales. Princeton: Princeton University Press, 1994.

———. "The Writing Lesson of 1381." In *Chaucer's England: Literature in Historical Context,* ed. Barbara Hanawalt, 201–21. Minneapolis: University of Minnesota Press, 1992.

Cullingford, Elizabeth Butler. "British Romans and Irish Carthaginians: Anticolonial Metaphor in Heaney, Friel, and McGuinness." *PMLA* 111 (1996): 222–39.

Curtis, E. *A History of Medieval Ireland.* London: Oxford University Press, 1938.

———. *Richard II [and the Submissions of the Irish Chiefs].* Oxford: Clarendon Press, 1927.

David, Alfred. "Chaucer's Edwardian Poetry." In *The Idea of Medieval Literature: New Essays on Chaucer and Medieval Culture in Honor of Donald R. Howard,* ed. James M. Dean and Christian K. Zacher, 35–54. Newark: University of Delaware Press, 1992.

———. "Gawain and Aeneas." *English Studies* 49 (1968): 402–9.

Davies, R. H. "Richard II and the Principality of Chester, 1397–9." In *The Reign of Richard II,* ed. F. R. H. Du Boulay and Caroline M. Barron., 256–79. London: Athlone, 1971.

Davies, R. R. *Domination and Conquest: The Experience of Ireland, Scotland, and Wales, 1100–1300.* Cambridge: Cambridge University Press, 1990.

de Certeau, Michel. *The Writing of History.* Trans. Tom Conley. New York: Columbia University Press, 1988.

Delany, Sheila. *Chaucer's* House of Fame: *The Poetics of Skeptical Fideism.* Chicago: University of Chicago Press, 1972.

———. "Geoffrey of Monmouth and Chaucer's *Legend of Good Women.*" *Chaucer Review* 22 (1988): 170–74.

De Lauretis, Teresa. *Technologies of Gender.* Bloomington: Indiana University Press, 1987.

Derrida, Jacques. *Of Grammatology.* Trans. G. C. Spivak. Baltimore: The Johns Hopkins University Press, 1974.

———. *The Post Card (from Socrates to Freud and Beyond)*. Trans. Alan Bass. Chicago: University of Chicago Press, 1987.

Desmond, Marilynn. *Reading Dido*. Minneapolis: University of Minnesota Press, 1994.

Dinshaw, Carolyn. *Chaucer's Sexual Poetics*. Madison: University of Wisconsin Press, 1989.

———. "Getting Medieval: Pulp Fiction, Gawain, Foucault." In *The Book and the Body*, ed. Dolores Warwick Frese and Katherine O'Brien O'Keefe, 116–63. Notre Dame, Ind.: University of Notre Dame Press, 1997.

———. *Getting Medieval: Sexualities and Communities, Pre- and Postmodern*. Durham, N.C.: Duke University Press, 1999.

———. "A Kiss Is Just a Kiss: Heterosexuality and Its Consolations in *Sir Gawain and the Green Knight*." *diacritics* 24 (1994): 205–26.

Dobson, R. B. *The Peasants' Revolt of 1381*. London: Macmillan, 1983.

Donaldson, E. Talbot. *Speaking of Chaucer*. New York: Norton, 1970.

Doyle, A. I. "English Books in and out of Court from Edward III to Henry VII." In *English Court Culture in the Later Middle Ages*, ed. V. J. Scattergood and J. W. Sherborne, 163–82. London: Duckworth, 1983.

Du Boulay, F. R. H. *Germany in the Later Middle Ages*. London: Athlone, 1983.

Duchêne, Hervé. *The Golden Treasures of Troy: The Dream of Heinrich Schliemann*. Trans. Jeremy Leggatt. London: Thames and Hudson, 1996.

Dvořáková, V. *Gothic Mural Painting in Bohemia and Moravia, 1300–1378*. Oxford: Oxford University Press, 1964.

Dyer, Christopher. "The Social and Economic Background to the Rural Revolt of 1381." In *The English Rising of 1381*, ed. R. H. Hilton and T. H. Aston, 9–42. Cambridge: Cambridge University Press, 1984.

Eckhardt, Carolyn D. "The Presence of Rome in the Middle English Chronicles of the Fourteenth Century." *Journal of English and German Philology* 90, no. 1 (1991): 187–207.

Federico, Sylvia. "The Imaginary Society: Women in the Rising of 1381." *Journal of British Studies* 40 (2001): 159–83.

Fehrenbacher, Richard William. Blood and Virtue: Representing Legitimacy/Legitimating Representation in Fifteenth-Century English Literature." Ph.D. diss., Duke University, 1992.

Ferster, Judith. *Fictions of Advice: The Literature and Politics of Counsel in Late Medieval England*. Philadelphia: University of Pennsylvania Press, 1996.

Finlayson, John. "Guido de Columnis' *Historia destructionis Troiae*, the *Gest Hystorial of the Destruction of Troy*, and Lydgate's *Troy Book*: Translation and the Design of History." *Anglia* 113 (1995): 141–62.

Fisher, John H. *John Gower: Moral Philosopher and Friend of Chaucer*. New York: New York University Press, 1964.

———. "A Language Policy for Lancastrian England." *PMLA* 107 (1992): 1168–80.

Fisher, Sheila. "Leaving Morgan Aside: Women, History, and Revisionism in *Sir Gawain and the Green Knight*." In *The Passing of Arthur: New Essays in Arthurian Tradition*, ed. Christopher Baswell and William Sharpe, 129–51. New York: Garland, 1988.

Fleming, John V. *Classical Imitation and Interpretation in Chaucer's* Troilus. Lincoln: University of Nebraska Press, 1990.

Fletcher, Robert Huntington. *The Arthurian Material in the Chronicles.* New York: Burt Franklin, 1966.

Foucault, Michel. "Of Other Spaces." *diacritics* 16 (1986): 22–27.

Fradenburg, Louise. *City, Marriage, Tournament.* Madison: University of Wisconsin Press, 1991.

———. "Rethinking Queenship." In *Women and Sovereignty,* ed. Louise Fradenburg, 1–13. Edinburgh: Edinburgh University Press, 1992.

Fradenburg, Louise, and Carla Freccero. "Caxton, Foucault, and the Pleasures of History." Introduction to *Premodern Sexualities,* ed. Louise Fradenburg and Carla Freccero, xiii–xxiv. New York: Routledge, 1996.

Frame, Robin. *The Political Development of the British Isles, 1100–1400.* Oxford: Oxford University Press, 1990.

———. "Thomas Rokeby, Sheriff of Yorkshire and Justiciar of Ireland." *Peritia* 10 (1996): 274–96.

———. "Two Kings in Leinster: The Crown and the MicMhurchadha in the Fourteenth Century." In *Colony and Frontier in Medieval Ireland: Essays Presented to J. F. Lydon,* ed. T. B. Barry, Robin Frame, and Katharine Simms, 155–75. London: Hambledon Press, 1995.

Friend, A. C. "Chaucer's Version of the *Aeneid.*" *Speculum* 28 (1953): 317–23.

Freud, Sigmund. *The Complete Letters of Sigmund Freud to Wilhelm Fliess, 1887–1904.* Ed. and trans. Jeffrey Moussaieff Masson. Cambridge, Mass.: Harvard University Press, 1985.

———. *The Standard Edition of the Complete Psychological Works of Sigmund Freud.* Ed. and trans. James Strachey. 24 vols. London: Hogarth, 1953–74.

Fyler, John M. *Chaucer and Ovid.* New Haven, Conn.: Yale University Press, 1979.

Galbraith, V. H. "Nationality and Language in Medieval England." *Transactions of the Royal Historical Society,* 4th ser., 23 (1941): 110–16.

———. "Thomas Walsingham and the St. Albans Chronicle." *English Historical Review* 4 (1932): 12–30.

Gasse, Rosanne. "Deiphebus, Hector, and Troilus in Chaucer's *Troilus and Criseyde.*" *Chaucer Review* 32 (1998): 423–39.

Gaunt, Simon. "From Epic to Romance: Gender and Sexuality in the *Roman d'Eneas.*" *Romanic Review* 83 (1992): 1–27.

Gay, Peter. *Freud: A Life for Our Time.* London: Dent, 1988.

Gerould, Gordon Hall. "King Arthur and Politics." *Speculum* 2 (1927): 33–51.

Giancarlo, Matthew. "Murders, Lies, and Storytelling: The Manipulation of Justice(s) in the Parliaments of 1397 and 1399." *Speculum* 77 (2002): 76–112.

Gillespie, James L. "Richard II: King of Battles?" In *The Age of Richard II,* ed. James L. Gillespie, 139–64. Stroud, Eng.: Sutton Publishing, 1997.

Gillingham, John. "The English Invasion of Ireland." In *Representing Ireland: Literature and the Origins of Conflict, 1534–1660,* ed. Brendan Bradshaw and Andrew Hadfield, 24–42. Cambridge: Cambridge University Press, 1997.

Given-Wilson, Chris. *The Royal Household and the King's Affinity: Service, Politics, and Finance in England, 1360–1413.* New Haven, Conn.: Yale University Press, 1986.

Grady, Frank. "The Boethian Reader of *Troilus and Criseyde*." *Chaucer Review* 33 (1999): 230–51.

———. "The Lancastrian Gower and the Limits of Exemplarity." *Speculum* 70 (1995): 552–75.

Gransden, Antonia. *Historical Writing in England*. Ithaca, N.Y.: Cornell University Press, 1982.

Green, Richard Firth. "King Richard II's Book Revisited." *Library*, 5th ser., 31 (1976): 235–39.

———. *Poets and Princepleasers*. Toronto: University of Toronto Press, 1980.

Griffith, Richard R. "The Political Bias of Malory's *Morte Darthur*." *Viator* 5 (1974): 365–86.

Grosz, Elizabeth. "Bodies—Cities." In *Sexuality and Space*, ed. Beatriz Colomina, 241–53. New York: Princeton Architectural Press, 1992.

Gruen, Erich S. *Culture and National Identity in Republican Rome*. Ithaca, N.Y.: Cornell University Press, 1992.

Guenée, Bernard. *States and Rulers in Later Medieval Europe*. Trans. Juliet Vale. Oxford: Blackwell, 1985.

Hall, Lewis Brewer. "Chaucer and the Dido and Aeneas Story." *Mediaeval Studies* 25 (1963): 148–59.

Hammond, Eleanor. "A Burgundian Copy of Chaucer's *Troilus*." *Modern Language Notes* 26 (1911): 32.

Hanning, Robert W. *The Vision of History in Early Britain*. New York: Columbia University Press, 1966.

Hanrahan, Michael. "The Seduction of *The Testament of Love*." *Literature and History*, 3rd ser., 7 (1998): 1–15.

———. "'A Straunge Succesour Sholde Take Youre Heritage': The *Clerk's Tale* and the Crisis of Ricardian Rule." *Chaucer Review* 35 (2001): 335–50.

———. "Teaching Textual Politics." *Studies in Medieval and Renaissance Teaching* 5 (1997): 50–57.

Henry, Avril. "Temptation and Hunt in *Gawain*." *Medium Aevum* 45 (1976): 187–99.

Hoy, James. "Chaucer and Dictys." *Medium Aevum* 59 (1990): 288–91.

Ingham, Patricia Clare, "'In Contrayez Strange': Colonial Relations, British Identity, and *Sir Gawain and the Green Knight*," *New Medieval Literatures* 4 (2001): 61–94.

———. "Marking Time: *Branwen, Daughter of Llyr* and the Colonial Refrain." In *The Postcolonial Middle Ages*, ed. Jeffrey Jerome Cohen, 173–92. London: Macmillan, 2000.

Ingledew, Francis. "The Book of Troy and the Genealogical Construction of History: The Case of Geoffrey of Monmouth's *Historia regum Britanniae*." *Speculum* 69 (1994): 665–704.

———. "Jerusalem, Babylon, Camelot: The Concept of the Court in the *Pearl* Poet." Ph.D. diss., Washington University, 1989.

James, Heather. *Shakespeare's Troy*. Cambridge: Cambridge University Press, 1997.

Jameson, Fredric. *The Political Unconscious: Narrative as a Socially Symbolic Act*. Ithaca, N.Y.: Cornell University Press, 1981.

Jarrett, Bede. *The Emperor Charles IV*. London: Eyre and Spottiswoode, 1935.

Jefferson, Lisa. "Two Fifteenth-Century Manuscripts of the Statutes of the Order of the Garter." *English Manuscript Studies* 5 (1995): 18–35.

Johnson, David J. *Southwark and the City*. Oxford: Oxford University Press, 1969.

Johnston, Dorothy. "Richard II and the Submissions of Gaelic Ireland." *Irish Historical Studies* 22 (1980): 1–20.

Jones, Richard H. *The Royal Policy of Richard II*. Oxford: Blackwell, 1968.

Justice, Steven. *Writing and Rebellion: England in 1381*. Berkeley and Los Angeles: University of California Press, 1994.

Kaske, R. E. "The *Aube* in Chaucer's *Troilus*." In *Chaucer Criticism*, ed. Richard J. Schoek and Jerome Taylor, 167–79. Notre Dame, Ind.: University of Notre Dame Press, 1961.

Keeler, Laura. *Geoffrey of Monmouth and the Late Latin Chroniclers, 1300–1500*. Berkeley and Los Angeles: University of California Press, 1946.

Keen, Maurice. "Chaucer's Knight, the English Aristocracy, and the Crusade." In *English Court Culture in the Later Middle Ages*, ed. V. J. Scattergood and J. W. Sherborne, 45–62. London: Duckworth, 1983.

———. *Chivalry*. New Haven, Conn.: Yale University Press, 1984.

Keiser, Elizabeth B. *Courtly Desire and Medieval Homophobia*. New Haven, Conn.: Yale University Press, 1997.

Kelly, Henry Ansgar. *Chaucerian Tragedy*. Cambridge: Cambridge University Press, 1997.

Kennedy, Edward D. "Malory's Use of Hardyng's *Chronicle*." *Notes and Queries* 214 (1969): 167–70.

Kingsford, Charles Lethbridge. *English Historical Literature in the Fifteenth Century*. New York: Burt Franklin, 1913.

Kipling, Gordon. "Richard II's 'Sumptuous Pageants' and the Idea of the Civic Triumph." In *Pageantry in the Shakespearean Theatre*, ed. David M. Bergeron, 83–103. Athens: University of Georgia Press, 1985.

Kiser, Lisa J. *Telling Classical Tales*. Ithaca, N.Y.: Cornell University Press, 1983.

Knapp, Ethan. "Bureaucratic Identity and the Construction of the Self in Hoccleve's *Formulary* and *La Male regle*." *Speculum* 74 (1999): 357–76.

Kruger, Steven F. *Dreaming in the Middle Ages*. Cambridge: Cambridge University Press, 1992.

Lacan, Jacques. *Feminine Sexuality: Jacques Lacan and the école freudienne*. Ed. Juliet Mitchell and Jacqueline Rose. Trans. Jacqueline Rose. New York: Norton, 1982.

———. *The Four Fundamental Concepts of Psycho-Analysis*. Ed. Jacques-Alain Miller. Trans. Alan Sheridan. Harmondsworth, Eng.: Penguin, 1977.

———. *Speech and Language in Psychoanalysis*. Trans. Anthony Wilden. Baltimore: The Johns Hopkins University Press, 1981.

Laclau, Ernesto, and Lilian Zac. "Minding the Gap: The Subject of Politics." *The Making of Political Identities*, ed. Ernesto Laclau, 11–39. London: Verso, 1994.

Lacoue-Labarthe, Philippe. *Typography: Mimesis, Philosophy, Politics*. Cambridge, Mass.: Harvard University Press, 1989.

Lagorio, Valerie M. "The Evolving Legend of St. Joseph of Glastonbury." *Speculum* 46 (1971): 209–31.

Laplanche, Jean, and Jean-Bertrande Pontalis. *The Language of Psychoanalysis*. Trans. Donald Nicholson-Smith. New York: Norton, 1973.

Lerer, Seth. *Chaucer and His Readers: Imagining the Author in Late-Medieval England*. Princeton: Princeton University Press, 1993.

Lewis, C. S. "What Chaucer Really Did to *Il filostrato.*" *Essays and Studies* 17 (1932): 56–75. Reprinted in *Chaucer's* Troilus: *Essays in Criticism,* ed. Stephen A. Barney, 37–54. Hamden, Eng.: Archon, 1980.

Lindenbaum, Sheila. "The Smithfield Tournament of 1390." *Journal of Medieval and Renaissance Studies* 20 (1990): 1–20.

Loomis, Roger Sherman. *Arthurian Literature in the Middle Ages.* Oxford: Clarendon Press, 1959.

———. "Geoffrey of Monmouth and Arthurian Origins." *Speculum* 3 (1928): 16–33.

Lukacher, Ned. *Primal Scenes: Literature, Philosophy, Psychoanalysis.* Ithaca, N.Y.: Cornell University Press, 1986.

Lynch, Kathryn. *The High Medieval Dream Vision: Poetry, Philosophy, and Literary Form.* Stanford, Calif.: Stanford University Press, 1988.

Machan, Tim William. "Textual Authority and the Works of Hoccleve, Lydgate, and Henryson." *Viator* 23 (1992): 281–99.

Mannheim, Karl. *Ideology and Utopia: An Introduction to the Sociology of Knowledge.* Trans. Louis Wirth and Edward Shils. New York: Harcourt, Brace, 1936.

Margherita, Gayle. *The Romance of Origins: Language and Sexual Difference in Middle English Literature.* Philadelphia: University of Pennsylvania Press, 1994.

Marin, Louis. *Utopics: Spacial Play.* Trans. Robert A. Vollrath. Atlantic Highlands, N.J.: Humanities Press, 1984.

———. *Utopiques: Jeux d'espaces.* Paris: Minuit, 1973.

Mathew, Gervase. *The Court of Richard II.* New York: Norton, 1968.

McAlpine, Monica. *The Genre of* Troilus and Criseyde. Ithaca, N.Y.: Cornell University Press, 1978.

McCall, John P. "The Trojan Scene in Chaucer's *Troilus.*" *English Literary History* 29 (1962): 263–75. Reprinted in *Chaucer's* Troilus: *Essays in Criticism,* ed. Stephen A. Barney, 101–14. Hamden, Eng.: Archon, 1980.

McCall, John P., and George Rudisill. "The Parliament of 1386 and Chaucer's Trojan Parliament." *Journal of English and Germanic Philology* 58 (1959): 276–88.

McFarlane, K. B. *Lancastrian Kings and Lollard Knights.* Oxford: Clarendon Press, 1972.

McKisack, May. *The Fourteenth Century: 1307–1399.* Oxford: Oxford University Press, 1991.

McRee, Benjamin R. "Unity or Division? The Social Meaning of Guild Ceremony in Urban Communities." In *City and Spectacle in Medieval Europe,* ed. Barbara A. Hanawalt and Kathryn L. Reyerson, 96–114. Minneapolis: University of Minnesota Press, 1994.

Middleton, Anne. "The Idea of Public Poetry in the Reign of Richard II." *Speculum* 53 (1978): 94–114.

———. "War by Other Means: Marriage and Chivalry in Chaucer." *Studies in the Age of Chaucer: Proceedings* 1 (1984): 119–33.

Minnis, Alistair J. *Medieval Theory of Authorship.* London: Scolar Press, 1984.

Mitchell, Shelagh. "Richard II: Kingship and the Cult of the Saints." In *The Regal Image of Richard II and the Wilton Diptych,* ed. D. Gordon, 110–34. London: Harvey Miller, 1998.

Mooney, Linne R. "Lydgate's *Kings of England* and Another Verse Chronicle of the Kings." *Viator* 20 (1989): 255–89.

Morgan, Philip. "Henry IV and the Shadow of Richard II." In *Crown, Government, and People in the Fifteenth Century*, ed. Rowena E. Archer, 13–26. Stroud, Eng.: Sutton, 1995.

Nightingale, Pamela. "Capitalists, Crafts, and Constitutional Change in Late Fourteenth-Century London." *Past and Present* 124 (1989): 3–35.

———. *A Medieval Mercantile Community*. New Haven, Conn.: Yale University Press, 1995.

Nolan, Barbara. *Chaucer and the Tradition of the Roman Antique*. Cambridge: Cambridge University Press, 1992.

Ormrod, W. M. "Government by Commission: The Continual Council of 1386 and English Royal Administration." *Peritia* 10 (1996): 303–21.

Otter, Monika. "'New Werke': *St. Erkenwald*, St. Albans, and the Medieval Sense of the Past." *Journal of Medieval and Renaissance Studies* 24 (1994): 387–414.

Palmer, J. J. N. *England, France, and Christendom, 1377–99*. London: Routledge and Kegan Paul, 1972.

———. "English Foreign Policy, 1388–99." In *The Reign of Richard II: Essays in Honour of May McKisack*, ed. F. R. H. Du Boulay and Caroline M. Barron, 75–107. London: Athlone, 1971.

Partridge, Stephen. "Questions of Evidence: Manuscripts and the Early History of Chaucer's Works." In *Writing after Chaucer: Essential Readings in Chaucer and the Fifteenth Century*, ed. Daniel J. Pinti, 1–26. New York: Garland, 1998.

Patterson, Lee. *Chaucer and the Subject of History*. Madison: University of Wisconsin Press, 1991.

———. "Chaucer's Pardoner on the Couch: Psyche and Clio in Medieval Literary Studies." *Speculum* 76 (2001): 638–80.

———. "Making Identities in Fifteenth-Century England: Henry V and John Lydgate." In *New Historical Literary Study*, ed. Jeffrey Cox and Larry J. Reynolds, 69–107. Princeton: Princeton University Press, 1993.

———. *Negotiating the Past*. Madison: University of Wisconsin Press, 1987.

Pearsall, Derek. "Chaucer and Lydgate." In *Chaucer Traditions: Studies in Honour of Derek Brewer*, ed. Ruth Morse and Barry Windeatt, 39–53. Cambridge: Cambridge University Press, 1990.

———. "Hoccleve's *Regement of Princes:* The Poetics of Royal Self-Representation." *Speculum* 69 (1994): 386–410.

———. *John Lydgate*. Charlottesville: University of Virginia Press, 1970.

———. *The Life of Geoffrey Chaucer*. Oxford: Blackwell, 1992.

Perroy, Edouard. *L'Angleterre et le grand schisme d'occident*. Paris: J. Monnier, 1933.

Pratt, R. A. "Chaucer and the Visconti Libraries." *English Literary History* 6 (1939): 191–99.

Prescott, A. J. "The Judicial Records of the Rising of 1381." Ph.D. diss., University of London, 1984.

———. "London in the Peasants' Revolt: A Portrait Gallery." *London Journal* 7 (1981): 125–43.

Raby, F. J. E. "Some Notes on Virgil, Mainly in English Authors, in the Middle Ages." *Studi Medievali*, new ser., 5 (1932): 359–71.

Reale, Nancy M. "'Bitwixen Game and Ernest': *Troilus and Criseyde* as a Post-Boccaccian Response to the *Commedia*." *Philological Quarterly* 71 (1992): 155–71.

Reeves, Marjorie. "History and Prophecy in Medieval Thought." *Medievalia et Humanistica* 5 (1974): 54–73.

Reinhold, Meyer. "The Unhero Aeneas." *Classica et Mediaevalia* 27 (1966): 195–207.

Réville, Andre. *Le Soulèvement des travailleurs d'Angleterre en 1381*. Paris, 1898.

Rickert, Edith. "King Richard II's Books." *Library*, 5th ser., 13 (1933): 144–47.

Ricoeur, Paul. "Ideology and Utopia as Cultural Imagination." In *Being Human in a Technological Age*, ed. Donald M. Borchert and David Stewart, 107–25. Athens: Ohio University Press, 1979.

Robertson, D. W. *Chaucer's London*. New York: Wiley, 1968.

———. *A Preface to Chaucer*. Princeton: Princeton University Press, 1962.

Root, R. K. *The Textual Tradition of Chaucer's* Troilus. London: Kegan Paul, 1916.

Rose, Jacqueline. *States of Fantasy: The Clarendon Lectures in English Literature, 1994*. Oxford: Clarendon Press, 1996.

Ross, Valerie. "Believing Cassandra: Intertextual Politics and the Interpretation of Dreams in *Troilus and Criseyde*." *Chaucer Review* 31 (1997): 339–56.

Rosser, Gervase. "London and Westminster: The Suburb in the Urban Economy in the Later Middle Ages." In *Towns and Townspeople in the Fifteenth Century*, ed. John A. F. Thomson, 45–61. Gloucester: Alan Sutton, 1988.

Roth, Michael S. *Psychoanalysis as History: Negation and Freedom in Freud*. Ithaca, N.Y.: Cornell University Press, 1987.

Ruff, Nancy K. "'Sely Dido': A Good Woman's Fame." *Classical and Modern Literature* 12 (1991): 59–68.

Sanderlin, George. "Two Transfigurations: Gawain and Aeneas." *Chaucer Review* 12 (1978): 255–58.

Saul, Nigel. "The Kingship of Richard II." In *Richard II: The Art of Kingship*, ed. Anthony Goodman and James Gillespie, 37–57. Oxford: Clarendon Press, 1999.

———. *Richard II*. New Haven, Conn.: Yale University Press, 1997.

———. "Richard II and Westminster Abbey." In *The Cloister and the World: Essays in Medieval History in Honour of Barbara Harvey*, ed. John Blair and Brian Golding, 196–218. Oxford: Clarendon Press, 1996.

———. "Richard II, York, and the Evidence of the King's Itinerary." In *The Age of Richard II*, ed. James L. Gillespie. 71–92. Stroud, Eng. Sutton, 1997.

Sayles, G. O. "Richard II in 1381 and 1399." *English Historical Review* 94 (1979): 820–29.

Scanlon, Larry. "The King's Two Voices: Narrative and Power in Hoccleve's *Regement of Princes*." In *Literary Practice and Social Change in Britain, 1380–1530*, ed. Lee Patterson, 216–47. Berkeley and Los Angeles: University of California Press, 1990.

Scase, Wendy. "'Now you see it; now you don't': Nation, Identity, and Otherness." *New Medieval Literatures* 4 (2001): 1–8.

Scattergood, V. J. "Literary Culture at the Court of Richard II." In *English Court Culture in the Later Middle Ages*, ed. V. J. Scattergood and J. W. Sherborne, 29–44. London: Duckworth, 1983.

Scherer, Margaret R. *The Legends of Troy in Art and Literature*. New York: Phaidon Press for the Metropolitan Museum of Art, 1963.

Schibanoff, Susan. "Criseyde's 'Impossible' *Aubes.*" *Journal of English and Germanic Philology* 76 (1977): 326–33.

Schlauch, Margaret. "Chaucer's Doctrine of Kings and Tyrants." *Speculum* 20 (1945): 133–56.

Schliemann, Heinrich. *Ilios: The City and Country of the Trojans.* London, 1880.

———. *Troja: Results of the Latest Researches and Discoveries on the Site of Homer's Troy.* London, 1884.

———. *Trojanische Alterhümer: Bericht über die Ausgrabungen in Troja.* Leipzig, 1874.

———. *Troy and Its Remains.* London, 1875.

Scott, Joan W. *Gender and the Politics of History.* New York: Columbia University Press, 1988.

Sherborne, J. W. "Aspects of English Court Culture in the Later Fourteenth Century." In *English Court Culture in the Later Middle Ages,* ed. V. J. Scattergood and J. W. Sherborne, 1–28. London: Duckworth, 1983.

———. "Charles VI and Richard II." In *Froissart: Historian,* ed. J. J. N. Palmer, 50–63. Woodbridge, Suffolk: Boydell, 1981.

———. "Richard II's Return to Wales, July 1399." *Welsh History Review* 7 (1975): 389–402.

Simon, Sherry. *Gender in Translation: Cultural Identity and the Politics of Transmission.* London: Routledge, 1996.

Simpson, James. "'Dysemol Daies and Fatal Houres': Lydgate's *Destruction of Thebes* and Chaucer's *Knight's Tale.*" In *The Long Fifteenth Century: Essays for Douglas Gray,* ed. Helen Cooper, 15–33. Oxford: Clarendon Press, 1997.

———. "The Other Book of Troy: Guido delle Colonne's *Historia destructionis Troiae* in Fourteenth- and Fifteenth-Century England." *Speculum* 73 (1998): 397–423.

Singerman, Jerome E. *Under Clouds of Poesy.* New York: Garland, 1986.

Sklar, Elizabeth S. "Guido, the Middle English Troy Books, and Chaucer: The English Connection." *Neophilologus* 76 (1992): 616–28.

Smith, D. Vance. "Irregular Histories: Forgetting Ourselves." *New Literary History* 28 (1997): 161–84.

Smith, L. Toulmin. *Expeditions to Prussia and the Holy Land made by Henry Earl of Derby.* London, 1894.

Spence, Sarah. *Rhetorics of Reason and Desire: Vergil, Augustine, and the Troubadours.* Ithaca, N.Y.: Cornell University Press, 1988.

Spiegel, Gabrielle M. *The Past as Text: The Theory and Practice of Medieval Historiography.* Baltimore: The Johns Hopkins University Press, 1997.

Srebnick, Walter. "*Sir Gawain and the Green Knight* and Late Medieval Aristocratic Culture." *Mid-Hudson Language Studies* 12 (1989): 12–23.

Stafford, Pauline. *Queens, Concubines, and Dowagers: The King's Wife in the Early Middle Ages.* Athens: University of Georgia Press, 1983.

Steel, Anthony. *Richard II.* Cambridge: Cambridge University Press, 1941.

Stevenson, Sharon. "Aeneas in Fourteenth-Century England." In *The Classics in the Middle Ages,* ed. Aldo S. Bernardo and Saul Levin, 371–78. Binghamton: Center for Medieval and Early Renaissance Studies, 1990.

Stow, George B. "Chronicles versus Records: The Character of Richard II." In *Documenting the Past: Essays in Medieval History Presented to George Peddy Cuttino*, ed. J. S. Hamilton and Patricia J. Bradley, 155–76. Woodbridge, Suffolk: Boydell, 1989.

———. "Richard II in Jean Froissart's *Chroniques*." *Journal of Medieval History* 11 (1985): 333–43.

———. "Richard II in Thomas Walsingham's Chronicles." *Speculum* 59 (1984): 68–102.

Strohm, Paul. *England's Empty Throne: Usurpation and the Language of Legitimation, 1399–1422*. New Haven, Conn.: Yale University Press, 1998.

———. *Hochon's Arrow: The Social Imagination of Fourteenth-Century Texts*. Princeton: Princeton University Press, 1992.

———. "'Lad with revel to Newegate': Chaucerian Narrative and Historical Meta-Narrative." In *Art and Context in Late Medieval English Narrative: Essays in Honor of Robert Worth Frank, Jr.*, ed. Robert R. Edwards, 170–94. Cambridge: D. S. Brewer, 1994.

———. "Passioun, Lyf, Miracle, Legende: Some Generic Terms in Middle English Hagiographical Narrative." *Chaucer Review* 10 (1975): 62–75.

———. "Politics and Poetics: Usk and Chaucer in the 1380s." In *Literary Practice and Social Change in Britain, 1380–1530*, ed. Lee Patterson, 83–112. Berkeley and Los Angeles: University of California Press, 1990.

———. *Social Chaucer*. Cambridge, Mass.: Harvard University Press, 1989.

———. "Storie, Spelle, Geste, Romaunce, Tragedie: Generic Distinctions in the Middle English Troy Narratives." *Speculum* 46 (1971): 348–59.

Tanner, Marie. *The Last Descendant of Aeneas: The Hapsburgs and the Mythic Image of the Emperor*. New Haven, Conn.: Yale University Press, 1993.

Tatlock, J. S. P. *The Legendary History of Britain*. Berkeley and Los Angeles: University of California Press, 1950.

Taylor, Andrew. "Anne of Bohemia and the Making of Chaucer." *Studies in the Age of Chaucer* 19 (1997): 95–119.

Taylor, John. *English Historical Literature in the Fourteenth Century*. Oxford: Clarendon Press, 1987.

———. "The French Prose *Brut*: Popular History in Fourteenth-Century England." In *England in the Fourteenth Century: Proceedings of the 1985 Harlaxton Symposium*, ed. W. M. Ormrod, 247–54. Woodbridge, Suffolk: Boydell, 1986.

———. "Richard II in the Chronicles." In *Richard II: The Art of Kingship*, ed. Anthony Goodman and James Gillespie, 15–35. Oxford: Clarendon Press, 1999.

Thrupp, Sylvia. *The Merchant Class of Medieval London, 1300–1500*. Ann Arbor: University of Michigan Press, 1948.

Torti, Anna. "From 'History' to 'Tragedy': The Story of Troilus and Criseyde in Lydgate's *Troy Book* and Henryson's *Testament of Cresseid*." In *The European Tragedy of Troilus*, ed. Piero Boitani. 171–98. Oxford: Clarendon Press, 1989.

Tout, T. F. *Chapters in the Administrative History of Medieval England*. 6 vols. Manchester: Manchester University Press, 1920–33.

Tuck, Anthony. *Richard II and the English Nobility*. London: Edward Arnold, 1973.

———. "Richard II and the House of Luxemburg." In *Richard II: The Art of Kingship*, ed. Anthony Goodman and James Gillespie, 205–29. Oxford: Clarendon Press, 1999.

Tuck, J. A. "Richard II and the Border Magnates." *Northern History* 3 (1968): 27–52.

Turville-Petre, Thorlac. *England the Nation: Language, Literature, and National Identity, 1290–1340.* Oxford: Oxford University Press, 1996.

Vale, Juliet. *Edward III and Chivalry: Chivalric Society and Its Context, 1270–1350.* Woodbridge, Suffolk: Boydell, 1982.

Vance, Eugene. *Mervelous Signals: Poetics and Sign Theory in the Middle Ages.* Lincoln: University of Nebraska Press, 1986.

Venuti, Lawrence. "The Destruction of Troy: Translation and Royalist Cultural Politics in the Interregnum." *Journal of Medieval and Renaissance Studies* 23 (1993): 197–219.

Walker, Simon. "Janico Dartasso: Chivalry, Nationality, and the Man-at-Arms." *History* 84 (1999): 31–51.

———. *The Lancastrian Affinity, 1361–1399.* Oxford: Clarendon, 1990.

Wallace, David. "Chaucer and the Absent City." In *Chaucer's England: Literature in Historical Context,* ed. Barbara Hanawalt, 59–90. Minneapolis: University of Minnesota Press, 1992.

———. *Chaucer and the Early Writings of Boccaccio.* Woodbridge, Suffolk: D. S. Brewer, 1985.

———. *Chaucerian Polity: Absolutist Lineages and Associational Forms in England and Italy.* Stanford, Calif.: Stanford University Press, 1997.

Watson, Nicholas. "Outdoing Chaucer: Lydgate's *Troy Book* and Henryson's *Testament of Cresseid* as Competitive Imitations of *Troilus and Criseyde.*" In *Shifts and Transpositions in Medieval Narrative: A Festschrift for Elspeth Kennedy,* ed. Karen Pratt, 89–108. Cambridge: D. S. Brewer, 1994.

Westover, Jeff. "Arthur's End: The King's Emasculation in the Alliterative *Morte Arthure.*" *Chaucer Review* 32 (1998): 310–24.

Wetherbee, Winthrop. *Chaucer and the Poets: An Essay on* Troilus and Criseyde. Ithaca, N.Y.: Cornell University Press, 1984.

———. "The Descent from Bliss: *Troilus* III, 1310–1582." In *Chaucer's* Troilus: *Essays in Criticism,* ed. Stephen A. Barney, 297–317. Hamden, Eng.: Archon, 1980.

White, Hayden. *Tropics of Discourse.* Baltimore: The Johns Hopkins University Press, 1978.

Wickham, Glynne. *Early English Stages, 1300–1660.* 2 vols. London: Routledge, 1959.

Wilkinson, B. "The Peasants' Revolt of 1381." *Speculum* 15 (1940): 12–35.

Wilson, Edward. "John Clerk, Author of *The Destruction of Troy.*" *Notes and Queries* 235 (1990): 391–96.

Wimsatt, James I. *Chaucer and His French Contemporaries.* Toronto: University of Toronto Press, 1991.

Withrington, John. "Caxton, Malory, and the Roman War." *Studies in Philology* 89 (1992): 350–66.

———. "King Arthur as Emperor." *Notes and Queries* 233 (1988): 13–15.

Žižek, Slavoj. "Beyond Discourse-Analysis." In *New Reflections on the Revolution of Our Time,* ed. Ernesto Laclau, 249–60. London: Verso, 1990.

———. *The Sublime Object of Ideology.* London: Verso, 1989.

Medieval Cultures

Volume 33
D. Vance Smith
Arts of Possession: The Middle English Household Imaginary

Volume 32
Edited by Sharon Farmer and Carol Braun Pasternack
Gender and Difference in the Middle Ages

Volume 31
L. O. Aranye Fradenburg
Sacrifice Your Love: Psychoanalysis, Historicism, Chaucer

Volume 30
Stephanie Trigg
Congenial Souls: Reading Chaucer from Medieval to Postmodern

Volume 29
Edited by Kathleen Ashley and Robert L. A. Clark
Medieval Conduct

Volume 28
D. Vance Smith
The Book of the Incipit: Beginnings in the Fourteenth Century

Volume 27
Edited by Glenn Burger and Steven F. Kruger
Queering the Middle Ages

Volume 26
Paul Strohm
Theory and the Premodern Text

Volume 25
David Rollo
Glamorous Sorcery: Magic and Literacy in the High Middle Ages

Volume 24
Steve Ellis
Chaucer at Large: The Poet in the Modern Imagination

Volume 23
Edited by Barbara Hanawalt and Michal Kobialka
Medieval Practices of Space

Volume 22
Michelle R. Warren
History on the Edge: Excalibur and the Borders of Britain, 1100–1300

Volume 21
Olivia Holmes
Assembling the Lyric Self: Authorship from Troubadour Song to Italian Poetry Book

Volume 20
Karen Sullivan
The Interrogation of Joan of Arc

Volume 19
Clare A. Lees
Tradition and Belief: Religious Writing in Late Anglo-Saxon England

Volume 18
David Matthews
The Making of Middle English, 1765–1910

Volume 17
Jeffrey Jerome Cohen
Of Giants: Sex, Monsters, and the Middle Ages

Volume 16
Edited by Barbara A. Hanawalt and David Wallace
Medieval Crime and Social Control

Volume 15
Kathryn Kerby-Fulton and Denise L. Despres
Iconography and the Professional Reader: The Politics of Book Production in the Douce "Piers Plowman"

Volume 14
Edited by Marilynn Desmond
Christine de Pizan and the Categories of Difference

Volume 13
Alfred Thomas
Anne's Bohemia: Czech Literature and Society, 1310–1420

Volume 12
Edited by F. R. P. Akehurst and Stephanie Cain Van D'Elden
The Stranger in Medieval Society

Volume 11
Edited by Karma Lochrie, Peggy McCracken, and James A. Schultz
Constructing Medieval Sexuality

Volume 10
Claire Sponsler
Drama and Resistance:
Bodies, Goods, and Theatricality in Late Medieval England

Volume 9
Edited by Barbara A. Hanawalt and David Wallace
Bodies and Disciplines:
Intersections of Literature and History in Fifteenth-Century England

Volume 8
Marilynn Desmond
Reading Dido: Gender, Textuality, and the Medieval "Aeneid"

Volume 7
Edited by Clare A. Lees
Medieval Masculinities: Regarding Men in the Middle Ages

Volume 6
Edited by Barbara A. Hanawalt and Kathryn L. Reyerson
City and Spectacle in Medieval Europe

Volume 5
Edited by Calvin B. Kendall and Peter S. Wells
Voyage to the Other World: The Legacy of Sutton Hoo

Volume 4
Edited by Barbara A. Hanawalt
Chaucer's England: Literature in Historical Context

Volume 3
Edited by Marilyn J. Chiat and Kathryn L. Reyerson
The Medieval Mediterranean: Cross-Cultural Contacts

Volume 2
Edited by Andrew MacLeish
The Medieval Monastery

Volume 1
Edited by Kathryn L. Reyerson and Faye Powe
The Medieval Castle

Index

Sylvia Federico has taught medieval literature at Washington State University and at the University of Leeds. She has published several articles on late-medieval literature and history.